# Adolescent Violence in the Home

*Adolescent Violence in the Home* examines a form of violence that has a profound impact on families but is often overlooked and frequently misunderstood: teen aggression and violence towards members of their family—especially parents. Violence in adolescents is often seen as the result of a mental health diagnosis, delinquency, or as a response to dysfunctional parenting, and though understanding a youth's mental health status or a parenting style can be helpful, complete focus on either is misplaced. *Adolescent Violence in the Home* uses a restorative framework, developed by the authors and in use in court systems and organizations around the world, to situate violent behaviors in the context of power and the intergenerational cycle of violence. Readers will come away from this book with a profound understanding of the social and individual factors that lead youth to use violence and how adolescent violence affects parents, and they will also learn about a variety of interventions that specifically address teen violence against parents.

**Gregory Routt**, MA, is codeveloper of Step Up, a counseling program in Seattle for teens that are violent with family members, and coauthor of the Step Up curriculum. The Step Up curriculum has been used in juvenile courts, family courts, and related agencies in the United States, Canada, England, and Australia. Prior to working with Step Up, Mr. Routt worked with adult perpetrators of domestic violence at Family Services Domestic Violence Treatment Program in Seattle and was codirector of the program. He has also worked as a chemical dependency counselor with inmates in Seattle's King County Jail.

**Lily Anderson**, MSW, is codeveloper of Step Up and a coauthor of the Step Up curriculum. She has worked in the field of domestic violence since 1978. From 1986 to 1998 she developed and coordinated a parent education program for Family Services in Seattle, where she authored two parenting curriculums, *Anger Management for Parents* and *Skills for Respectful Parenting*. In 1997, she coauthored *Helping Children Who Have Experienced Domestic Violence: A Guide for Parents*, a curriculum for parents of children who have experienced domestic violence that is being used nationwide in perpetrator and survivor programs.

# Adolescent Violence in the Home

## Restorative Approaches to Building Healthy, Respectful Family Relationships

GREGORY ROUTT AND LILY ANDERSON

Routledge
Taylor & Francis Group

NEW YORK AND LONDON

First published 2015
by Routledge
711 Third Avenue, New York, NY 10017

and by Routledge
2 Park Square, Milton Park, Abingdon, Oxon, OX14 4RN

*Routledge is an imprint of the Taylor & Francis Group, an informa business*

*Library of Congress Cataloging-in-Publication Data*
Routt, Gregory.
 Adolescent violence in the home : restorative approaches to
building healthy, respectful family relationships / Gregory Routt,
Lily Anderson. — 1 Edition.
 Includes bibliographical references and index.
 1. Youth and violence.  2. Families.  3. Interpersonal relations.
I. Anderson, Lily.  II. Title.
 HQ799.2.V56.R68  2014
 303.60835—dc23  2014000890

ISBN: 978-0-415-82900-7 (hbk)
ISBN: 978-0-415-82901-4 (pbk)
ISBN: 978-0-203-51799-4 (ebk)

Typeset in Minion
by Apex CoVantage, LLC

Printed and bound in the United States of America by Publishers Graphics,
LLC on sustainably sourced paper.

# Contents

# Preface

> I never know what his mood will be like when he comes home. I start to worry even before he even comes in the door. I avoid talking to him about anything that might trigger another outburst. He calls me names, screams and yells, breaks things and terrifies everyone in the house. The other day he pushed me. I don't know what to do. I love him, but I just can't take it anymore . . .

Susan is not talking about an abusive husband; she is talking about her teenage son. For most people, Susan's story is shocking to hear. It goes against the grain and defies the natural order. However, it is a familiar story to countless other parents who are facing abuse from their adolescent children. Fearing your own child might hurt you, hearing your son or daughter call you degrading and humiliating names, and feeling threatened and intimidated by your teenage child is a daily experience for millions of parents.

We have been listening to stories like Susan's every working day for over 15 years. Our continual involvement with families like hers has given us knowledge and understanding about the experiences of teens who are abusive and violent, and the parents who are trying to care for them. Families come to us with a wide diversity of backgrounds, circumstances, and challenges. Regardless of their differences, they all have one thing in common—a teen who is physically and emotionally hurting family members and a parent who does not know what to do about it.

Embarrassment and shame create a veil of secrecy around this type of family abuse. Parents feel disgraced by their child's behavior and don't want others to know their child acts this way, and even worse, that they cannot control them.

When parents do tell others about the abuse, most people find it very hard to believe. It runs contrary to all our beliefs about how a parent-child relationship should be. Parents are supposed to be in charge and have authority, and if they don't, most people believe they must be doing something terribly wrong. Many think the parent is simply being a "pushover" and is too permissive; others think the parent must be abusive and the teen is fighting back. Well-meaning friends and family give parenting advice, such as "don't let him get away with that. You need to let him know who the boss is." Such responses discourage parents from seeking the help they and their child desperately need.

Families facing this issue pose serious social policy problems. Juvenile courts throughout the country confront these cases on a daily basis. Police agencies differ on what they perceive their responsibility to be in these cases. The parent's job performance is affected by the emotional stress and work time missed attending court hearings and other meetings that are tied to violence at home. Siblings, especially younger ones, can have negative developmental and psychological consequences by being the direct targets of violence or simply by being exposed to violence in their home. Mental health clinicians struggle with finding an effective way to address adolescent violence and often direct the course of treatment to related issues, but not the abuse or violence itself. Child protection agencies lack a clear policy regarding who is responsible for addressing this kind of family violence. Social policy makers are simply unaware the problem exists at all.

The lack of awareness is in part due to the dearth of information about abused parents. We have found that students in schools of social work, psychology, or criminology rarely learn about adolescent violence in the home. In looking at the literature and learning about the advocate training of domestic violence agencies in the United States, we have seen that they rarely include information about adolescent violence, even though it is a concern for survivors of domestic violence. Books in the United States that offer a depth of understanding and speak to a diverse audience are nonexistent. Barbara Cottrell, a Canadian researcher, broke ground in 2001 with her study, *Parent Abuse: The Abuse of Parents by Their Teenage Children,* the first publication to speak directly to this issue. Another title, *Power and Compassion* by Jerome Price, offers valuable advice to family therapists. *Adolescent-to-Parent Abuse* by Amanda Holt is an outstanding addition to the literature. With our backgrounds in family and domestic violence, psychology, counseling, and social work, we hope to begin to fill this gap.

We have learned, through getting to know each teen and parent, and much trial and error, an array of strategies that work for most families regardless of their varied histories and circumstances. We have also learned about the warning signs of abuse that can help parents and teens take action early to head off more serious acts of violence. For parents, certain behaviors are red flags that their teen is escalating. For teens, a new perspective on the impact that abuse can have on family members can lead to genuine change. We have learned how to help parents reestablish boundaries and leadership in the home, while at the same time reconnecting with their teens in more positive, healthy ways. Most importantly, we have learned ways to engage teens in investigating their own behavior and taking responsibility to change it.

We came to our work with this special group of teens and parents in 1997 in King County, Washington (the Seattle area), when we took part in developing an intervention program called Step Up within the juvenile court system for youth with domestic violence charges against parents. It's important to note that these were not teens who were assaulting family members who had abused them (although this often happens). Youth served by this intervention are those who are the primary perpetrators of violence in the home.

The number of King County juvenile domestic violence cases in 1997 was staggering. Approximately 800 to 900 juvenile domestic violence cases were referred to the court every year, with 85 percent being violence against a family member and 65 percent of the victims, parents. These were most often situations where a parent called the police during a violent incident by their teen. Some parents were afraid to have their teen released home from detention because they feared for their safety. The need to address this critical issue resulted in the development of a specialized program for these youth and parents.

At the time, there were no other programs that focused on youth violence in the home. There was little research on this issue and no treatment models to guide us. In spite of considerable research into youth aggression, we found that virtually none of it looked at youth who physically assaulted their parents. From our first contacts with these families, we realized many of the assumptions that even researchers had about these youth and parents were inaccurate. We came to the conclusion that we would have to draw on our past experience in the field of family violence, and that our best resource was likely to be the parents and youth we would be serving. And, indeed, what we learned from the families ultimately shaped our intervention strategies.

Our experience in adult domestic violence with offenders and survivors and parent education is the foundation for our work with teen violence in the home. Lily worked in a variety of capacities with survivors of domestic violence, facilitated a parent's anger management program, authored an anger management and parenting skills curriculum for parents who were abusive with their children, and coauthored a curriculum for parents whose children witnessed domestic violence. Greg facilitated treatment groups for men who were arrested for domestic violence. We were well acquainted with the dynamics and behaviors of family and intimate partner violence. But children abusing parents was new territory.

We knew we had a lot to learn and were faced with many unanswered questions. What dynamics are operating when a teen abuses his or her parent? When a parent is afraid of his or her teen, how is it different from intimate partner violence? Most importantly, what helps an adolescent change abusive and violent behavior?

What helps a parent cope with the violence in the home and parent a child she is afraid of? How can we help teens and parents work together to learn respectful family relationship skills and restore their relationships? The search for answers to these questions led to some unique ways of intervening with these families.

Our biggest challenge in designing an intervention was meeting the needs of both teens and parents. For youth, our intervention initially relied on three sources: cognitive-behavioral strategies, some elements of the Duluth Model's domestic violence approach, and restorative practice. Cognitive-behavioral skills-based strategies made sense because the last 40 years of research on violence and aggression has taught us an important lesson: the best predictor of violence is found by looking at the thoughts and feelings that comprise a person's decision-making process (Bierman, 2007; Farrington, 2007). A person who uses violence perceives, understands, and interprets difficult and conflict-laden situations in a very different way than the person who chooses nonviolent actions. And cognitive-behavioral interventions have been proven effective in the treatment of aggression and violence (Heyman & Slep, 2007). In our own work with men who used violence against their partners, we helped them take steps to understand their internal process—beliefs, thinking, and feelings, along with learning skills to change unhelpful or damaging beliefs and thoughts. Using a similar model with youth, we were confident they could learn about the links between their own thoughts, feelings, and actions and how they have some control in the process, leading to more respectful behaviors.

The Domestic Abuse Intervention Project (DAIP) from Duluth, Minnesota, transformed adult batterer intervention by implementing a comprehensive vision of victim safety. DAIP was instrumental in developing coordinated community responses that created systematic monitoring and tracking of domestic violence cases, developed best practice policies and protocols for intervention agencies, encouraged networking among community domestic violence agencies, and supported a community infrastructure for victim safety. It also developed a comprehensive curriculum for intervening with domestic violence offenders that has become known as the Duluth Model and is based on a feminist cognitive-behavioral approach (Mederos, 2002).

The Duluth Model made accountability for using abuse and violence towards intimate partners an important step in helping adult men change, and in a supportive environment, we felt accountability could be a powerful experience for youth as well. To help teens become accountable, we revised the Duluth Model's Power and Control Wheel and the Equality Wheel to fit teen-parent relationships, renaming them Abuse/Disrespect Wheel and Mutual Respect Wheel. The wheels have become important tools in helping youth understand the difference between abusive and respectful behaviors with family members. By using the wheels, youth could both acknowledge accountability for hurtful behavior and also be motivated to learn new skills that would support nonviolence with family members.

Since the revised wheels included nonviolent, respectful behaviors, youth could use these wheels to identify these behaviors in addition to abusive ones, and so the wheels became tools for a strength-based approach to behavior change.

Using the revised Power and Control/Equality Wheels with parents and teens together led to a "restorative" approach that helped transform their relationship. When teens are directly accountable to parents for their hurtful behavior, they are taking the first steps towards rebuilding their relationship, replacing a parent's fear and anger with trust and respect. Parents also feel their teens are genuinely changing when they hear their teens talk about how destructive abusive behavior is to their relationship.

Restorative practice has its roots in restorative justice, which originated in the 1970s (Daly, 2006). It questioned the effectiveness of simply punishing a wrong-doer when addressing crime and introduced the radically new idea of helping perpetrators understand the effects of their behavior on the victims of their crimes. When there is a personal relationship between a perpetrator and victim, restorative reconciliation process can restore the relationship. Over the last 10 years, restorative justice concepts have expanded to areas outside of criminal justice, into the helping professions, schools, organizations, and even whole towns.

The principles of restorative practice parallel an internal process of moral development that all human beings experience. We are all born with an involuntary, biological response when we witness another person in distress. This response is empathy in its most basic form. We learn more highly developed empathetic responses from our parents throughout our childhood, and when we reach adulthood, most of us have internalized a highly developed empathetic sensitivity. The restorative practices we use trace the same steps in the development of empathy that are universal to us all.

Our work with families is a multilayered approach, weaving together cognitive-behavioral therapy and skill development, in a restorative practice framework, with family safety and respectful family relationships at the center. We apply our practice in a group setting with parents and teens together in a multifamily group, along with separate teen and parent groups. A group approach has many features that contribute to success for families—peer and parent support and feedback, role-playing, observing others practice skills, and most importantly, the power of a group of people to whom each participant is held accountable, and who support and praise each member's efforts and progress. The restorative elements of this model are strengthened in a group setting, as well. However, the essentials of this practice have a broad application beyond a group setting. They can also be applied to individual counseling and family therapy sessions.

The book is divided into two sections. The first provides an overview for understanding adolescent violence in the home where parents are the primary victims. It is relevant to a general audience from different disciplines concerned about the broad social consequences of the problem. As a form of family violence, adolescent violence has similarities and differences with other types of violence in the home. Physical and emotional abuse is discussed in some detail in order to lay the groundwork for understanding the dynamics at work in these families. Factors that put youth at risk for using violence are presented in a developmental context.

The second section describes our intervention model for helping families move through a restorative process from abuse, violence, anger, fear, and powerlessness to nonviolence, understanding, empathy, trust, and respect. We will outline the stages of intervention, beginning with safety and building a framework for safe communication and accountability. Strategies for helping youth increase self-awareness and take responsibility for their own change process through setting weekly goals and self-evaluation of progress will be explained. How to help parents move from being the target of violence to a leadership role in a respectful and peaceful household will be discussed. The restorative practice described above incorporates evidence-based cognitive-behavioral practices that are used in other programs and therapies that address youth aggression. While practitioners may be familiar with some of these practices, we have adapted them specifically for these families. As with any form of family violence, the path towards a more respectful home often begins with support from outside the family that sets the stage to begin work for reconciliation in a safe environment.

## Terminology

We use the word "parent" to refer to any caregiver of the adolescent. The "parent" may include grandparents, foster parents, aunts, uncles, or other family members or friends who are the caretaker for the teen.

Throughout the book we use terms such as "victimized parents" and "abusive teens." These terms are used in the interest of helping the reader understand this issue and not to stereotype the parents or teens. The use of the term "victimized parent" in no way implies helplessness, but simply identifies a parent who is the target of aggression. We never refer to parents as "victims" or teens as "abusers" in our work with them. From our experience, the parents and teens come from a wide variety of economic, religious, and ethnic backgrounds. Neither parents nor teens fit into any "personality type" and cannot be easily categorized. The words "victimized" and "abusive" make the book more readable and are used instead of cumbersome phrases. We have at times used the term "intimate partner violence" to describe domestic violence with adults who are in an intimate relationship.

We have taken great care in removing any details from the testimony of parents and teens that would reveal their identity. The case vignettes are fictitious and each one is a composite based on the actual experiences of many different families.

We developed the model described in this book during our work with King County's Step Up program. Readers who are interested in more information about Step Up can find a complete summary of the program at www.kingcounty. gov/courts/step-up.aspx.

## References

Bierman, K. (2007). Anger and aggression: a developmental perspective. In T. A. Cavell & K. T. Malcolm (Eds.), *Anger, aggression, and interventions for interpersonal violence* (pp. 215–238), Mahwah, NJ: Lawrence Erlbaum Associates.

Cottrell, B. (2001). *Parent abuse: the abuse of parents by their teenage children.* Ottawa: Health Canada.

Daly, K. (2006). The limits of restorative justice. In D. Sullivan & L. Tifft (Eds.), *The handbook of restorative justice* (pp. 134–145), New York: Routledge.

Farrington, D. F. (2007). Origins of violent behavior over the life span. In D. J. Flannery, A. T. Vazsonyi, & I. D. Waldman (Eds.), *The Cambridge handbook of violent behavior and aggression* (pp. 19–48), Cambridge, UK: Cambridge University Press.

Heyman, R. E., & Slep, A.M.S. (2007). Therapeutic treatment approaches to violent behavior. In D. J. Flannery, A. T. Vazsonyi, & I. D. Waldman (Eds.), *The Cambridge handbook of violent behavior and aggression* (pp. 602–617), Cambridge, UK: Cambridge University Press.

Holt, A. (2013). *Adolescent-to-parent abuse.* Bristol, UK: Polity Press.

Mederos, F. (2002). Changing our visions of intervention—the evolution of programs for physically abusive men. In E. Aldarondo & F. Mederos (Eds.), *Programs for men who batter* (pp. 1–23), Kingston, NJ: Civic Research Institute.

Price, J. (1999). *Power and compassion.* New York: Guilford Press.

# Acknowledgments

The clinical work reported in this book was undertaken when we were employed as social workers for King County's Department of Judicial Administration. Meg Crager, King County's Domestic Violence Program Manager, and Kaki Dimock, the At Risk Youth Program Manager in King County's juvenile court, conceived the idea of a program for youth who were arrested for domestic violence against parents. We are particularly grateful to Meg Crager for her insight, encouragement, dedication, and leadership in initiating this intervention. We acknowledge the support of Judge Bobbie Bridge; Paul Sherfey, Chief Administrative Officer of King County Superior Court; Mark Wirschem, Programs Manager; and Bruce Knudson, Juvenile Court Services Director, while the program was being established. Barb Miner and Teresa Bailey, King County Judicial Administration directors, have offered the program much-needed support in difficult economic times. Mary Taylor, our supervisor, has been a great advocate for Step Up.

The three members of the Victim Advocate's Office in the King County's Prosecutor's Office, Stephanie Trollen, Alyssa Schultz, and Rebecca Steiner offer support to victimized parents and collaborate with us on a daily basis. Judge Phillip Hubbard advocated for Step Up after the program's funding was cut. We are grateful to Bill Meyers, our clinical consultant, for his thoughtful comments and insights. We appreciate the referrals from and collaboration with the juvenile court's administration, probation staff, and the diversion program staff. We want to thank the King County Council for their support of our work with the citizens of King County.

We were honored to host three guests from abroad who were interested in our work. Two Winston Churchill Fellowship recipients, Jo Howard from Australia and Lynette Robinson from the United Kingdom, came during the summer of 2010 to learn about our approach and they have generously shared their experiences with colleagues after returning to their respective countries. In 2013 Dr. Rachel Condry from University at Oxford in England travelled to Seattle to meet with us, Step Up parent and teen program participants, and our court's judges and court staff.

We have colleagues in other parts of the United States and abroad who have given us support and inspiration: Hans Giller and Amy Lenz in Toledo, Ohio; Christal Ireland, David Nix, Shannon Hartnett, and Wendy Nussbaum in Dupage, Illinois; and Patti Morris in Peoria, Illinois.

In Australia, Mary McKenna, Rosalie O'Conner, Jeanette Stott and all of the other Walking on Eggshells Project team members with Relationships Australia who developed Step Up South Australia; Jo Howard and her staff who developed Keeping Families Safe at Peninsula Health in Melbourne. In England Paul Morris, Amanda Holt, Helen Bonnick, and Caroline Miles.

Kristie Kujawski first suggested that we write a book and gave us priceless feedback on our manuscript. We appreciate changes Anna Moore, our editor at Routledge Press, suggested after reading the proposal. Nancy Wick, our editor from Enlightened Edits, made invaluable comments that greatly improved this book.

We are especially grateful to the many teens and parents who have taught us about their lives, and how to best help them build nonviolent, respectful relationships.

# one
# Adolescent Violence in the Home

## An Uncharted Territory

The names he calls me ... Oh, they just make me feel disgusted ... I can't repeat them to you. Then an hour later he acts like nothing happened.

I have a bruise on my arm from where she pushed me into the table. I've been wearing long sleeves to hide it for 3 weeks. What would people think?

He really scares me sometimes just with the look on his face. I have to be careful what I say to him. We all walk on eggshells when he is home. You never know what will set him off.

These are the words of parents who are talking about their teenage children. The words of these parents show the anxiety, guilt, and helplessness abused parents experience almost every day. While all parents have these feelings at times, abused parents are living in a different world where they routinely face verbal attacks and physical violence. They are sometimes afraid for themselves and often fear for the safety of their other children, but they are also afraid for their teen. "What will happen to my son if he keeps acting this way?" "Should I have seen something when he was younger that led to this?" "What can I do to stop him from acting this way?" "I don't want his younger brothers and sisters to start doing the same things he's doing."

Yet, when parents do seek professional help, they find that the problem is often not addressed. Parents will say, "We have been in family counseling for over a year and we never really talk about my son's abusive behavior." It is common even for experts who specialize in family violence to disregard the reports from abused parents. Such responses silence parents and keep them from seeking the help they and their child desperately need.

## Three Parents, Three Stories

As we noted in the preface, we have been listening to parents like these and trying to help them make sense of what is happening in their homes for 15 years, and we have learned that every story is both different and the same. Here is Marla's account of what happened with her son Daniel:

> I never know what Daniel will be like when he comes home from school. He went straight to his room and sat down at the computer. I said hello, but he didn't say anything. I used to try to read his father's moods like I'm doing with Daniel now. I could never really figure out his father, Richard, though, and it feels the same with Daniel.
>
> It's been four years since I first called the police on Daniel's dad. He had been kicking Daniel in the stomach with his heavy boots. Daniel's face was getting pale and blank. I had gone to the hospital a couple of times after Richard punched me in the face and slammed my head into the wall. The second time Richard attacked me, Daniel led his brother and sister out the back window to the neighbor's house. I was so proud of him.
>
> Even though we were free of Richard, Daniel's father, I couldn't help thinking that at any minute Richard would march in to tell the kids to stop laughing so loud or not to get the popcorn on the floor. Unfortunately, even within the first week, Daniel began to order his brother and sister around and I felt a knot in my stomach.
>
> I went into Daniel's room to remind him about the counseling appointment. I told him we needed to leave in 10 minutes. After a few minutes, I returned to Daniel's room to tell him to turn off the computer. He just ignored me and continued to play his game so I pressed the off button. Daniel turned toward me and called me a "fucking whore." I reacted quickly and I slapped his face. It was the same thing Richard used to call me and now I was hearing it again from my son. Daniel told me to get out of his room. I said "we need to go."
>
> Daniel picked up a hockey stick that was leaning against his computer table and held it above his head, like he was going to hit me. I ran from the room and he went outside and smashed the back window of the car with the hockey stick. Daniel had come full circle. Just a few months ago he swore he would never be like his dad. Now he was acting just like him. I decided to call the police. I couldn't believe I was doing this.

This story is typical of many we have heard from parents. Marla was dealing with a volatile teen whose violence was escalating, but was frustrated at every turn when she tried to do something about it. The mental health agencies she called suggested more of the same individual counseling he had been doing that had not helped because he didn't disclose what was really going on at home. Plus he often refused to go and she couldn't make him. The domestic violence agencies she was going to for support had been a great help to her but couldn't provide help to her son. She even tried calling Child Protective Services, and she was told they could only serve children who were abused, not parents. When she called the police, they made her feel like she should be a stronger parent, telling her she should "put her foot down, and discipline him more strictly," even suggesting corporal punishment. Marla felt that no one really asked her about how the violence was affecting her and her other children, and when people did ask, her response was not taken seriously. No one really understood what she was going through.

Unlike Daniel, Tanisha didn't grow up in a violent home, and yet, her mother Michelle reported to us that Tanisha was becoming increasingly belligerent and moving towards violence:

Tanisha is 14 years old and we have always been very close until about a year ago when she started spending more time with her friends. Her father and I separated when she was 7 and she sees her father once a month. During this last school year, Tanisha's grades started dropping and she had an in-school suspension for skipping classes. What bothers me the most, though, is Tanisha and a couple of her friends have been hanging out with a group of older boys who are 18 or 19 years old. Right away I told her they were too old for her and she couldn't see them. Tanisha lied to me about being with them after I said that. I am really worried about what they do and where they're going. I grounded her when I found out she was lying to me about seeing them. Now, I realize I can't really stop her. We argue about it all the time.

My parents disciplined me by spanking and slapping me when I was a child. I decided I would never do that to my kids. During the last year as I began to confront Tanisha more about her contact with these older boys, she started swearing at me, calling me foul names, and making really disgusting comments to me. When I grounded Tanisha for the bad language she used, she became more threatening. You know, like getting close to me, getting in my face, pushing past me, throwing things, kicking doors and walls. Finally, one night when I stood in the doorway to stop Tanisha from leaving the house at 11:30 at night, she pushed me out of the way so hard I fell into a table and then she ran out the front door.

Michelle is facing very different issues from Marla. Daniel seems to be taking the role of his abusive father in Marla's household, while Tanisha is just trying to be with her friends. Daniel may have been influenced by his father's behavior in ways he is not fully aware of, while Tanisha is just acting like some of the tough girls she sees at school. However, given what Daniel and Tanisha are doing at home to their mothers, how different are they really? Their behavior may have come from a different source but it's playing out in a similar way.

Let's look at one more family:

> Maureen and I adopted Gabe when he was about a year old and today he is 13. I work as an accountant for a construction business and Maureen is a nurse. Gabe is currently in a special education program for students with behavioral problems in the local middle school. Since he has been in middle school, he has been unable to attend mainstream classes due to his behavior. He was disruptive in class, disturbed other students, and challenged the teacher's authority.
>
> Gabe does not have many friends. He is socially isolated and unpopular. He reacted aggressively to his classmates' teasing and was suspended from school twice for fighting. When Gabe was in grade school, he worked with a therapist and his behavior seemed to improve at home and at school. Gabe had been prescribed medication to stabilize his mood and took it regularly. Gabe still had outbursts: he would yell, swear, and kick or punch walls. By age 11, he would sometimes have two-hour periods when he would yell, argue, and sometimes cry when he was told to turn off the TV or the computer or when we would simply say "no" to something. Overall though, he seemed to be getting better. We don't always agree on how to handle Gabe. I feel he needs very strict rules and consistent consequences, especially when he's violent. I think Maureen is too easy on him. She wants to reason with him about his behavior and get him to agree to make changes.
>
> We were confident Gabe would continue to improve and grow out of his difficult behavior. When he got to middle school, he refused to attend counseling and stopped taking his medication. Then he started directing more of his aggressiveness at us, especially Maureen. He would hit her and threaten her when he didn't get his way. He doesn't do these things to me as much, but when I would step in when he was starting to attack his mother, he would physically challenge me and he has hit me a number of times. Finally, we decided to call the police. We didn't know what else to do.

John and Maureen have a very different child than either Marla or Michelle. Unlike Daniel, he hasn't grown up in a violent home, and unlike either of the others, he's been violent from an early age. In fact, the three children don't seem to have much in common with each other. Their personalities, interests, and backgrounds are very different. However, all the parents are struggling with abuse that is directed towards them and looking for relief from the chaos at home.

## What the Numbers Tell Us

The problem of violence and abuse by children towards parents is widespread, and the numbers are much larger than most people imagine. Research on parent

abuse shows significant numbers of families each year are affected by teen violence at home. One of the few research reports from the mid-1970s estimated
millions of parents were abused each year by their teenagers (Cornell & Gelles,
1982). These numbers only include reports of specific kinds of physical violence,
like hitting, and not the wide range of other kinds of physical violence. Unfortunately, the lack of research on parent abuse prevents the public from recognizing
it as an important social issue.

Furthermore, these numbers don't reflect the widespread emotional abuse
towards parents that is endemic to anyone facing physical abuse. The name-
calling, threats, humiliation, and extensive property destruction are all part of an
abusive relationship (Ganley, 1989). The pattern of emotional abuse reinforces
and supports the physical abuse, but also carries its own destructive psychological punch apart from the physical violence. Among women who are survivors of
abuse from a partner, about half report that emotional abuse causes the greatest
harm (Follingstad et al., 1990). When we talk to parents, they agree that emotional
abuse often feels as destructive as physical abuse.

## A Blind Spot for Professionals

When we give workshops about adolescent to parent violence, some professionals
think we are ignoring an obvious fact: teens that we are describing as violent are
simply protecting themselves from an abusive and violent parent. It's true that
some adolescents are victims of violence and abuse by parents (Haber & Toro,
2009), and by appealing for recognition of parent abuse, we in no way mean to
diminish the pain and suffering of teens who are abused by parents. Public recognition of parent violence towards adolescents is lacking in much the same way
adolescent to parent violence lacks recognition. Child abuse laws were passed to
protect young children, and while these laws are meant to protect adolescents, in
reality adolescents who experience violence at home often have little protection
and face long-term developmental problems. But although we recognize violence
can be enacted both ways in parent-teen relationships, our focus is teens who are
not currently being abused and who initiate violence against parents and family
members.

Adolescent violence towards parents can also be confusing for professionals
because teens are not consistently argumentative, belligerent, and confronta-
tional. Parents report their teens able, kind, and considerate some of the time, yet
become violent at other times. Teachers report they are respectful and helpful in
their classrooms. Parents of their teen's friends see them as model children when
they are in their homes. These youth are seldom the schoolyard bullies most people think they might be and are not consistently aggressive towards peers. Outside
of their families, these youth are often not necessarily conspicuous for their hostility or malevolence towards others.

## Patterns of Abuse

Youth who are violent in the home can develop different patterns of abuse. Some youth have never used physical violence against a parent, but they use an array of verbal attacks and demeaning comments to assert power. Other youth have assaulted their parent one time and felt they crossed a line they shouldn't have, and return exclusively to emotional attacks. Still others have physically assaulted a parent many times. Youth who develop a pattern of abuse have adopted a belief that, at least in some circumstances, "might makes right" and that verbal and physical attacks are legitimate.

In spite of the differences among youth who are violent at home, we can say they share some qualities: they are less able to manage difficult emotions like irritability, anger, and frustration, and their decision-making process restricts them to more aggressive solutions when they have conflicts with family members. No easy answers exist to help us understand these youth, but we do know many of them have influences in their lives that make it more likely they will choose abuse and violence. The most apparent factor, to be discussed later, is exposure to violence at home. Growing up with violence can have a powerful, lasting effect on the way we respond emotionally and cognitively to difficult situations. Other factors that can influence a youth towards using aggressive behavior include being victimized physically and emotionally, being affected by drugs or alcohol, and having a mental health diagnosis.

Parents talk about "walking on eggshells" when their teen gets upset. They don't want to say or do something that will "set them off." Their adolescent children are described as having "Jekyll and Hyde" personalities because they can be pleasant one minute and unbearable the next (Edenborough et al., 2008). Parents are left feeling confused and hurt and don't know what to do about the problem.

## Parent Abuse Is Unique

The description above should sound familiar to those of us who have some understanding of domestic violence, but we believe that abused parents are different from other survivors of violence at home. To explain how, we need to begin by talking about power.

Power relations lie at the heart of family and interpersonal violence, and often social and cultural norms support the power that one person has over another in these close relationships (Gelles & Straus, 1988; Tew & Nixon, 2010). Sometimes power in relationships is inherently oppressive. For instance, in patriarchal societies men have more power and influence than women, and men are socialized to take charge in intimate relationships. In Western societies for centuries, legal, literary, historical, and religious writings sanctioned the use of physical violence by husbands against wives (Dobash & Dobash, 1979).

Research on family violence concludes "wife abuse" happens more often when power is concentrated in the hands of the husband (Straus, Gelles & Steinmetz, 1980). Violence against women is one of the consequences of unequal power in patriarchal societies.

In other cases, power is part of a role one person is playing in relation to another person. For instance, a parent has more power than an infant and a middle-aged adult has more power than his or her elderly, Alzheimer's-stricken parent. In these cases, power is part of a caring, nurturing, and protective role one person is playing in relation to another, and social norms support the power of one person over another in order to fulfill responsibilities for care. However, the use of power in these relationships can become oppressive and abusive if misused. Three family violence researchers conclude, "In addition, power differentials often exist among family members: Children are subordinate to parents, elderly parents may be subordinate to their adult children, and wives may be subordinate to husbands. The result is that the powerless sometimes become targets of aggression" (Barnett, Miller-Perrin & Perrin, 2005, p. 4). Both types of power described above are given some measure of social support.

Parent abuse doesn't fit this model. Social and cultural norms give parents more power than adolescent children in families, for important reasons. Parents control the family's resources, like money, power, status, decision making, and even the right to use violence. Considerable social pressure is exerted on parents to take charge in families with the expectation that parents will control family matters, including their children. Parents who are not "in control" of their teenagers feel derided and rejected. In spite of these widely held social and cultural norms that support parental power in the family, teen violence and abuse against their parents is widespread. One report concluded adolescent aggression towards a parent is "an explicit marker of power struggles in the authority relationship" (Evans & Warren-Sohlberg, 1988). Teens who use violence against their parents don't have the support of traditional social and cultural norms that, for instance, adult males do when they use violence against their female partners. Other social norms may support abuse and violence, but they are not part of the role of a child in a family.

A second reason parent abuse is radically different from other kinds of abuse is that, in spite of the violence, parents are inextricably bound to their teens by their parental commitment to raise and guide them. Parents continue to be legally and morally responsible for their child, even after parents are victimized. Victims of partner abuse have the possibility and sometimes the resources to separate from their abuser. Great efforts are made to find safe places for victims of partner abuse, and victim advocates spend much of their time developing safety plans for survivors of violence. On the other hand, parents in most cases want desperately to develop a closer relationship with their child, not a more distant one, even after being abused. Parents do not want no-contact orders or protection orders that would require long-term separation from their child. Even in cases where parents must temporarily separate from their abusive child, they eventually want to work towards a closer connection with them. Most parents' first concern is getting help for their teen so that the violence and abuse will stop and the relationship can be restored.

Finally, a third important difference is parents' concern for their child's future relationships. Parents often seek help outside their family, even calling the police, in part because they are worried their child will abuse other people in their future family and intimate relationships. Often mothers who are victims of domestic violence are seeing their children repeat the same violence their father used against her. They are worried their child will use violence in their future relationships.

In a foreword to the 2002 *World Report on Violence and Health* (Dahlberg & Krug, 2002, p. ix), Nelson Mandela noted that the suffering caused by violence "is a legacy that reproduces itself, as new generations learn from the violence of generations past, as victims learn from victimizers, and as the social conditions that nurture violence are allowed to continue. No country, no city, no community is immune from it." We would add no family or interpersonal relationship is immune from it either. The act of one person intentionally hurting another person has a ripple effect from one person to the next and from one generation to the next. Parents of abusive youth and, especially mothers, witness the transmission of this legacy of violence to the next generation.

## Parent Abuse Is Different from Partner Abuse

While in the next few chapters we will describe physical and emotional forms of abuse that parallel adult domestic violence, adolescent to parent violence should not be conflated with adult intimate partner violence. There are significant differences between the two. Intimate relationships where one adult is using a pattern of abuse towards the other adult are often characterized by possessiveness, jealousy, intrusiveness, and attempts to isolate the other person from others in their social world. At first, specific behaviors can be very subtle and difficult for the victim to identify. They often develop slowly. When these kinds of abusive tactics are successful, the victim withdraws from others and becomes more and more isolated. The lack of support and the isolation makes them vulnerable to control by the abuser. While these dynamics may be common for intimate partner abuse, they are not for adolescent to parent abuse.

Economic abuse and sexual abuse are two forms of abuse that are particularly relevant to the dynamics of intimate partner abuse. While youth behave in ways that are very costly for their parents, such as destroying property or stealing money and using credit cards, we would not consider these behaviors the same as economic abuse in an intimate partner relationship because the outcome of these behaviors does not lead to the control of the family finances. In adult relationships, the outcome of behaviors associated with economic abuse is restricting the freedom and independence of the intended victim and making them financially dependent on the abuser. In our experience youth do not behave this way.

Sexual abuse, like economic abuse, is an attempt to control an intimate other; it represents one of the most viciously intrusive forms of abuse. When youth verbally attack their mothers using sexual references or sexualized language, they are certainly engaging in a kind of sexual harassment or abuse. While this language is an attempt to sexually degrade and humiliate their mothers, it does not include the threat or use of coercive physical sexual abuse. We have never encountered any parent or youth who gave any indication that physical, sexual abuse has occurred or found evidence to suggest that it exists.

## Parent Abuse Is Similar to Other Abuse

Although parent abuse is unique in some ways, it resembles other types of violence in close relationships in that it is a pattern of behaviors directed at achieving compliance or control in a relationship (Ganley, 1989; Pagelow, 1984). Emerge, a domestic violence agency in Boston, defines domestic violence as "forcing one's partner to do something that they don't want to do or preventing them from doing what they want to do" (Emerge, 2011). In other words, parent abuse, like intimate partner violence, is not a group of random, discrete behaviors the teen just happens to act out; the behaviors are linked together and have the effect of usurping his or her parent's power in the family. Although adolescence is a time when teens learn to navigate a way between their perceived needs and their parent's limits, most teens find avenues that lead to independence and autonomy in a healthy, nonviolent way. Some teens use abuse or violence in isolated and extreme circumstances. Others, however, develop patterns of abuse and violence that undermine a parent's decision-making authority. While adult male batterers demand control in many areas of their partner's life, a teen's demand for control is usually limited to what is relevant to his or her current situation. As we will discuss later, parents face abuse and violence when they are simply carrying out the more difficult parts of parenting an adolescent, like limit setting and imposing consequences.

Victimized parents, as many victims of family violence, experience a range of abusive tactics on a regular basis. Typically, the abuse occurs as a part of a continuum from emotional and verbal abuse to physical assaults and threats to kill. When teens use the range of behaviors between physical violence and emotional abuse, they are usually trying to get what they want by dominating and controlling their parent. The routine use of yelling, name-calling, put-downs, property destruction, and assault makes it impossible to adequately parent a child. Many parents are familiar with behaviors in isolation, but when they are used together and often, the impact is debilitating for parents. Even the fear that a child might use violence or carry out a verbal tirade leads parents to second-guess their parenting decisions.

Finally, family violence in all its forms, including parent abuse, is hidden from public view. One of the first popular books that summarized the results of a nationwide study on family violence is titled *Behind Closed Doors* (Straus, Gelles & Steinmetz, 1980). One of the few books on sibling abuse is called *Sibling Abuse: Hidden Physical, Emotional, and Sexual Trauma* (Wiehe, 1997), and this author refers to sibling abuse as an "undetected problem." Other authors who write about family violence use similar phrases, like "behind the curtain," that describe the social invisibility of family violence. When statistics on the recorded cases and incidence of child abuse, elder abuse, or abuse of women are published in official reports, the authors often preface their remarks by cautioning the reader that the numbers in the report do not reflect the "true extent of the problem" or they give the reader only an "approximate idea of its true dimensions" (Garcia, 2003).

The secrecy of parent abuse may lead to some parental reactions that seem strange to those who haven't experienced such violence. In some cases, victimized parents themselves don't recognize violent behavior from their sons and daughters as abuse, or in other cases, they feel responsible for the abuse and try to excuse it. At first, some try to ignore the severity of the behavior, in the hope that it will go away. Others explain it away as something they have to live with as a part of their children's mental health or trauma reaction. Many parents feel the violence is their fault because they didn't parent well enough or allowed their child to be abused or exposed to domestic violence. Still other parents believe their child is going through a phase that he or she will outgrow. We will discuss these parent reactions in greater detail in Chapter 2.

## What We Know

Parent abuse has been described as one of the most taboo of all forms of family violence (Edenborough, Jackson, Mannix & Wilkes, 2008; Stewart, Jackson, Wilkes & Mannix, 2006; Straus, Gelles & Steinmetz, 1980). It has garnered the least interest in research and practically no funding for intervention or support for parents. Two family violence scholars (Gelles & Cornell, 1985, p. 96) get to the heart of the matter: "The idea of children attacking their parents is so foreign to our conceptions of parent-child relations that it is difficult for most of us to believe that such behavior occurs." Social attitudes about the people involved in parent abuse and the other forms of family violence are a barrier to solving this problem. However, there is some history of research into the subject.

Adolescent violence against parents was first documented in an article entitled, "Battered Parents: A New Syndrome," which appeared in the *American Journal of Psychiatry* in 1979. Two practitioners—a physician and a psychologist—who specialized in working with violent adults, adolescents, and families at the University of Maryland hospital began a pilot project with a small group of assaultive adolescents and their parents. When they discovered some of the youth were targeting their parents, the authors felt compelled to write about the disturbing trend they were witnessing. The message in the final paragraph was that health professionals need to identify and treat this distinct form of family violence (Harbin & Madden, 1979). Unfortunately, their plea fell on deaf ears. The only reference to adolescent to parent violence in the popular press during this time was in an obscure quote in a 1981 *U.S. News and World Report* magazine article by Stanley Wellborn, that focused on "troubled teens." The quote from the article echoes the concern expressed above,

> "Parent abuse" is also becoming evident in the courts, where parents seek restraining orders against their belligerent children. Deputy Inspector Thomas Gallagher of the New York Police Department youth-services section—a father of seven—says flatly: "Some parents are afraid of their own children."
>
> (p. 42)

For many years after the initial 1979 article, surprisingly few research articles appeared on the topic of parent abuse, and in many of those that were published, the results were inconsistent and even contradictory (Walsh & Krienert, 2007; Kennair & Mellor, 2007). A brief look at some of the results reveals how difficult this topic is to grasp. The prevalence of youth violence towards parents in these early studies ranged widely, from 5 percent to 29 percent of all families (Agnew & Huguley, 1989; Browne & Hamilton, 1998; Bobic, 2004; Cornell & Gelles, 1982; Cottrell & Monk, 2004; Evans & Warren-Sohlberg, 1988; Kratcoski, 1985; Livingston, 1986; Paulson, Coombs & Landsverk, 1990; Peek, Fischer & Kidwell, 1985). A recent review of the literature covering more than 30 years of research doesn't even attempt to identify a prevalence rate (Hong et al., 2012).

The research does not agree on some basic demographics, such as the gender of the victimizers and victims. While most studies indicate boys are responsible for most of the violence (Agnew & Huguley, 1989; Cornell & Gelles, 1982; Evans & Warren-Sohlberg, 1988; Langhinrichsen-Rohling & Neidig, 1995; Laurent & Derry, 1999; Paulson et al., 1990), others show both boys and girls participate in the violence (Cottrell, 2001; Walsh & Krienert, 2009; Gebo, 2007; Nock & Kazdin, 2002). Many studies pointed to mothers as the most likely victims (Paulson, Coombs & Landsverk, 1990; McCloskey & Lichter, 2003; Agnew & Huguley, 1989; Edenborough et al., 2008; Evans & Warren-Sohlberg, 1988; Ibabe, Juareguizar & Diaz, 2009), but one study found fathers were the primary victims (Peek, Fischer & Kidwell, 1985).

Research on significant family factors repeated the incongruous conclusions described above. Some studies indicate white, European American families experience more violence than African American families (Agnew & Huguley, 1989; Charles, 1979; Nock & Kazdin, 2002), while other researchers indicate no differences (Cornell & Gelles, 1982; Paulson et al., 1990). Some find violence most common among families of middle or higher socioeconomic status (Charles, 1986; Paulson, Coombs & Landsverk, 1990; Nock & Kazdin, 2002), while others see it as a lower income phenomenon (Cottrell & Monk, 2004). Social class seems to have little influence for another group of researchers (Agnew & Huguley, 1989; Paulson et al., 1990; Peek et al., 1985).

Discussion of family functioning in the research often obscured the relationships between youth and parents in these families. "Weak emotional bonds," "overly permissive parenting," and "patterns of parentification" serve as causes for violence among many of the early researchers. But do these features come before the onset of youth violence and help generate it? Or are they part of its aftermath? For some researchers, these terms confounded causes of violence with its consequences. In the coming chapters, abused parents themselves will give the reader a more nuanced and complete understanding of their family relationships. We will also include relevant research in our discussion of teens and parents.

## Beyond Academia: The View from Abroad

Much like the United States, researchers from Spain, France, England, Japan, New Zealand, Canada, and Australia have published articles in professional journals that speak to a very limited audience. However, unlike the United States, interest in some of these countries has moved beyond the narrow confines of the academic arena to professionals who encounter these families. Health Canada, a government health agency, offered the first book (Cottrell, 2001) on parent abuse to the public. The New Zealand Family Violence Clearinghouse (2007) and the Australian Domestic and Family Violence Clearinghouse (Bobic, 2004) both list parent abuse on their family violence fact sheets and link readers to professional articles about adolescent to parent violence. The Ministry of Social Development in New Zealand makes parent abuse part of their nationwide campaign, called "It's Not OK" (2012), to end all forms of family violence. A community agency in Melbourne, Australia, published a 22-page, full-color pamphlet entitled, "Adolescent Violence to Parents" (Friend, Howard & Parker, 2008) that gives information ranging from a description of abusive behaviors to suggestions for parents and family members on how to respond to adolescent violence. The Queensland Centre for Domestic and Family Violence Research (2009), also in Australia, identifies parent abuse as a form of family violence and developed materials for the general public.

From Australia and England we now have examples of research that moves beyond traditional academic interest. Interviews of 185 mothers of abusive children resulted in a qualitative study that contextualized the experience of becoming a victimized parent. These women in their own words described how their experience was minimized and devalued by those around them and how little opportunity they had for changing their situation (Edenborough et al., 2008). Another qualitative study on child to mother violence that was also based on interviews with mothers revealed that violence, fear, and shame were central features of their parenting experience (Jackson, 2003). A third study interviewed 60 mothers in three different age groups and interviewed them again five years later (Stewart,

Burns & Leonard, 2007). The study initially focused on these women's experiences with aging, but as the interviews progressed, many of these mothers revealed they were victims of violence from their children. In each of these studies, mothers spoke directly about their experience as victims of their children's violence.

Three unique reports, again from Australia and England, are based on parent experiences of adolescent violence in the family. A public phone-in about adolescent violence in the home was held in November 2008 in Adelaide, Australia, and respondents were asked about specific violent behaviors, the impact of the violence on family members, what assistance was sought, and suggestions for addressing the problem. The report contains an abundance of detail that allows the reader to get an intimate look at these families from the inside (McKenna, O'Conner & Verco, 2010). The second report came from Family Lives, a national charity in England that publically advocates for parents on a variety of family issues including adolescent violence. Parentline Plus, a program created by Family Lives, has been reporting for years about the overwhelming number of calls about teen violence that they receive on their confidential helpline. In 2011, Family Lives issued an update to a 2010 report entitled, *When Family Life Hurts: Family Experience of Aggression in Children* (Family Lives, 2011). The update alone analyzed almost 40,000 calls of a duration of 20 minutes or more over a one-year period and concluded the vast majority of callers were concerned about their child's aggression at home. It's a story that had national significance since it first appeared in *The Observer* in 2000 (McVeigh, 2000) and also in the *BBC News Magazine* in 2009 (Winterman, 2009). The third report of parent experiences relied on two online message boards to glean firsthand accounts of violence from parents' posted messages and revealed narratives of powerlessness and hopelessness (Holt, 2011). These three reports offer a unique opportunity to understand adolescent violence and speak to the need for public support.

Finally, a heightened awareness among professionals has led to national conferences in England and Australia that have brought together justice officials, researchers, practitioners, and policy makers who are trying to develop new interventions and change public policy (Condry, 2013; Wise, 2013). Two internet sites in England, Holes in Walls and APV (Adolescent to Parent Violence Project), are exclusively devoted to parent abuse. Excellent programs in both of these countries have been developed to address this problem (No to Violence, 2013; Holt, 2013).

The United States needs to catch up to the efforts that have been made in other countries, as described above. Parents who are abused by their adolescent children deserve the attention that other victims of family violence receive. They should not be overlooked by the public, researchers, or members of the social service and public policy communities as they are today. While considerable progress has been made in effective response to other forms of family violence, such as elder abuse, intimate partner violence, and child abuse, adolescent violence towards parents has not been recognized as a serious issue deserving of such attention.

## Summary

Even for those familiar with family and domestic violence, parent abuse is uncharted territory. Parents are overwhelmed by feelings of guilt, anxiety, and helplessness, and professionals are often at a loss about how to respond. The lack of community support for abused parents compounds an already devastating predicament for these parents. Professionals can support abused parents when they understand how their situations are both similar to and different from other forms of family violence. By shedding light on their situation, we can begin to understand how to help these families.

## References

Agnew, R., & Huguley, S. (1989). Adolescent violence toward parents. *Journal of Marriage and the Family*, 51, 699–711.

Barnett, O., Miller-Perrin, C. L., & Perrin, R. D. (2005). *Family violence across the lifespan*. Thousand Oaks, CA: Sage.

Bobic, N. (2004). Adolescent violence towards parents. Topic paper from Australian Domestic and Family Violence Clearinghouse. Retrieved from http: www.adfvc.unsw.edu.au/PDF%20files/adolescent_violence.pdf

Browne, K. D., & Hamilton, C. E. (1998). Physical violence between young adults and their parents: associations with a history of child maltreatment. *Journal of Family Violence*, 5(4), 59–79.

Charles, A. V. (1986). Physically abused parents. *Journal of Family Violence*, 1(4), 343–355.

Condry, R. (2013). APV conference, September 23, 2013, St. Hilda's College, University of Oxford, England. Retrieved from http://apv.crim.ox.ac.uk/apv-conference-23-september-2013/

Cornell, C. P., & Gelles, R. J. (1982). Adolescent-to-parent violence. *Urban Social Change Review*, 15(1), 8–14.

Cottrell, B. (2001). *Parent abuse: the abuse of parents by their teenage children*. Ottawa: Health Canada.

Cottrell, B., & Monk, P. (2004). Adolescent-to-parent abuse: a qualitative overview of common themes. *Journal of Family Issues*, 25(8), 1072–1095.

Dahlberg, L. L., & Krug, E. G. (2002). Violence-a global health problem. In E. G. Krug, L. L. Dahlberg, J. A. Mercy, A. B. Zwi, & L. L. Lozano (Eds.), *World report on violence and health* (pp. 1–21), Geneva, Switzerland: World Health Organization.

Dobash, E. R., & Dobash, R. (1979). *Violence against wives*. New York: Free Press.

Edenborough, M., Jackson, D., Mannix, J., & Wilkes, L. M. (2008). Living in the red zone: the experience of child-to-mother violence. *Child and Family Social Work*, 13, 464–473.

Emerge. (2011). Domestic Violence FAQ page. Retrieved September 15, 2011, from www.emergedv.com

Evans, E. D., & Warren-Sohlberg, L. (1988). A pattern of analysis of adolescent abusive behavior toward parents. *Journal of Adolescent Research*, 3(2), 201–216.

Family Lives. (2011). When family life hurts: family experience of aggression in children. Retrieved from http://pelorous.totallyplc.com/public/cms/209/432/256/391/the_aggression_report_2011_family_lives.pdf?realName=2xCtiO.pdf

Follingstad, D. R., Rutledge, L. L., Berg, B. J., Hause, E. S., & Polek, D. S. (1990). The role of emotional abuse in physically abusive relationships. *Journal of Family Violence*, 5, 107–210.

Friend, D., Howard, J., & Parker, T. (2008). *Adolescent violence to parents.* South Melbourne, Australia: Inner South Community Health Center.

Ganley, A. L. (1989). Integrating feminist and social learning analyses of aggression: creating multiple models for men who batter. In P. L. Caesar & L. K. Hamberger (Eds.), *Treating men who batter* (pp. 196–235). New York: Springer Publishing.

Garcia, E. (2003). Social visibility and tolerance to family violence. *Psychology in Spain,* 7(1), 39–45.

Gebo, E. (2007). A family affair: the juvenile court and family violence cases. *Journal of Family Violence,* 22, 501–509.

Gelles, R. J., & Cornell, C. P. (1985). *Intimate violence in families.* Beverley Hills: Sage.

Gelles, R. J., & Straus, M. (1988). *Intimate violence.* Beverley Hills: Sage.

Haber, M. G., & Toro, P. A. (2009). Parent-adolescent violence and later behavioral health problems among homeless and housed youth. *American Journal of Orthopsychiatry,* 79(3), 305–318.

Harbin, H., & Maddin, D. (1979). Battered parents: a new syndrome. *American Journal of Psychiatry,* 136, 1288–1291.

Holt, A. (2011). 'The terrorist in my home': teenagers' violence towards parents—constructions of parent experiences in public online message boards. *Child and Family Social Work,* 16(4), 454–463.

Holt, A. (2013). *Adolescent-to-parent abuse: current understanding in research, policy and practice.* Bristol, UK: Policy Press.

Hong, J. S., Kral, M. J., Espelage, D. L., & Allen-Meares, P. (2012). The social ecology of adolescent-initiated parent abuse: a review of the literature. *Child Psychiatry and Human Development,* 43, 431–454.

Ibabe, I., Jaureguizar, J., & Dias, O. (2009). Adolescent violence against parents: is it a consequence of gender inequality? *The European Journal of Psychology Applied to Legal Context,* 1 (1), 3–24.

It's Not OK. Campaign from the Ministry of Social Development in New Zealand. Retrieved January 12, 2012, from www.areyouok.org.nz/files/Parent_abuse_forweb.pdf

Jackson, D. (2003). Broadening constructions of family violence: mothers' perspectives of aggression from their children. *Child and Family Social Work,* 8, 321–329.

Kennair, N., & Mellor, D. (2007). Parent abuse: a review. *Child Psychiatry and Human Development,* 38, 203–219.

Kratcoski, P. C. (1985). Youth violence directed towards significant others. *Journal of Adolescence,* 8, 145–157.

Krug, E. G., Dahlberg, L. L., Mercy, J. A., Zwi, A. B., & Lozano, L. L (Eds.). (2002). *World Report on Violence and Health.* Geneva, Switzerland: World Health Organization.

Langhinrichsen-Rohling, J., & Neidig, P. (1995). Violent backgrounds of economically disadvantaged youth: risk factors for perpetrating violence? *Journal of Family Violence,* 10(4), 379–398.

Laurent, A., & Derry, A. (1999). Violence of French adolescents towards their parents. *Journal of Adolescent Health,* 25(1), 21–26.

Livingston, L. R. (1986). Children's violence to single mothers. *Journal of Sociology and Social Welfare,* 13(4), 920–933.

McCloskey, L. A., & Lichter, E. (2003). Childhood exposure to marital violence and adolescent aggression: psychological mediators in the cycle of violence. *Journal of Interpersonal Violence,* 18, 1–23.

McKenna, M., O'Connor, R., & Verco, J. (2010). *Exposing the dark side of parenting: A report of parents' experiences of child and adolescent family violence.* Regional Alliance Addressing Child & Adolescent Family Violence in the Home, South Australia.

McVeigh, T. (2000). Families at war as spoilt teens hit out. *The Observer*, April 8, p. 7.

New Zealand Family Violence Clearinghouse. (2007). Overview of Family Violence Fact Sheet. Retrieved May 5, 2013, from www.nzfvc.org.nz/sites/nzfvc.org.nz/files/factsheet-overview-1.pdf

Nock, M. K., & Kazdin, A. E. (2002). Parent-directed physical aggression by clinic-referred youths. *Journal of Clinical Child Psychology*, 31(2), 193–205.

No to Violence. (2013). Adolescent violence in the home: mapping the Australian and international service system. Retrieved August 18, 2013, from http://ntv.org.au/wp-content/uploads/121115-AVITH-report.pdf

Pagelow, M. D. (1984). *Family violence*. New York: Praegar.

Paulson, M. J., Coombs, R. H., & Landsverk, J. (1990). Youth who physically assault their parents. *Journal of Family Violence*, 5(2), 121–133.

Peek, C. W., Fischer, J. L., & Kidwell, J. S. (1985). Teenage violence toward parents: a neglected dimension of family violence. *Journal of Marriage and the Family*, 47(4), 1051–1058.

Queensland Centre for Domestic and Family Violence Research. (2009). Adolescent-to-Parent Abuse—The Facts. Retrieved May 15, 2013, from www.noviolence.com.au/public/factsheets/adol2parweb.pdf

Sellick-Lane, L. (2004). King County Prosecutor's Office, Juvenile Division Report. (unpublished report).

Sheehan, M. (1997). Adolescent violence—strategies, outcomes and dilemmas in working with young people and their families. *Australian and New Zealand Journal of Family Therapy*, 18(2), 80–91.

Stewart, M., Burns, A., & Leonard, R. (2007). Dark side of mothering role: abuse of mothers by adolescent and adult children. *Sex Roles*, 56, 183–191.

Stewart, M., Jackson, D., Mannix, J., & Lines, K. (2004). Current state of knowledge on child-to-mother violence: a literature review. *Contemporary Nurse*, 18, 199–210.

Stewart, M., Jackson, D., Wilkes, L. M., & Mannix, J. (2006). Child-to-mother violence: a pilot study. *Contemporary Nurse*, 21(2), 297–310.

Straus, M., Gelles, R., & Steinmetz, S. (1980). *Behind closed doors*. Garden City, NY: Anchor Books.

Tew, J., & Nixon, J. (2010). Parent abuse: opening up a discussion of a complex instance of family power relations. *Social Policy & Society*, 9(4), 579–589.

Walsh, J. A., & Krienert, J. L. (2007). Child-parent violence: an empirical analysis of offender, victim and event characteristics in a national sample of reported incidents. *Journal of Family Violence*, 22, 563–574.

Walsh, J. A. & Krienert, J. L. (2009). A decade of child-initiated family violence: comparative analysis of child-parent violence and parricide examining offender, victim, and event characteristics in a national sample of reported incidents, 1995-2005. *Journal of Interpersonal Violence*, 24, 1450–1477.

Wellborn, S. (1981). Troubled teenagers. *U.S. News and Report*, December 14, pp. 40–43.

Wiehe, V. R. (1997). *Sibling abuse: hidden physical, emotional, and sexual trauma*. New York: Sage.

Winterman, D. (2009). Abused by their children. *BBC News Magazine*, November 23.

Wise, S. (2013). Be kind to your mother: adolescent violence on the rise. *ProBono Australia*. Retrieved May 15, 2013, from www.probonoaustralia.com.au/news/2013/02/be-kind-your-mother-adolescent-violence-rise

## two
# Physical Abuse

I can't believe I'm sitting here with a black eye. My daughter came home at 3:00 am and all I did was ask her why she was so late. I was so worried something happened to her.

Last night David was talking to his mother about his failing grades. I heard his voice get louder and I went to see what was going on. He was yelling at his mother and was walking towards her. I got between her and David and he pushed and hit me.

Each one of these parents is baffled by their teen's behavior. None of the parents' demands are unusual, but all of them have witnessed an escalation in their teen's behavior from being disrespectful to physically abusive over a few months and sometimes years. Fear has crept into their decisions about how to respond. At times, their relationship with their teens is close and enjoyable. During these times, they feel hopeful that the abuse was just a phase that has come to an end. Unfortunately, for many it is just the high point in the roller coaster existence they are living with their teen. Just when they are feeling confident to venture into talking with their teen about difficult topics, such as curfews and homework, there is another outburst of violence towards them or others in the family.

## Defining Physical Abuse

The most common definition of violence is physical force used against another person. Physical force can range from pinching and slapping to hitting with a fist or threatening with a weapon. When researchers investigate family violence, they don't just ask people general questions about "physical abuse" or "violence" in their family. They ask about specific types of forceful behaviors that family members use against each other to determine the severity and extent of violence in a family (Gelles, 1979). Let's start with some examples that demonstrate the range of violent behaviors used against parents.

> My daughter had hit me before so when she started yelling and walking towards me, I grabbed her by the arms to stop her. When I did, she bit my arm until it bled. I had a deep bruise on that spot for a month.
>
> I had a bandage wrapped around my finger because it was sprained and I was supposed to keep it straight so it would heal. I was trying to separate my son from his brother since they were starting to argue and I didn't want them to fight. He grabbed my sprained finger and bent it back until it broke.
>
> He was so mad that I took his iPod away, he pushed me with all his might into the wall. One side of my face and my arm hit the wall and I bounced back until I lost my balance and fell down. The next day I had a black eye and a big bruise on my arm.

Physical abuse of a parent can be defined as any behavior that intends to physically hurt or harm that parent (Dahlberg & Krug, 2002). The legal system uses the term physical assault or battery to describe physical abuse. As you can see from the examples above, harm done to the parent often results in some physical injury, but not always. Some parents are assaulted one time and others face routine physical assaults that may be weekly or once every few months. In still other circumstances the intention to hurt or harm is in the eyes of the victim. For instance, when a teen's behavior starts escalating and parents or other family members are afraid they are going to get hurt, according to the law in some jurisdictions in the United States that behavior is considered assaultive, even though there is no physical contact.

> He didn't realize he even hurt me until later. I know he didn't mean to do it.
>
> She gets so upset she doesn't realize what she's doing. I know she doesn't really want to hurt me.
>
> His dad and I just separated and he's really mad about it. Last night he slapped me and said he was going to kill me. I don't think he really wants to hurt me. I have hidden all the knives though.

We hear parents say their child didn't really intend to hurt them and youth also say they didn't really set out to injure their parent. So how can we say physical abuse is a behavior that intends to hurt someone? First, even though youth may not have intended to cause their parents an injury, they certainly intended to use force. Most people who use violence in an interpersonal relationship don't calculate the precise way they are going to injure the other person. Secondly, when youth do use force against their parents, they often do not think of it or define it as "violence" at the time they are committing the act. So intentionality doesn't mean a youth has made a calculated plan to injure their parent. It simply means they used force against their parent (Dahlberg & Krug, 2002).

## When Physical Abuse Begins

When we inquire about what age the violence began, there seem to be three different types of reports: since early childhood, during the teen years, or at an age when the child experienced a particular life experience that was difficult or traumatic. Physical violence can begin in different stages of a child's development. Some teens have exhibited violent behavior since they were very young, while others begin using violent behaviors during their adolescent years. Let's consider these three examples:

Alex has used violence with people around him since he was young. Even when he was in day care, Alex used to punch and kick some of the other kids when he got mad and one time he even stabbed another child with scissors. His mother, Brenda, has put a great deal of time and effort into learning ways to parent that would help Alex with his aggressive behavior. Alex has been in counseling off and on since grade school, along with various rounds of psychotropic medications recommended by psychiatrists and pediatricians. For periods of time, even a couple of years, Alex's behavior improved. In middle school, however, the violence and aggression returned and with his increased size and strength, his mother found she was afraid of him. He was acting much like he used to when he was little when she would tell him "no"—with arguing and yelling escalating to pushing, shoving, and throwing things as she held her ground. Alex's mother became fearful for the safety of herself and her younger children. He has been living at his grandparents for a month due to his behavior. He is close to his grandparents and knew it was temporary, so he was cooperative with them. He is coming home now but his mother is afraid.

Dakota hit his mother tonight. She had told him she would take his cell phone away if his grades didn't improve. Dakota's mother is alone in enforcing the rules at home ever since his dad moved out of the house after being arrested for domestic violence. When his dad was still at home, Dakota was protective of his mother, even trying to stop his dad from hurting his mom. Since Dad left, Dakota has been using some of the same behaviors his dad used with his mom, such as putting her down, swearing at her, and even hitting her. During his visits with his father, Dakota's complaints about his mother, such as that she's unreasonable and hard to live with, are reinforced by the degrading comments his father makes about her. Today a report from the school came in the mail showing he had the same poor grades as his previous report. When his mother was simply trying to enforce the rule they discussed about his grades and his phone, she asked him to hand it to her. He refused and she tried to grab it from him. He punched her arm and pushed her down. Dakota's brother came into the room to help her; Dakota jumped on him and tried to strangle him. Dakota punched him five or six times in the face. Dakota's sister called the police when she heard her mother being hit.

Jared was raised in a closely knit family for the first eight years of his life. His mother was able to stay at home with him all day until he started school, and his father couldn't wait to get home from work to play with him. When Jared was eight, his father was sent to fight in Iraq. Over the next three years, Jared saw his father only three times when he returned home for month-long furloughs. Each time his father left for Iraq, Jared would isolate himself in his room, but he also became increasingly aggressive towards his mother. His mother thought Jared was influenced by his father's yelling, swearing, and threats directed at her during the furloughs. She also admitted she stayed in her bedroom for long periods of time after he went back to Iraq, sometimes sleeping or just not wanting to be around anyone. There were times she could not stop herself from crying after telephone conversations with Jared's father. When Jared was 11, he hit his mother when they were arguing about chores. Jared is now 13 and his mother reports he has hit her every couple of months over the past two years.

Alex used violence against both his peers in school and family members. Violent behavior has been a chronic, pervasive problem for him in which any frustrating situation can lead to an outburst of aggression towards others. On the other hand, for Dakota, violence began in adolescence and only at home. He responds with violence in situations typical of conflict for teens and parents. Confiscation of a cell phone would likely elicit anger from many teens; however, most would not resort to physical violence. Jared's violence, which started before adolescence, seems to coincide with a devastating loss of daily contact with his father, fear for his father's life, and his mother's reactions to this situation.

## Seriousness of Physical Abuse

The physical assault of parents differs from intimate partner physical assault. First, few parents are killed by their teenage children. In the few recorded cases of parricide, the child perpetrators have either had serious mental health problems or have been victims of severe physical abuse (Heide, 1995). Second, some data indicate physical assaults of parents are less onerous than in adult domestic violence. The assaults on parents don't often reach the degree of physical injury that female victims of domestic violence experience (Evans & Warren-Sohlberg, 1988; A. Schultz, King County Prosecutors Office, personal communication, October 15, 2011). Finally, fewer assaults against parents involve the use of weapons than is true in adult domestic violence cases. (A. Schultz, King County Prosecutors Office, personal communication, October 15, 2011).

However, assaults by teens towards their parents can be serious. Cornell and Gelles (1982, p. 13) report, "While the rate of overall violence directed at parents by children 10 to 17 years of age is lower than the rates of overall violence between other family members, the rate of severe, or what could be called abusive violence was nearly as high as the rates of child and spouse abuse." Approximately 3 percent of the adolescents were reported to have kicked, punched, bit, "beat up," or used a knife or gun against a parent. While this percentage appears quite small, when it is projected to the total number of adolescents between 10 and 17 living in two-parent households, it means that in 1981, as many as 900,000 parents were being seriously abused each year.

In King County 12 percent of domestic violence cases in juvenile court reach the level of a felony charge. In addition, many parents are afraid to have their teenagers return home after being arrested for assaulting a family member, and some parents in King County go so far as to refuse to pick up their teens from detention because they fear more violence when their teen returns home. In some cases, juvenile court judges make a decision not to release a youth because of the court's concern for the safety of family members.

## Prevalence of Physical Abuse Towards Parents

In 1975 the *National Family Violence Survey*, a comprehensive nationwide study on violence in the family, was conducted using a sample of 2,143 families (Straus, Gelles & Steinmetz, 1981). Each of the randomly chosen families was interviewed about all types of abuse that were occurring in their home. The final report showed four different types of abuse that American families were experiencing at that time. Today most people are familiar with two types of family violence: child abuse and domestic violence between adults. A third, lesser known type of violence was abuse between siblings. The fourth type of violence was parent abuse.

This study became the basis for a widely distributed book on family violence, and it reported that over a period of one year, 18 percent of parents were victims of physical violence by their children at least one time (Straus et al., 1981). To find out how many parents were being physically abused by adolescent children, researchers looked only at the portion of the 2,143 families that had children between the ages of 10 and 17. From this group of 608 families, they identified parents who were hit by their child at least one time in the previous year. From this sample of parents, the researchers projected across the nation the number of parents who are hit by their adolescent children. The results of the survey were startling. Two and a half million parents were struck each year by their adolescent children and 900,000 parents were victims of severe violence. They concluded that 10 percent of the teens in the United States between the ages of 10 to 17 years old were physically violent with their parents (Cornell & Gelles, 1982).

Looking back at this study today, we realize the results are conservative. First, the interviewers asked only about parents who were "hit" by their children at least one time in the previous year. Other types of physical assaults were not included. Second, not all parents were asked about being hit since only one parent was interviewed in each family. Finally, one child in each family was interviewed, even when there was more than one child in the family. The authors (Straus et al., 1981, p. 119) make a startling revelation about the results of their research: "Almost one out of five of the children in this study had hit the parent we interviewed in the year we asked about. Since we interviewed mothers in half the families, and fathers in the other half of the families, the number of children who had hit a parent during the year might actually be double. This means that one out of every three children between the ages of 3 and 17 hit their parents each year."

In addition, the definition of abuse did not include other types of abuse that often accompany physical abuse in a relationship. After interviewing hundreds of families we have served and recording their abuse history, we know that the parents in this study were more than likely experiencing other kinds of abuse such as verbal attacks, threats, and property destruction. Furthermore, our familiarity with the experiences of abused parents leads us to believe that a significant number of these 608 parents were probably assaulted more than once during that year, and very likely in previous years. Like intimate partner violence, one-time assaults by a teen towards his or her parent are rare. Finally, this study only included two-parent families, which are less likely to have incidents of parent abuse (Routt & Anderson, 2011). As the first real study of its kind in the United States, this was a sound beginning approach to developing an understanding of family violence. However, from what we have learned, we know it is only part of the story.

Harbin and Madden (1979, p. 1288) were the first to write about "battered parent syndrome," defining it as "physical assaults or verbal and non-verbal threats of physical harm," but they had no estimate on prevalence. Agnew and Huguley (1989) took data from the *National Survey of Youth* collected in 1972 and concluded between 9.2 percent and 11.7 percent of all adolescents had assaulted their parents at least once in the previous three-year period. Most other family violence researchers agree the number of teens who assault their parent ranges somewhere between 7 percent and 13 percent (Evans & Warren-Sohlberg, 1988; Kratcoski, 1985; Paulson, Coombs & Landsverk 1990; Peek, Fischer & Kidwell, 1985; Browne & Hamilton, 1998; Bobic, 2004; Pagani, Tremblay, Nagin, Zoccolillo, Vitaro & McDuff, 2004).

The prevalence of parent abuse can be measured in other ways. Since assault is a crime, and some parents do call the police, law enforcement has some data on parent assault. In 2004, the FBI compiled data from law enforcement agencies in 30 states on a variety of crimes including assaults among family members. They concluded that half (51 percent) of the juvenile domestic assault offenders victimized a parent (Snyder & McCurley, 2008). A review of juvenile probation records involving youth who were violent against family members in a central Illinois county revealed over 80 percent of the victims were parents or other adults in a parenting role (Kethineni, 2004). Another study cited a report from Western New York indicating over 9 percent of all family violence in 1998 was committed by a child against a parent (Judge, 2005). In 1994 Massachusetts examined adolescents who had a restraining order issued against them for a 10-month period from September 1992 through June 1993. Family members were victims in 42 percent of these cases and 76 percent of the family members were parents (Cochran, Brown, Adams & Doherty, 1994).

Some people who bemoan the decline in family values may think parent abuse is particular to American children, but evidence from other countries shows parents outside the United States are also targets of their adolescent's violence. A small sample of studies and reports from the United Kingdom, Australia, Canada, France, Spain, Israel, Japan, South Africa, New Zealand, and South Korea document parent abuse in other countries as well (Kumagai, 1983; Laurent & Derry, 1999; Omer, 2004; Ibabe & Jaureguizar, 2010; Hong, 2006; Gallagher, 2004; Cottrell & Monk, 2004; Lee & Kim, 2010; Parent24, 2011; Condry & Miles, 2012). In Japan, one author (Kozu, 1999, p. 50) notes, "Filial violence (i.e., physical attacks on parents by their children) is the first type of domestic violence that has been brought to the attention of the general public and sensationalized as a social problem since the early 1970's." Canada (Cottrell, 2001) has published a booklet for parents and professionals that provides information about parent abuse. Family violence agencies in Australia are leaders in developing materials for the general public about how to respond to adolescents who use violence at home (Friend, Howard & Parker, 2008; Parent Link, 2014). Parentline Plus, a national charity that offers support to parents in the United Kingdom, analyzed calls to its helpline between October 2007 and June 2008 and found 30 percent of its calls concerned physical aggression at home from children, often towards parents. El Pais, a Spanish newspaper, reported the alarming increase in children's aggression towards parents since 2000 in their Fiscalias de Menores (family courts) (Brown, 2010). In 2007, these courts had 2,683 cases and in 2008 the number increased to 4,200. Parent abuse is indeed a worldwide problem.

Parent abuse is significantly underreported. Parents have repeatedly told the authors their call to get help with a violent teen was a last resort, an act of desperation and a call they never thought they would make. One of the main reasons that parents are hesitant to report abuse is the shame and humiliation they feel when they do tell someone about their situation. People who have not had experience with parent abuse often minimize the violence towards parents or blame the parent. Victimized parents who want help for their teens and for themselves often feel there is no place to turn and choose not to tell anyone. Researchers agree the number of cases of parent abuse is underreported and there are many more incidents of violence towards parents than the data shows (Pagelow, 1984; Cornell & Gelles, 1982; Price, 1996).

## Siblings

When a teen is violent at home, parents are concerned for their own safety, but sometimes they are even more concerned about the safety of their other children.

> I can take care of myself when my son starts blowing up, but I worry about my nine-year-old daughter. I'm afraid he'll hurt her too. He's already started calling her a "bitch" and acts like he's going to slap her. I think it's just a matter of time before he actually does it.
>
> My youngest son calls me at work because his older brother is hitting and punching him. I really get scared—sometimes I have to leave work to go home because of it.
>
> When my two boys start hitting each other they are hard to separate. The smaller one has gotten hurt before, so I try to get in the middle to stop them. They'll just keep punching away and I've gotten hurt trying to keep them apart.

When asked about other family members who are victimized, about 40 percent of parents reveal brothers and sisters are also being physically assaulted by the teen. If only families with more than one child are included, that number jumps to 60 percent. Violence against siblings is particularly concerning for parents who desperately try to protect their more vulnerable children from being attacked and hurt. When the parent feels unable to protect the younger sibling from the abuse, her authority is undermined, striking at the core of the parent role of protector and provider.

Sibling abuse by itself is one of the most prevalent forms of violence in the family (Straus et al., 1981) and, like parent abuse, is a hidden form of family violence (Wiehe, 1997; Caffaro & Caffaro, 1998). Violence against siblings does reach the seriousness of a crime in some families. Figures from the King County Prosecutor's Office reveal an average of 15 percent of all victims of juvenile domestic violence are brothers and sisters of teen perpetrators. In cases where there's been an arrest, siblings are the primary victims of violence.

Physical abuse of parents and siblings can take three different patterns. In our interviews, parents are usually the primary targets of abuse from their adolescent youth and the other, usually younger children, are secondary targets. With most siblings, the violence usually doesn't reach the severity it does with the parent and it doesn't happen as often. In other cases, though, the siblings are the primary targets and they are unable to protect themselves against the routine violence from their stronger brother or sister. Parents in these families are sometimes assaulted in their attempt to protect the targeted children. Finally, in still other cases, siblings share equal responsibility in initiating violence towards each other and neither sibling is a "primary aggressor" or the sole victim. Again, the parent may get hurt when trying to stop the violence between adolescent children who are hurting each other.

## Power and Control in Parent Abuse

A common question asked is "why do teens do these things to their parents?" Most people cannot imagine cursing at their parents when they were younger, much less hitting them. There is not one answer to the question of why a teen is violent towards a parent. We will discuss the combination of factors that leads a teen to use violence in another chapter. We do know that most often the abuse or violence occurs when teens are responding to a parent setting a limit, such as saying "no" to a request, or telling them to do something they don't want to do. In that moment, the violence is a tactic of power to compel the parent to change his or her mind.

As we noted in Chapter 1, adolescent to parent violence is a form of power, and we want to continue the discussion by first looking at two schools of thought about power in the family (Dempsey, 2006). Social science academic research is the source of much of what is known today about the types of violence in the family: child abuse, sibling abuse, spousal abuse, and elder abuse. Murray Straus, Richard Gelles, and Susan Steinmetz were some of the first researchers to identify parents as victims of abuse in the family (Straus et al., 1981). This research views domestic and family violence as the outcome of dysfunctional attempts by family members to resolve conflicts, and the research identifies a variety of variables to explain family violence. They define family violence by simply recording acts of violence one family member uses against another.

Feminist researchers and domestic violence activists challenged academic researchers by focusing on the social context for acts of violence (Pence & Paymar, 1993). They regarded intimate partner violence as an example of the pervasiveness of patriarchy and sexism as structural inequalities and as a way that gender inequality between men and women was sustained. (The academics regard patriarchy as only one of many variables when explaining violence in the family.) Furthermore, feminists regarded the immediate context of acts of violence as essential to understanding them. For instance, when one brother hits another, were they play-fighting or hurting each other? If a woman hit her partner, was she defending herself from an attack, retaliating from a previous attack, or initiating an attack? For feminists, the context is foundational in determining whether an act of physical force is violent or not.

Adolescent to parent violence can in part be explained as another assertion of power and control over women. In most cases, mothers are victims of their son's physical violence, and verbal attacks often degrade mothers as women. Mothers who are survivors of domestic violence report to us they often hear the same humiliating language and witness the same behavior from their youth as they experienced from their former abusive partners. Male identity as a patriarchal construct is defined as being in control in intimate relationships. While this is only one form of masculinity, male entitlement and privilege is socially supported and boys from a young age often feel pressured and encouraged to behave in ways that model power and control (Connell, 1995). However, gender inequality offers only part of the explanation. Youth are attacking their mothers as parents who hold the power in the family.

Richard Gelles and Murray Straus (1988, p. 82) write, "Power, power confrontations, and perceived threats to domination, in fact, are underlying issues in almost all acts of family violence." An imbalance of power is inherent in a parent-child relationship, and teens often feel dependent and powerless at some point during their adolescence. They want to make their own decisions and follow their own rules. Abusive teens use violence to rectify this imbalance. Abusers in other relationships share these same feelings. Dependency and the relative feeling of powerlessness have been identified as important characteristics of lesbian batterers (Renzetti, 1992), for example. Renzetti (1992, p. 117) concluded, ". . . batterers are individuals who feel powerless and use violence as a means to achieve power and domination in their intimate relationships." Abusive heterosexual men have some of the same feelings of helplessness, powerlessness, and inadequacy in their relationships and use violence in response to these feelings (Gelles & Cornell, 1985). One researcher (Finkelhor, 1983) asserts that one of the common features of all forms of family violence is that it occurs as a response to perceived powerlessness on the part of the abuser. The perception of powerlessness is a common theme among individuals who use coercive tactics in family relationships.

While some of the abusive behaviors used by a teen may be similar to those of an abusive intimate partner, a teen's use of controlling tactics towards a parent also differs in important ways. In an adult intimate relationship, the abuser uses a variety of tactics to exert control over his partner's life (Bancroft, 2002). Some men control particular aspects of their partner's life and other men exert control that touches every aspect of their partner's life. For instance, some men might tell their partner how to dress and who their friends should be. Others might prevent them from having a credit card or even a job. One man we worked with would check his partner's receipts to see when she was at the store, how much money she spent, and where she went to shop. Men feel entitled to use these control tactics and, in fact, believe they are acting in the best interests of their partners. Women who experience the full range of controlling tactics often report profound impacts on their physical and mental health and their personal sense of well-being and self-esteem. Teens coerce parents to get something they want rather than to restrict their parent's freedom and independence. While the impact can be personally debilitating and disturbing, parents don't often experience the same degree of distress that survivors of domestic violence commonly describe.

## Parents' Response

How do parents respond to physical abuse from their adolescents? The following are some of the ways parents respond in the moments following a physical attack by their teen. There are different responses over time with repeating incidents of violence that will be discussed in a later chapter.

### Denial

Most parents search for some sort of explanation for the violence, trying to find a reason to make sense of it. It is not easy to accept that your child would actually assault you and finding an explanation is an understandable reaction for any parent. We all want to know that our children are not "bad." There is always a reason for every behavior. In the quest for an explanation, conclusions are drawn, such as, he is mad about his dad leaving, she is stressed at school, or he has bipolar disorder. Such conclusions may absolve the child of responsibility for the harm done by the behavior. Unintentionally, the child integrates a belief that "I am not responsible for my violence." Here are some of the reactions we have heard from parents in denial:

> It's only happened a few times. I know he doesn't mean to hurt me. My girlfriend was shocked to see the bruise on my arm where he hit me. She thinks I need to wake up about what's going on. She just doesn't understand my son.
>
> It's just normal sibling rivalry. His little sister is no angel; she's always provoking him. I guess she learned her lesson when he slapped her.
>
> He has threatened me with a knife. I know he would never really hurt me. But I have hidden all the knives, just to be sure.

### Taking Responsibility for the Violent Behavior

Parents often feel that their child's violence is a result of something they did wrong, that they parented poorly, or are responsible for hardships their child has endured such as abuse by their father or exposure to domestic violence. It is a natural response for a parent to take responsibility for a child's behavior; after all, it is a parent's job to raise their kids to behave, follow rules, and do what is right. Anytime children make mistakes or are having a difficult time, most parents on some level feel responsible. The feeling of self-blame makes it difficult to hold a child responsible for any misbehavior, but it is particularly difficult when the behavior is violence.

> The divorce has been hard on her and I've been really stressed so I can see why she's throwing things. I'm just afraid since she's been threatening me more lately. I wish I could do something.
>
> I know he has anger problems from living with his dad who was abusive with me. I shouldn't have let him be around his dad so much. I know it's my own fault he's like this. So, I try to just let it go. What else can I do?

## Shock and Surprise

One of the strongest reactions many parents describe after the first time their youth hit them is shock and surprise. Many say that they couldn't even think about how to respond because of how unexpected and unbelievable it was.

> I couldn't believe what was happening. I was in shock. I couldn't believe he was doing this to me. I just screamed at him.
>
> I've never been so hurt and mad at the same time. I was yelling at my son to stop and crying at the same time. How can he do this to me?

## Protecting Themselves

As you would expect anyone to do, the immediate response for many parents who were being physically assaulted was to protect themselves.

> My daughter swung at me, so I pushed her down. I sat on her until she calmed down. I've been through this before and I didn't want to get any more bruises on my arm from her punches.
>
> I do whatever I can to get away from him when he starts yelling and getting too close to me. Last week I locked myself in the bathroom for an hour until he calmed down.

## Separating Themselves

The feeling of powerlessness leads some parents to get away from their abusive teen so they can protect themselves. They go to the first place they can that puts a wall between themselves and their child, like their bedroom or the bathroom. Other parents leave their house to go to a friend's house or they go for a drive just to get away. Younger siblings are a concern for parents too. They worry their younger children will get hurt or will be influenced by their abusive teen, so parents separate their younger children from their abusive sibling.

> He hit me before, so when he did it again, I ran out the back door and got into the car. I drove around for an hour while he calmed down.
>
> He really started to escalate and since he hit me before, I ran out of the house. I was in my pajamas so I looked kind of foolish when the neighbors saw me.
>
> When I heard him punching the wall in his room, I got his younger brother and went next door.

## Avoidance

Parents find one way of coping with their teen's violence is to avoid having contact with them. Sometimes this means being in physically separate places in their home and in other cases, just not communicating with them when they are together.

> He'll come in the house and go straight to his room. I have to admit I feel relieved when he does that. I only talk with him about things that are absolutely necessary. So many conversations lead to yelling and cursing at me I just don't want to talk to him.
>
> I used to ask him about school to make sure he was keeping up with his assignments, but he would always start with foul names and slamming doors. If he would just do his work, I wouldn't get on him about school. I got tired of being called a "fucking bitch" so I don't bring up the subject anymore.

## Protecting Their Other Children

Parents who are assaulted by their teens are also concerned about the safety of their other children. Some youth who assault their parents also assault their siblings. Sometimes siblings are assaulted at the same time a parent is being assaulted and at other times, siblings are the primary target. In still other cases, violence between siblings is mutual and neither sibling is a clear aggressor. In all these cases, the potential for harm is great and most parents try to stop violence when they can. Some parents are assaulted when they try to stop violence between their teen children.

> I don't leave my son home alone with the younger children. They don't get along and I'm afraid he'll hurt them.
>
> For a while I was getting calls at work from my daughter who was crying that her brother wouldn't stop hitting her and teasing her. I tell her to go to her friend's house to get away from him.
>
> My younger kids are afraid of my oldest son. Sometimes he plays with them and is very sweet. When he gets frustrated with them, he calls them names and hits them. Whenever he yells at me, they hide in their room. I'll get in the car with the younger ones when he gets crazy.

## Calling the Police

In most cases, calling the police is a last resort. Some parents feel their teen's violence breaks a special trust with them and they have no choice but to call the police. Parents who call the police report feeling desperate and hopeless about what to do about their son or daughter's behavior. Usually, by the time a parent calls the police there have been multiple incidents of violence over a period of time. Most parents say it was the most difficult thing they ever had to do.

> I wanted him to know he can't hit me. When the police first came to the door, I told them what he did and they needed to talk to him. My son ended up getting arrested.
>
> I was so mad. I knew if I didn't call the police, I might hurt him.
>
> I warned him in the past that I would call the police the next time he hit me. I knew I had to follow through, otherwise I'd be making empty threats.
>
> I had to call. I was terrified. I thought, "I need help before someone is killed . . ."

## Fighting Back

Some parents respond by fighting back, especially if they feel the need to protect themselves or others, feel cornered or angry, or feel the need to show they are not powerless. Fathers will return the physical attack, especially if it is a son, to show them they will not take it, and put fear into the youth to "never try that again." Other fathers will intervene on an attack by the teen towards the mother by grabbing him and pushing him up against the wall. Anger prompts some mothers to respond by slapping or pushing back. Feelings of powerlessness after enduring the abuse over time may result in parents one day deciding they are not taking it anymore, and they hit back. Most parents express remorse about their behavior when they fight back, understanding that it does not help the situation and actually makes it worse.

> I'm not going to let my own kid hurt me. You've got to be kidding. I've never spanked them and now they think they can do this to me. I hit her after she hit me.
>
> He was going after his mother so I shoved him up against the wall before he could do anything. I wrestled him to the floor.
>
> She grabbed my hair and yanked down hard. I hit her so she would let my hair go.

## Summary

Physical violence towards parents by their own adolescent children is a widespread problem, nationally and internationally. The violence can be serious and occurs frequently in many homes, ranging widely in circumstances and familial issues. In some respects, the experiences and responses of parents vary, but in other ways they are strikingly similar. Parents feel afraid, hopeless, and helpless about what to do. Systems of care have not yet developed a coordinated response to meet the needs of these youth and parents in a helpful way. We can begin by taking the problem seriously, listening to parents and believing them.

## References

Agnew, R., & Huguley, S. (1989). Adolescent violence toward parents. *Journal of Marriage and the Family*, 51, 699–711.

Bancroft, L. (2002). *Why does he do that?* New York: G. P. Putnam's Sons.

Bobic, N. (2004). Adolescent violence towards parents. Topic paper from Australian Domestic and Family Violence Clearinghouse. Retrieved from http://www.adfvc.unsw.edu.au/PDF%20files/adolescent_violence.pdf

Brown, K. (2010). Living with teenage violence. *Therapy Today*, 21(10), 11–15.

Browne, K. D., & Hamilton, C. E. (1998). Physical violence between young adults and their parents: associations with a history of child maltreatment. *Journal of Family Violence*, 5(4), 59–79.

Caffaro, J., & Caffaro, A. C. (1998). *Sibling abuse trauma.* New York: Routledge.

Cochran, D., Brown, M. E., Adams, S. L., & Doherty, D. (1994). *Young adolescent batterers: a profile of restraining order defendants in Massachusetts.* Boston: Massachusetts Trial Court, Office of Commissioner of Probation.

Condry, R., & Miles, C. (2012). Adolescent to parent violence and youth justice in England and Wales. *Social Policy and Society*, 11(2), 241–250.

Connell, R. W. (1995). *Masculinities*. Berkeley: University of California Press.

Cornell, C. P., & Gelles, R. J. (1982). Adolescent-to-parent violence. *Urban Social Change Review*, 15(1), 8–14.

Cottrell, B. (2001). *Parent abuse: the abuse of parents by their teenage children*. Ottawa: Health Canada.

Cottrell, B., & Monk, P. (2004). Adolescent-to-parent abuse. *Journal of Family Issues*, 25(8), 1072–1095.

Dahlberg, L. L., & Krug, E. G. (2002). Violence—a global health problem. In E. G. Krug, L. L. Dahlberg, J. A. Mercy, A. B. Zwi & L. L. Lozano (Eds.), *World report on violence and health* (pp. 1–21), Geneva, Switzerland: World Health Organization.

Dempsey, M. M. (2006). What counts as domestic violence? A conceptual analysis. *William & Mary Journal of Women and the Law*, 12(2), 301–333.

Evans, E. D., & Warren-Sohlberg, L. (1988). A pattern of analysis of adolescent abusive behavior toward parents. *Journal of Adolescent Research*, 3(2), 201–216.

Finkelhor, D. (1983). Common features of family abuse. In D. Finkelhor, R. Gelles, G. Hotaling, & M. Straus (Eds.), *The dark side of families: current family violence research* (pp. 17–28), Beverley Hills: Sage.

Friend, D., Howard, J., & Parker, T. (2008). *Adolescent violence to parents*. South Melbourne, Sidney: Inner South Community Health Service.

Gallagher, E. D. (2004). Parents victimized by their children. *Australian and New Zealand Journal of Family Therapy*, 25(1), 1–12.

Gelles, R. J. (1979). *Family violence*. Beverley Hills: Sage.

Gelles, R. J., & Cornell, C. P. (1985). *Intimate violence in families*. Beverly Hills, CA: Sage.

Gelles, R. J., & Straus, M. A. (1988). *Intimate violence*. New York: Simon & Schuster.

Harbin, H., & Maddin, D. (1979). Battered parents: a new syndrome. *American Journal of Psychiatry*, 136, 1288–1291.

Heide, K. M. (1995). *Why kids kill parents: child abuse and adolescent homicide*. Thousand Oaks, CA: Sage.

Hong, K. M. (2006). Impacts of rapid social and family changes on the mental health of children in Korea. *Psychiatry Investigation*, 3(1), 6–25.

Ibabe, I., & Jaureguizar, J. (2010). Child-to-parent violence: profile of abusive adolescents and their families. *Journal of Criminal Justice*, 38, 616–624.

Judge, C. (2005). Parental abuse by adolescents and the need for juvenile family violence courts in the state of New York. Retrieved from www.law.buffalo.edu/family_law/student_research/parental_abuse.pdf

Kethineni, S. (2004). Youth-on-parent violence in a central Illinois county. *Youth Violence and Juvenile Justice*, 2(4), 374–394.

Kozu, J. (1999). Domestic violence in Japan. *American Psychologist*, 54(1), 50–54.

Kratcoski, P. (1985). Youth violence directed toward significant others. *Journal of Adolescence*, 8, 145–157.

Kumagai, F. (1983). Filial violence in Japan. *Victimology*, 8, 173–194.

Laurent, A., & Derry, A. (1999). Violence of French adolescents towards their parents. *Journal of Adolescent Health*, 25(1), 21–26.

Lee, J., & Kim, J. Y. (2010). The effects of family violence on South Korean adolescents who abuse their parents, and the moderating effects of problem-solving. Abstract. Presented at the Society for Social Work and Research 14th Annual Conference, January 15, 2010, Hyatt Regency Embarcadero Center, San Francisco, CA. Retrieved from http://sswr.confex.com/sswr/2010/webprogram/Paper13171.html

Omer, H. (2004). *Nonviolent resistance: a new approach to violent and self-destructive children*. New York: Cambridge University Press.

Pagani, L. S., Tremblay, R. E., Nagin, D., Zoccolillo, M., Vitaro, F., & McDuff, P. (2004). Risk factor models for adolescent verbal and physical aggression toward mothers. *International Journal of Behavioral Development*, 28(6), 528–537.

Pagelow, M. D. (1984). *Family violence*. New York: Praeger.

Parent Link. (2014, March). ACT Government Publication No 14/0125. Retrieved from www.parentlink.act.gov.au/parenting-resources/parenting-guides/young-people/abuse-to-parents

Parent24. (2011). Retrieved from http://www.parent24.com/Teen_13–18/development_behavior/Could-your-teen-abuse-you

Paulson, M. J., Coombs, R. H., & Landsverk, J. (1990). Youth who physically assault their parents. *Journal of Family Violence*, 5(2), 121–133.

Peek, C. W., Fischer, J. L., & Kidwell, J. S. (1985). Teenage violence toward parents: a neglected dimension of family violence. *Journal of Marriage and the Family*, 47(4), 1051–1058.

Pence, E., & Paymar, M. (1993). *Education groups for men who batter: the Duluth model*. New York: Springer Publishing.

Price, L. A. (1996). *Power and compassion: working with difficult adolescents and abused parents*. New York: Guilford.

Renzetti, C. M. (1992). *Violent betrayal*. Thousand Oaks, CA: Sage.

Routt, G., & Anderson, L. (2011). Adolescent violence towards parents. *Journal of Aggression, Maltreatment and Trauma*, 20, 1–19.

Ryan, R. G., & Wilson, D. (2010). NGA Tukitanga Mai Koka Ki Tona Ira: Maori mothers and child to mother violence. *Nursing Praxis in New Zealand*, 26(3), 25–35.

Simmons, R. (2002). *Odd girl out*. New York: Harcourt.

Snyder, N. H., & McCurley, C. (2008). Domestic assaults by juvenile offenders. *Juvenile Justice Bulletin*, Office of Juvenile Justice and Delinquency Prevention, US Department of Justice.

Straus, M., Gelles, R., & Steinmetz, S. (1981). *Behind closed doors*. Garden City, NY: Anchor Books.

Wiehe, V. (1997). *Sibling abuse*. Thousand Oaks, CA: Sage.

# three
# Emotional Abuse

I work as a nurse in a large hospital. I really love my job and feel good that I'm helping people in need. Patients tell me all the time they appreciate what I do for them. My supervisors praise my work. My co-workers feel like we work as a team. When I go home, everything changes. My son calls me degrading and insulting names. I've never talked like that to him. His father used to say some of the same things to me, but I left him because I didn't want my son to start saying the same things. I thought my son would respect me for leaving his father since he didn't like him either. Now when I try to talk to my son about his insults, he threatens me. Sometimes he'll even punch a wall or break something. I can't believe he's doing and saying some of the same things his father did. I thought it would be different at home when his father left. He has just stepped into his father's shoes.

This mother feels she is under her son's thumb. When he wants something or when she says "no" to something he wants, he postures and gets in her face in a threatening way. She said the names he called her left her feeling dirty. He has never hit or punched her, and he makes a point of saying this to her when she tells him to stop being a bully. At first she tried to ignore him and not show any reaction when he said these things to her, hoping he would stop. Later she realized even the subtle reactions she had to his verbal attacks encouraged him to do it more. At times when she was exhausted, she gave in to his demands.

The old saying, "sticks and stones will break my bones, but names will never hurt me," is a lesson that elders have been trying to teach children for generations. When parents say this, they hope their children will just ignore the names used against them and dismiss the bad feelings they might have. While it's true that even a negative response to name-calling can encourage the person to do it more, ignoring the emotional pain doesn't mean it has no effect. While most of us can ignore an occasional name or insult, heavy doses of emotional abuse can have profound long-term negative effects. Emotional abuse results in emotional distress, undermines confidence and self-esteem, and erodes a parent's capacity to function as a parent (Loring, 1994).

In this chapter, parents will talk about how repeated emotional and verbal abuse affects them. They will describe the demeaning language, the intimidating looks and gestures, and hurtful names their children use. Parents will also talk about the destruction of property in their household that creates a climate of fear, such as a teen punching a hole in the wall or repeatedly slamming a cabinet door until it breaks. Finally, they will talk about how the abuse damages the bonds between them and their child.

## Defining Emotional Abuse

Emotional abuse is more difficult to define than physical abuse. Physical violence is unmistakably abusive and harmful, especially when someone is physically hurt. To most people the word violence conjures up images of a physical attack and "family violence" or "domestic violence" is commonly viewed as one spouse or family member hitting and punching another. No one would ever argue physical violence is justified except in extreme circumstances such as when one is in danger. Given time to reflect, most people who have physically hurt someone realize they have done something wrong.

Emotional abuse, on the other hand, can be more elusive and more difficult to define. A verbal attack like using a foul name or a threat to kill is an obvious example of an emotionally abusive behavior. However, a more understated word or comment can be devastating to one person, while someone else might simply ignore it. Some words or gestures may threaten or demean a parent, but how or why may not be obvious to a bystander. A calmly stated sarcastic comment can be just as hurtful or scary as someone screaming in your face, depending on the circumstances, the people involved, and the source of the conflict. Not using any words at all, like being intentionally silent or withholding information, can be an insidious form of abuse. So while many examples of emotional abuse are easily recognized, others are not (Elgin, 2000).

Let's look at a few examples of emotional abuse.

I can tell when my son is getting irritated by the sharper edge in his voice and by the way he says things very slowly. It's a sign for me that something worse is about to happen. It's like he's telling me I better do what he wants or else. When I don't give in, he'll act like he's going to punch me and stop his fist about an inch in front of my face. When I flinch, he'll laugh and say he's just joking.

Some days my daughter comes in the door and goes to her room without saying anything. The way she walks and closes her door tells me if I need to watch out when she comes out of her room. If I ask her something when she's in a bad mood, she answers with venom, "get out of my face, bitch."

Sometimes he talks to me like an abusive husband. Like yesterday we were driving home from the store. He criticized how I drove, when I put my blinker on, how I didn't speed up when the light was changing, the route I chose to drive home, how slow I was driving, what station I played on the radio. He went on and on. And he does this kind of running commentary on my life all the time.

It's the constant swearing that gets to me. My 15-year-old says "fuck" all the time. When I wake him up in the morning, its "fuck you" and "get out of my fucking room." When I drive him to school, I'm a "fucking bitch." His 8-year-old sister is a "fuck head." I try to talk to him about it and it's "shut the fuck up, bitch." I hate to say it, but I don't like to be around him at all.

Professionals use a variety of definitions and terms for emotional abuse. It has been called psychological maltreatment, verbal abuse, mental abuse, symbolic aggression, and nonphysical abuse (Mouradian, 2000). The US Department of Justice (2012) defines emotionally abusive traits as provoking fear by intimidation; threatening physical harm to self, partner, children, or partner's family or friends; destroying of pets and property; and forcing isolation from family, friends, school, or work. In 1996, Health Canada asserts that emotional abuse is motivated by urges for "power and discontrol," and defines emotional abuse as including rejecting, degrading, terrorizing, isolating, corrupting/exploiting, and "denying emotional responsiveness" (Thompson & Kaplan, 1996). The National Network to End Domestic Violence (2013) defines emotional abuse as: constant put-downs or criticisms, name-calling, "crazy making," acting superior, minimizing the abuse or blaming you for their behavior, threatening and making you feel fearful, isolating you from family and friends, excessive jealously, accusing you of having affairs, and watching where you go and to whom you talk. The federal Child Abuse and Prevention Act of 1974 (Child Welfare Information Gateway, 2011) identified emotional abuse as "mental injury." Some professionals for research purposes define it more narrowly as a very specific group of behaviors (Straus, 1979), and other professionals who are interested in educating the public define it more broadly to show its harmful effects (Pagelow, 1984).

## Prevalence of Emotional Abuse

The prevalence of emotional abuse towards parents is difficult to determine since there is little agreement on how to document it. Among researchers, harm to family members is usually defined by physical assaults, not emotional abuse, although a few have tried to record emotional abuse. Family Lives, a national charity in England, issued a 2010 report based on 205 web surveys of parents. Thirty-seven percent of the parents reported swearing and aggressive language by their teen, 27 percent reported property destruction and almost 70 percent reported "angry outbursts." Another report issued by 4Children (2012), a national charity in the United Kingdom, also documented emotional abuse in families. In this survey of over 1,000 parents, 54 percent thought verbal insults in families were common, 18 percent thought property destruction was typical, and 17 percent responded that "threatening and intimidating" language was normal.

## Emotional Abuse and the Law

The legal system defines particular forms of abuse as violations of the law. On the one hand, physical assaults are clearly illegal since a case can be made against an assailant who physically hurts another person. On the other hand, a person who merely threatens physical violence with words, actions, or gestures can also be charged with an assault even though the perpetrator makes no physical contact with the victim. Property destruction and harassment are the most common examples of our definition of emotionally abusive behavior that violates the law. When a teen punches a hole in the wall, kicks a door off its hinges, or breaks something, he or she can be charged with a crime. When the teen verbally threatens to physically hurt or kill a parent or destroy property, "harassment" is the legal term used. In some instances, property destruction and harassment can feel just as threatening and intimidating to parents as physical violence, but the teen has made no physical contact with them. Unfortunately, when an act of emotional abuse leaves no physical evidence, like a verbal threat, and no documentation exists other than the victim's report, a crime is difficult to prove.

The most far-reaching definition of emotional abuse is, "any behavior that is harmful to another person's well-being" (Tolman, Rosen & Wood, 1999). Well-being is more than personal happiness or a positive outlook; it is a state of balance or equilibrium in a person's life (Dodge et al., 2012). Family relationships support personal development and serve as an emotional resource in the face of life's challenges; these relationships are a core feature of well-being that is threatened by emotional abuse.

While a person thoughtlessly blurting out a cruel name in an argument may be a passing incident, the effect of repeated name-calling over time can inflict irreparable damage to a relationship that is a critical part of a person's well-being.

## Physical Abuse Is Linked to Emotional Abuse

Physical abuse rarely occurs without emotional abuse. Emotional attacks are often a prelude to physical violence. Commonly, a conflict begins with emotional abuse, such as swearing, name-calling, or degrading language directed at the parent, and may escalate to a physical assault. Destroying property is a form of emotional abuse, since it inflicts fear, and it too may accompany a physical assault. In most cases, physical abuse and emotional abuse are part of a single violent event.

> When the yelling starts, I never know how it is going to end because the physical violence always starts there.

Physical abuse in the past multiplies the impact of emotional abuse because of the fear one might be hit again.

> About a month ago my son hit me. It started with arguing, and when he couldn't get me to agree with him he flared up and started yelling at me and calling me names and swearing. All of a sudden he just slugged me. I couldn't believe it. Ever since then, when he starts yelling I tighten with fear that he is going to get physical again.

The memory of physical violence remains strong when parents hear their son or daughter threaten to hurt or kill them or when they hear their teen break a hole in the wall in the next room.

> Ever since my daughter physically attacked me I get scared when I hear her start to escalate and hit things or throw things. The other day she threatened to kill me. In the past I wouldn't have been afraid—I just figured she is really mad and saying things that don't make sense. Now I'm not so sure. It's scary. And it really makes it hard to be a parent when you're afraid of your own child. I get knots in my stomach when I have to say no about something. I don't know how she's going to react.

As is the case with adult domestic violence, the abuse is a continuum that usually begins with verbal and emotional assaults that escalate to physical. This repeating cycle puts the victim in a continuous state of not knowing what will happen next, what kind of mood the person will be in, and where a conflict will lead. Parents "walk on eggshells" and are hesitant and fearful when they need to do their job as a parent by setting limits and standing firm.

## Research on Adolescent Violence

Research on adolescent violence towards parents identifies emotional abuse as a broad range of behaviors. Barbara Cottrell (2001, p. 8) defines emotional abuse as "the deliberate use of psychological means to manipulate, control and hurt parents." Another writer includes an additional dimension by defining it as "taking advantage of a parent's weakened emotional state and playing on a parent's fear or guilt" (Price, 1996). When a researcher (Holt, 2011) from the United Kingdom interviewed abused parents, they described two styles of emotional outbursts as abusive. A "lit fuse" (or "ticking time bomb"), the first style, is a teen that blows up in an instant without the slightest bit of warning and puts parents on edge thinking about when the next blow up will happen. Living with a "Jekyll and Hyde," the second style, describes a teen who switches between considerate and respectful one moment and hurtful the next depending on the situation. Again, parents never know when one or the other will appear.

Natasha Bobic (2004, p. 2), an Australian researcher, identifies emotional abuse towards parents as "maliciously playing mind games, trying to make the parent think he or she is crazy; making unrealistic demands on parents, such as insisting they drop what they are doing to comply with their demands; lying, running away from home and staying away all night; making manipulative threats, such as threatening to run away, commit suicide or otherwise hurt themselves without really intending to do so; and controlling the running of the household." Some of these examples are part of normal teenage behavior. "Making unrealistic demands" is common for any teenager, but when unrealistic demands are made in the context of an array of other abusive behaviors, they become part of the abuse pattern. Threatening self-harm, running away, or suicide are signs of a seriously troubled teen, but when these statements are made to manipulate and control a parent, they also become part of a pattern of abuse.

When harming someone's well-being is more than just an isolated event and becomes a pattern, it crosses over into abuse. Regarding teen abuse towards parents, we regard emotional abuse as a pattern of nonphysical attacks or assaults that are an attempt to degrade, demean, control, coerce, or dominate a parent or family member (Tolman, 1992; McKinnon, 2008). Often, it is an attack on a parent's integrity, character, or personality, but it can also take the form of overt threats and scare tactics. Using this definition, emotionally abusive behaviors can extend from subtle gestures to harsh language to threats to kill to destroying things. The list of behaviors can be overwhelming and everyday use makes them especially corrosive to family relationships.

With domestic violence or family violence, using emotional abuse habitually becomes the way one person tries to establish power over another person. A regular pattern of degrading personal statements, hurtful sarcastic comments, threatening postures, and belittling responses is an attempt to put the targeted family member in a subservient position. Emotional abuse undermines everyday conversations since the mutuality inherent in simply listening and responding to another person can become difficult and even impossible. The more complex communication skills like negotiation and compromise are out of the question when one person is emotionally attacking another person. Many parents have reported the verbal attacks and threats from their teen force them into a power struggle where they have to go to battle every time a problem comes up if they want to be heard. So while many people have used some form of emotional abuse in isolated instances, the regular use of verbal attacks and emotional abuse becomes the default mode for the person who addresses conflicts by bullying and overpowering another person.

## Key Points About Emotional Abuse

### Verbal Abuse Is More Than Words

A verbal attack is the words used in an aggressive statement that is insulting or threatening. However, the way a verbal attack is delivered is just as important as the words chosen and sometimes is more important than the words themselves. Many communication experts agree that, "the meaning conveyed by your body language is much more powerful than the meaning conveyed by your words" (Elgin, 2000). The tone, intensity, and sound of a statement can make the difference between a simple request and a threatening demand. The most sophisticated forms of verbal abuse are conveyed by the emphasis particular words are given in a statement. Gestures, movements, and noises are additional ways a threatening or hurtful message is communicated. Parents report that although their children have never used physical violence, the edge in their voices, their profanity, and their facial expressions are very frightening. Will he or she hit me the next time?

### Emotional Abuse Versus Physical Abuse

The impact of emotional abuse is difficult to access, but no one disputes it can have serious and long-term effects. For most people, the thought of physically assaulting a parent is very difficult to imagine and represents the most extreme act of disrespect. Since verbal attacks are precursors to physical violence, emotional abuse is often considered less pernicious than a physical attack. In interviews with parents, we hear about youth who have only used verbal abuse, and these parents feel their situation hasn't gotten that bad yet. While this may be true for some parents, not all feel the same.

In exploring the relationship between verbal, emotional, and physical abuse, one researcher used communication theory to analyze material she gathered during in-depth interviews with 20 parents of abusive teens, 7 men and 13 women (Eckstein, 2004). She examined the parent-teen interaction patterns in these families and tracked the development of abuse beginning with simple verbal abuse to high intensity emotional and physical attacks. These parents came to some very clear conclusions: emotional abuse was more "damaging and hurtful" than physical abuse. They reported the pain left an indelible emotional scar. As one parent stated, "The physical could hurt you more, but the emotional is going to last the longest" (Eckstein, 2004, p. 375). Even in cases where the verbal and emotional abuse does not lead to more physically destructive behavior, the atmosphere in a home filled with verbal attacks is toxic and unhealthy.

## Emotional Abuse Enhances Physical Abuse

Physical abuse directed towards an intimate partner or family member often begins with some form of verbal abuse (Gelles, 1987; Infante, Sabourin, Rudd, & Shannon, 1990). Adolescents who physically assault a parent often begin with a verbal attack (Eckstein, 2004). These attacks come when the teen is asking for permission to do something, go somewhere, or wants something from their parents. Verbal attacks can also be a part of a power struggle between teens and their parents when the conflict moves beyond an immediate demand to a more direct challenge to the parent's authority to decide family rules and norms.

Physical violence against a parent is often used when verbal abuse doesn't work. Youth will move from verbal to physical abuse to get the response they want. Time and again, parents report they are more afraid of their teen's verbal attacks after a physical attack than before. The physical attack confirms the threats a teen makes to parents to hurt them and forces parents to consider a physical attack when they feel threatened.

These parent responses underscore an important point when we try to understand abuse and violence; we sometimes analyze a particular incident by separating the physical abuse from the emotional abuse. For our understanding, separating them may be helpful. However, victims often remember an incident simply as a horrible, degrading, hurtful experience. So the next time a threatening word is used or even a simple hostile gesture is made, the emotional memory of previous attacks returns. The word and gesture become echoes of the previous experience of attacks. And if the word and gesture are used at the same time, they reinforce each other so the impact is enhanced and magnified.

## Adolescent Emotional Abuse Versus Intimate Partner Emotional Abuse

Emotional abuse by youth towards their parents and by adults towards their intimate partners give rise to fear, humiliation, and many other difficult feelings. However, the attacks towards parents can be distressing in different ways. On the one hand, adults in intimate partner relationships who are emotionally abused report having feelings of worthlessness, hopelessness, a lack of self-confidence, and a damaged self-concept as human beings because their attacker enjoys an intimate relationship with them. Equality, which is the basis for a successful healthy adult relationship, is destroyed by emotional abuse. On the other hand, although parents may have similar feelings as those in intimate partner relationships, they experience these feelings more as parents who are responsible for their child's development and well-being. When teens are emotionally hurtful to their parents it impacts their personal sense of efficacy as a parent. They feel they have failed as a parent. Most parents feel the behavior of their children is a reflection of them as a parent. Some parents who have been abused by their partner and their child have said that the abuse by their child is more devastating.

The types of emotional abuse described below don't take place in isolation of each other. Different kinds of abuse are used in a single incident and they are also used in the many incidents that make up the history of abuse. Invariably, when a parent tells us about an act of violence like a youth breaking a door down, the youth's tirade began with several minutes of verbal attacks and foul language that escalated to threatening statements. And in turn, the threatening statements led to the property damage. So the verbal attack, the threatening statements, and the broken door are all part of a single incident that is experienced by the targeted family member as one event. Only in extremely rare cases would this kind of incident be a onetime event, since this level of violence is always the result of an escalating pattern of abusive behaviors.

We have divided emotional abuse into primary and secondary tactics. Primary tactics are used regularly, sometimes on a daily or weekly basis, while secondary tactics that can be particularly harmful to parents are not used as often. The discussion of emotional abuse highlights the behaviors parents and youth have described most often in our work with them, but is not meant to be exhaustive of all emotionally abusive behaviors.

## Primary Tactics

### Insults and Humiliation

Name-calling and put-downs are the most common forms of emotional abuse directed at family members. It is not uncommon for abused parents to be called names or hear some kind of put-down every day by their teen. We understand small children who are upset might call their mother or father "ugly," "stupid," or "butt-heads," and while these words might concern parents, they are viewed as an emotional outburst, not a personal attack. Teens use names and put-downs that are more personally degrading, intended to humiliate and demean their parents as people and as parents. Parents who are targets of name-calling receive a regular reminder of their debased status in the family.

> My daughter calls me a fucking bitch even at times when she doesn't seem to be mad at me. It feels like a dagger she's throwing at me when I hear it.
>
> When I went out on a date recently and got dressed up, he made an ugly comment about what I was wearing and said I looked like a "whore."
>
> I must hear the word "bitch" a hundred times a day. From the time I wake him up until the time I tell him to go to bed, he calls me "bitch" and sometimes "fucking bitch." I hate hearing it.

Another form of verbal abuse is an attack that ridicules, derides, or mocks another person. The statements below are examples of how teens use personal characteristics to demean and degrade their parents by questioning their worth and value. Teens use personal weaknesses they see in their parents to attack them. In a healthy relationship, we feel safe that people who care about us will offer support when we need it and not use our vulnerabilities as a way to attack us. While children might thoughtlessly make comments about their parents, the idea that they would regularly use a personal trait in a verbal attack can be particularly dismaying.

> My son tells me I'm a slob and an ugly bitch and I'll never go on a date again. The other day I was putting on lipstick and he said, "That won't help your ugly ass." I've tried to talk to my son about these comments, but when he's upset he says very personally degrading things. It hurts me to hear that and I worry about what he'll say to his girlfriend when he gets mad at her.
>
> The last time my daughter and I had a fight she called me a fat fucking pig and said I was disgusting. She didn't know how I could look at myself in the mirror. I know I'm overweight and I'm trying to work on it so it really hurts when she says that. I understand she was mad and wanted to go out with her friends, but for her to attack me like that worries me about who she's becoming.
>
> When I ask my son where he's going and who he's going out with he gets mad at me. He says I don't have any friends because I'm such a bitch. He calls me a "loser," "stupid," and "a worthless bitch" all the time. I hear this stuff constantly from him, every day.

## Threats and Intimidation

Feeling safe with your family in your home is taken for granted by most parents. While most young people have some negative feelings towards their parents during their adolescence, these feelings don't often lead to a regular pattern of emotional attacks. Simple requests from a youth can escalate to verbal demands and when parents ask more questions, young people sometimes use outright verbal threats to hurt their parents combined with displays of intimidating body language: raising closed fists, shoving, standing in doorways.

> First I hear the swearing, then if he's really mad, I get the "I'm going to slit your throat" or "cut your face off" and after that he's in my face, bumping and pushing me, saying, "You think I'm going to hit you, don't you?"
>
> When I tell him to stop the foul language, he gets into the "What are you going to do about it, faggot, you don't scare me." I'm his father so I'm not going to fight with him, but he tries to provoke me into something physical.
>
> My older son threatens my eight-year-old all the time. When they're in the same room, I hear him saying he going to "kick his ass," "fuck him up," "break his face." My little one tries to be strong, but I know he's afraid.
>
> I never know how she is going to react. We were driving down a busy street and she was yelling at me. Then she grabbed the steering wheel and we went over the curb and up onto the sidewalk. I'm glad no one was walking by.
>
> I found some pot in a knapsack he takes to school and wanted to talk to him about it. After some yelling, he came at me with a knife, put me in a headlock, and wrestled me to the floor. I got away and he stabbed some family pictures on the wall. Then he grabbed one of my dogs by the head and threatened to stab it. He pointed a knife right at its head.

## Constant Arguing

Parents feel disempowered when they can't have frank and open discussions with their children. Daily verbal interaction between children and adults allows children to develop sophisticated reasoning skills and gets them to think through the decisions they make. It's not that parents need to get their children to agree with them all the time, but it's important that with their parents' help, children think through the consequences of their decisions. Disagreement and conflict is normal, but abused parents feel like the arguing between them and their child is more about the power their child is trying to assert over them and not the actual subject they are discussing.

He argues with everything I say. No matter what it is. I'm fighting a constant battle with him over the silliest things. It isn't just that he disagrees with me because I would understand that but it's the way he discounts anything I have to say. He'll say things like "That's a stupid thing to say," or "That's the dumbest thing I've ever heard." His arguing often leads to yelling, swearing, and threats. Recently he started slamming doors. I get so exhausted I just don't want to have a conversation with him anymore.

My daughter always argues with me. When I ask her to do something or maybe suggest something, she argues about it and never considers what I have to say. I have to be careful about what I say to her or sometimes decide not to say anything unless I want to put up with an argument that usually involves swearing, yelling, and her getting right in my face.

## Property Damage

Property damage is a sign that teens have moved beyond verbal abuse and their behavior is becoming more heinous. Sometimes an object the teen breaks has special significance for the parent and at other times, breaking something is another way of threatening and intimidating a parent. Property damage is often part of an event that includes a series of abusive behaviors that are intended to get something a youth wants. The cost of making repairs is an additional burden to parents.

We've been evicted twice because of the holes my two sons have put in the walls of the apartments we've lived in. I don't know what I'll do if they keep it up. We won't have any place to live.

I was so afraid after I told her she couldn't go out that I ran into my bedroom and locked the door. She stabbed the door with a butcher knife over and over again. She kept saying she wanted to kill me all the while she was doing it.

I keep my door locked because he'll take things out of my room. When I went to work, he broke my door down and took some money I had in my drawer. When I got home, he told me that's what happens when I lock my door and I better not do it again. He didn't have to break the door, but I think he was just trying to scare me and take my money.

## Criticizing, Blaming, Harassing, and Accusing

While most teens like to debate and use their newly acquired reasoning skills, parents report to us a variety of abusive tactics teens use to get their way. Parents feel badgered when their teens criticize them constantly about the most insignificant details of their lives. Some youth constantly blame their parents for circumstances their parents have no control over or for situations the youth are actually responsible for. When teens want something, they sometimes torment and harass their parents until they hear the answer they want. Parents also report some teens repeatedly accuse them of intentionally trying to make their life more difficult. Criticizing, blaming, harassing, and accusing can also become an implied threat and feel intimidating when the teen is swearing, yelling, and using menacing body language.

> He criticizes me about everything I do. Like yesterday when I picked him up from school, he criticized me for driving too slow, the way I went home, the station I had on the radio, how I switched lanes. He works himself up and then starts swearing and calling me a "stupid bitch." It just never stops.
>
> Earlier in the week, I told my son he and his sister were going to start sharing the computer. He started arguing about it and I could see where things were going. I went to my bedroom and he followed me to the door. I closed the door and he stood there for at least an hour, pounding on the door and yelling at me the whole time.
>
> When I told her she couldn't see her boyfriend and had to stay home, she started yelling and swearing at me, and then got in my face and pushed against me. When I tried to walk outside, she stood in the doorway and held a knife toward me, so I went to my bedroom where I could lock myself in. She stood there for about an hour kicking the door and yelling at me.

## Secondary Tactics

### Economic Abuse

When teens use economic abuse, they are rarely trying to control their parent's lives by restricting their parents' access to money as adults do to their partners in abusive relationships. Stealing credit cards, household property, and money shows contempt for parental authority, but the prime motivation is usually to access money. A teen's destructive behavior can also incur huge costs on a parent's budget and adds even more emotional stress to an already difficult relationship. Most parents can understand personal, verbal attacks, but stealing adds a dimension of conscious intent that takes parents aback.

> He has taken my phone and laptop and sold it. I have to lock my electronics up in my car so he doesn't take them and sell them. I can't keep anything around the house that he can steal.

My daughter has used my credit card number and taken my credit card to buy things. I've had my credit rating ruined because of her doing this.

He tells me how to spend money and what I should buy. Like he complains about the car I bought which is a used, small car. He says if I did what he said, I'd be able to use less money and give him more spending money. It's like he's taken over his father's role and he feels like he's entitled to tell me how to spend my own money.

## Threats of Self-Harm

When teens threaten suicide or to put themselves in a dangerous situation, they can be using emotional abuse if they are doing it to get what they want or to get their parent to do something. These threats are emotional blackmail. Offering to help teens with their emotional distress, like taking them to a hospital emergency room, is a way of addressing a potentially dangerous situation without giving in to their demands.

He's under a lot of stress at school and then I ask him about it. First he tells me to fuck off. Then he says he going to kill himself and I won't have to worry about him. I took him to the emergency room the last time he said that and he admitted he was just trying to freak me out.

Especially when I tell her she can't go out with her boyfriend, she blows up and says she going to kill herself. She gets so emotional, I worry she might actually do it. When I asked her about it once, she said she'd just like to see my face when I saw her dead on the floor.

## Reporting Parents

A false allegation of child abuse from a teen can be devastating to a parent. Parents fear they will be labeled as abusive and unfit parents and that that will elicit sympathy for their youth's violence from government authorities. Parents also feel the government is working against them and see an investigation of child abuse as another example that their parental rights are being taken away.

When I said I was going to call the police the next time he hit me, he told someone at school that I was hitting and threatening him. Child Protective Services came to my house and I feel like a criminal.

When I walked to the phone after he kicked me, he grabbed it and called the police himself. He told them I was hitting him. The police came and acted like I was the criminal.

## Emotional Abuse Towards Siblings

The effects of abuse on other children in the family is often more important to parents than the abuse directed at them and motivates parents to seek help outside their family. Siblings of emotionally abusive teens are affected in two ways. First, they are exposed to the abuse and violence between their sibling and their parent. Some of the effects children experience when they are exposed to adult domestic violence may be similar to the exposure to abuse towards parents. Second, siblings can be direct targets of emotional abuse.

> I won't leave my son home alone with my younger children. He makes horrible threats to them all the time. I don't think he'll do the things he says but I'm still afraid he'll hurt them.
>
> My daughter looks up to her older brother. I worry because one moment they'll be laughing and playing together and the next, he's yelling at her, telling her she's fat and stupid and he's been so angry that he's even choked her. She's lost some her feistiness. She spends more time alone in her room than she used to.
>
> My two sons team up against me. I have to battle two of them.

## Parent Responses to Emotional Abuse

### Fear and Anxiety

"Walking on eggshells" is one of the most common phrases we hear parents say when they are asked about how they feel about their relationship with their teen. Some parents live in a state of tension and dread about what might happen next. They listen and look for cues in their teen's voice or body language for what might become the next storm. Parents' anxiety is experienced on different dimensions. From day to day and sometimes from hour to hour, parents worry about when the next outburst will happen and what their teen will do next. They worry the next incident will be worse than the last. Even parents who initially report they do not fear their youth also report they have hidden all the knives in the house or lock their bedroom door at night.

> I lock my bedroom door at night and put a chair against it. When he's upset, he says he'll kill me. I'm not afraid he'll actually do it, but when he's angry, I'm not sure what he'll do.

When my son yells at me, my stomach tightens just like when his dad was living here. My son has hit me before, so I have to really think about how to get out of the house when he escalates.

## Sadness-Disappointment

Parents who experience a pattern of abuse from their teen feel a sense of loss. Many parents describe a warm and close relationship when their teen was younger. Now they use phrases like "I feel like I've lost my son, or "I wish I had my daughter back," since there are only glimpses of the younger child of their memories. They fear the closeness and intimacy they had is gone forever.

## Emotional Fatigue

Being emotionally attacked takes a toll on self-esteem and confidence, especially as a parent. Constantly defending yourself to your teen who blames you for everything is exhausting, even when you know you are not responsible for everything they say. Parents cannot relax, be themselves, and enjoy the simple pleasures of being a parent when they have to be so careful about everything they say and do. Parents' energy is sapped by being on guard for signs of a mood change that might lead to swearing and name-calling.

I work all week so when we get to the weekend and he starts all the slamming doors, swearing, the attacks on me, sometimes I just tell him to get out and tell him to do whatever he wants to do. I get exhausted from hearing all the vile language he throws at me. My sister says I'm rewarding him for being this way, but I need a break from it.

Sometimes I just numb myself. I try to ignore all the verbal crap I hear from her, and put on a happy face, but I feel myself going into a dark hole anyway.

I'm a single parent and I'm finding it more difficult to get through the day without feeling very, very hopeless. I'll just go to my bedroom sometimes and stare out the window.

## Anger and Attacking Back

Parents worry about their angry responses and aggressiveness towards their youth. When we ask them how they have responded to the abuse, some parents admit they have screamed, yelled, threatened, and sometimes hit their youth. When parents react in these ways, they know what they are doing is counterproductive and want to find a way to stop. With some parents, their negative emotions have gotten the best of them and with others, they are simply trying to find ways to get their teen to stop the abuse.

> I only did this once, but I called him some of the same names he called me and thought he might feel what it's like for me to be called foul names. Nothing positive came out of it because he just laughed at me.
>
> I've slapped her before for calling me some pretty horrible names. She watched herself for a while and then just started back a few weeks later where she left off.
>
> One night he was walking toward his mother yelling at her and I stepped in to stop him from getting too close to her. He bumped me so I pushed him into the wall. He's got to know who's in charge here.

## Feeling Incompetent

Parents' self-confidence is tied to their ability to support and care for their children. Parents identify strongly with their role as a parent and the emotional demands that a child can put on a parent can be overwhelming. Violence can be a devastating blow to a parent's self-worth.

> He says I'm not a good parent and sometimes I think he's right because I should be able to figure out how to get him to stop all the names and yelling obscenities. I know he doesn't really mean it in that way, but I don't know anyone else who has to put up with what he's doing.
>
> I've tried everything, whether it's counseling or just sitting down to talk with him. I'll even ask him what I should do differently, but he always goes back to talking like he's in charge and when I tell him I'm the parent he escalates. I try so hard, but I still feel like a failure.

## Summary

Emotional abuse serves as a constant reminder to parents that their relationship with their child is severely damaged. It is a thread that ties seemingly isolated events into a larger pattern of hurt. A tone of voice, a cold stare, or a particular choice of words reminds parents of where they stand with their child. Emotional abuse can be more hurtful than physical abuse.

# References

4Children (2012). The enemy within. Retrieved March 13, 2013, from http://www.4children. org.uk/Resources/Detail/The-Enemy-Within-Report

Bobic, N. (2004). Adolescent violence towards parents. Topic paper from Australian Domestic and Family Violence Clearinghouse. Retrieved April 11, 2011, from http://www.adfvc.unsw.edu.au/PDF%20files/adolescent_violence.pdf

Child Welfare Information Gateway (2011). *Definitions of child abuse and neglect.* Washington, DC: US Department of Health and Human Services, Children's Bureau.

Cottrell, B. (2001). *Parent abuse: the abuse of parent by their teenage children.* Ottawa: Health Canada. Retrieved June 10, 2010, from http://www.canadiancrc.com/parent_abuse.aspx

Department of Justice. (2012). What is domestic violence? Retrieved March 30, 2012, from http://www.ovw.usdoj.gov/domviolence.htm

Dodge, R., Daly, A., Huyton, J., & Sanders, L. (2012). The challenge of defining wellbeing. *International Journal of Wellbeing, 2*(3), 222–235. doi:10.5502/ijw.v2i3.4

Eckstein, N. (2004). Emergent issues in families experiencing adolescent-to-parent abuse. *Western Journal of Communication,* 68(4), 365–388.

Elgin, S. H. (2000). *The gentle art of verbal self-defense at work.* New York: Prentice Hall Press.

Englander, E. K. (2007). *Understanding violence.* Mahwah, NJ: Lawrence Erlbaum and Associates.

Family Lives. (2010). When family life hurts: family experience of aggression in children. Retrieved October 21, 2012, from http://familylives.org.uk/media_manager/public/209/Documents/Reports/When%20family%20life%20hurts%202010.pdf

Gelles, R. J. (1987). *Family violence.* Beverly Hills: Sage.

Holt, A. (2011). 'The terrorist in my home': teenagers' violence towards parents— constructions of parent experiences in public online message boards. *Child and Family Social Work,* 16(4), 454–463.

Infante, D. A., & Rancer, A. S. (1995). Argumentativeness and verbal aggressiveness: a review of recent theory and research. *Communications Yearbook,* 319–351.

Infante, D. A., Sabourin, T. C., Rudd, J. E., & Shannon, E. A. (1990). Verbal aggression in violent and nonviolent marital disputes. *Communication Quarterly,* 38(4), 361–371.

Loring, M. T. (1994). *Emotional abuse.* New York: Lexington Books.

McKinnon, L. (2008). Hurting without hitting: non-physical contact forms of abuse. Stakeholder Paper 4 from Australian Domestic Family Violence Clearinghouse. Retrieved from www.adfvc.unsw.edu.au

Marshall, L. L. (1994). Physical and psychological abuse. In W. R. Cupach & B. H. Spitzberg (Eds.), *The dark side of interpersonal communication* (pp. 281–311), Hillsdale, NJ: Lawrence Erlbaum Associates.

Mouradian, V. E. (2000). Abuse in intimate relationships: defining the multiple dimensions and terms. *National Violence Against Women Prevention Research Center.* Retrieved from https://www.musc.edu/vawprevention/research/defining.shtml

National Network to End Domestic Violence. (2013). Forms of Abuse. Retrieved May 15, 2013, from http://www.nnedv.org/resources/stats/gethelp/formsofabuse.html

Pagelow, M. D. (1984). *Family violence.* New York: Praeger.

Price, J. (1996). *Power and compassion.* New York: Guilford Press.

Straus, M. (1979). Measuring intrafamilial conflict and violence: the conflict tactics (CT) scale. *Journal of Marriage and the Family,* 45, 633–644.

Thompson A. E., & Kaplan C. A. (1996). Childhood emotional abuse. *British Journal of Psychiatry*, 168(2), 143–148.

Tolman, R. M. (1992). Psychological abuse of women. In R. T. Ammerman & M. Hersen (Eds.), *Assessment of family violence: a clinical and legal sourcebook* (pp. 291–310). New York: John Wiley & Sons.

Tolman, R. M., Rosen, D., & Wood, G. C. (1999). Psychological maltreatment of women. In R. T. Ammerman & M. Hersen (Eds.), *Assessment of family violence: a clinical and legal sourcebook*. 2nd ed. (pp. 322–335), Hoboken, NJ: Wiley Publishers.

# four
# Understanding Parents and Families

Parents are often perplexed by their children's aggressive behavior. "Why is he doing this to us?" is a question we hear over and over. Parents begin by scrutinizing every aspect of their child's life in search of a reason for the violence. They often look at themselves as failed parents, but are not really sure where they went wrong. Each new round of verbal attacks or destroyed property leads to more searching and more unanswered questions.

Parents want the abuse to stop, but nothing they do seems to work. Often, giving consequences for abusive behavior only leads to more abuse from the child and then more consequences from the parent. Many parents feel like they have entered a cycle of abuse with no end in sight. Over a period of weeks and months the escalation of responses and counterresponses from the parent and child threatens to break the bond between the two. When we first talk to parents on the telephone or in interviews, we hear resignation, sadness, and anger in their voices. They've tried disciplining their child in every way they could think of. They have often sought out advice from books, therapists, and trusted family members without success.

This chapter explores the effects of abuse on their role as parents and on their family. Some parents are more vulnerable to abuse than others. Parents respond to the violence in a variety of ways. No profile exists for abused parents. Readers will get a sense of what it's like to live in a home with a child who uses violence and abuse. We'll set the stage by looking at some of the social beliefs and attitudes that limit parents who seek help outside their family.

## Abused Parents Lack a Profile

A common belief among professionals and researchers is that certain types of parents become targets of abuse or that there is a profile of abused parents. We've had sustained personal contact with hundreds of parents who have sought help for themselves and their families. One lesson we've learned from this work is the astonishing variety of parents who seek help. We've met couples in long-term marriages, single mothers, parents of adopted children, separated and divorced parents, and grandparents raising their children's children. Doctors, garbage men, psychiatrists, store clerks, nurses, truck drivers, teachers, lawyers, and social workers have sought services. Parents across all religious, ethnic, racial, and income boundaries have called us for help. Parents who were raised in Ireland, Burundi, and Taiwan were a part of one group session. The same group had a lesbian couple who adopted a child at birth and a single mother who had a disability. Parents with advanced educational degrees sit next to parents who never finished high school. We've also had parents of gay and transgender youth. The common tie between them is the violence and abuse by their children in their homes.

## Mothers as Victims

However, while both fathers and mothers are targets of youth violence, mothers are victims in far greater numbers. Parents seeking help for their families are referred to us from community agencies or from juvenile court mandates, or sometimes, the parents call us themselves. Most referrals are mothers who report they are victims of violence. Parents make calls to the police from many different municipalities in our area, and consistently, most calls are from or about mothers. Our court makes contact with every victim when the prosecutor has received a police report that a youth has committed a domestic violence offense. Again, mothers have consistently been victims in larger numbers than fathers.

Researchers confirm mothers as the most common victims when teens are violent in the home (Paulson, Coombs & Landsverk, 1990; McCloskey & Lichter, 2003; Agnew & Huguley, 1989; Edenborough, Jackson, Mannix & Wilkes, 2008; Evans & Warren-Sohlberg, 1988; Ibabe & Jaureguizar, 2010; Haw, 2010). Our own data documents mothers were the primary victims in 72 percent of the families referred to us over a four-year period (Routt & Anderson, 2011), and after conducting more extensive interviews with these families, 83 percent of these mothers were primary victims of violence at times apart from the specific incident that led to the court referral. The only report of fathers as the more likely victims of adolescent abuse is suspect (Peek, Fischer & Kidwell, 1985). When teen participants in the study were asked about hitting their parent, no distinction was made between teens who initiated hitting and teens who were responding to a violent parent. Since it's the only study to assert fathers as the primary victims, it only underscores mothers as the focus of abuse.

While fathers may be at risk for more serious injury than mothers (Condry & Miles, 2013), even when a father is reported to be the primary victim in an emergency call to the police, mothers are still the primary target in the household. In our examination of records from the prosecutor's office that covered a four-year span, 25 percent of the victims were fathers or male partners. However, in our interviews with these parents, we discovered that mothers were targets of abuse most of the time, apart from the incident that led to police involvement. In many of these cases, the father or male partner was simply protecting the mother of the teen from another attack and was not the primary target. Men acting in the role of protector are not usually hurt to the same degree as when mothers are assaulted. Also, men do not feel the same degree of intimidation and fear as mothers when they are verbally attacked. Fathers may express a great deal of concern and anxiety about their sons' and daughters' abusive behavior, but do not feel as bullied and badgered as mothers. In interviews, teens often say they would never use the same degree of abuse or violence toward their fathers as they do towards their mothers.

A mother who is the victim of her intimate partner's emotional and physical attacks can be vulnerable to becoming the victim of violence from her son or daughter. Simply observing violence against a parent is an obvious way that a child can learn the potential powerful impact of violence. A more insidious and sometimes longer-lasting impact is hearing a mother being belittled, called stupid and incompetent, degraded, insulted, and blamed for everything that goes wrong at home. When an abuser demeans a mother by treating her as a child rather than as a parent, her child loses respect for her authority and is likely to disregard her requests and rules. When she sets firmer limits and becomes more insistent, the child may use the same behaviors and language his or her father used against the mother. Unlike physical abuse that may be an isolated event, these daily messages are learned over a period of time and are constantly reinforced. They become the groundwork for the child to abuse his or her mother.

Mothers may more often be the victims of abuse from their youth due to two special roles mothers play in the family in addition to their role of caretaker. Mothers in distressed families are more engaged with difficult youth in the family than fathers, and as a result, mothers receive more of the difficult behavior used by youth than fathers. As a result, mothers in their role as "crisis manager" are more often the targets of abuse (Patterson, 1980). Youth are also more emotionally attached to their mothers than their fathers (Markiewicz, Lawford, Doyle & Haggart, 2006). Teens look to their mothers for security and safety during stressful life transitions, like the transition from childhood to adolescence, but also when particular difficulties arise in their lives. Most youth simply expect more of their mothers than their fathers and even demand more of their mothers to get their emotional needs met.

## Parents' Emotional Response to Abuse

In the previous chapters, we discussed some of the immediate responses that parents had to the violence and abuse. This section describes the more enduring emotional reactions to their youth's behavior.

### Fear

Parents who are targets of abuse and violence are often afraid to set limits with their children. Parents are fearful and anxious about where to draw the line with their children when they have to worry about their own safety. They feel futile and ineffective as parents when they cannot set curfew times, expectations about school, or household rules. Even in cases where parents and teens have some positive interactions, parents report they live in fear of another bout of violence when they decide to enforce a rule they set for their teen.

Parents often use the phrase "walking on eggshells" when describing the way they feel when they are around their children. Anyone who has lived in a violent home knows this feeling. An outburst happens so quickly and so unpredictably that everyone has to be careful so they don't "set off" the abusive person. Victims try to anticipate what might happen if they say or do something so the abusive person doesn't get upset and doesn't escalate to more violence. It means constantly rewording things you might say or rethinking what you do to bypass a conflict. Parents and siblings of an abusive youth live in this state of fear.

### Avoidance

Avoidance is one of the survival strategies parents use when they are "walking on eggshells." Parents feel if they confront an issue directly with their teenage child, they are in danger of a verbal or physical assault. So parents avoid talking about important issues like poor grades or curfew to minimize conflict. It can also mean having as little physical contact as possible to keep conflict to a minimum. Parents talk to us about how they sometimes don't like to be in the same room with their child because they are afraid a conflict will start. Both "walking on eggshells" and avoidance destroy a parent's ability to parent their child.

### Anger

Parents are not always able to stay calm and rational when responding to their teen's abuse and violence. The tension created by the fear and anxiety of living with an abusive teen sometimes leads parents to react in unhealthy ways. Some parents we interviewed talk about yelling at or slapping their children, throwing things, or slamming doors. One of the first parents we interviewed was a survivor of domestic violence whose son began to use many of the same vile words and phrases his father used towards her. Her immediate reaction was to slap him. From the outside looking in, these parents appear abusive and may look like the reason their children act the way they do. Some teens will use these episodes to justify their violence. When parents have a chance to think about their responses to their teen's violence, they know they haven't responded well. These same parents often realize they are contributing towards a violent home when they react in these ways.

## Powerlessness

Parents frequently relay feelings of being held hostage and straight-jacketed by their youth's abuse. Parents feel controlled and sometimes dominated. They cannot fulfill their responsibilities as legal and moral caregivers of their children when they live in fear of being verbally attacked or physically hurt. They cannot effectively parent when they feel helpless and have to second-guess every decision they make about their children. Parents and siblings feel like they don't have a home anymore because they have to be so careful about what they say and do when an abusive teen is in the home. Powerlessness is common to all victims of family violence, including parent abuse.

## Isolation

Victimized parents feel isolated in a number of ways. Most parents who were interviewed felt they could not talk to friends or family members about their youth's violence. Books on parenting rarely mention violent youth and parenting classes do not discuss children who use abuse and violence. Since these youth are often not violent outside their families, teachers or other adults who come into contact with these youth often do not see any signs of an abusive or violent teenager. People outside the family find it hard to believe they could do the things their parents are describing. When people have not heard about actual cases of parent abuse, they often think parents are calling the police when their teenage children are just doing normal teenage things. Even when they realize something dangerous is happening at home, therapists and counselors are often at a loss to help parents who are victims of youth who are assaultive.

## Shame

Parents have a strong sense of shame about the violence in their homes. One source of shame comes from their own sense of failure as parents. All parents feel responsible for their children, even abusive children, and think they should be able to control them. The singular bond between a parent and child makes it difficult for parents to separate themselves from their children. Parents naturally want to teach their children the skills they will need to face any problem.

When children face difficulties, parents often wonder if they have prepared them adequately. They feel if they were good parents, they should have foreseen the hurdle their child is facing. Parents have this feeling even when their child is using violence and abuse against them. They often question their own abilities for not anticipating this behavior and think they must have in some way caused it.

Another source of shame is the viewpoints of people who are not familiar with adolescent violence in the home. Parents feel people who have no experience with teen violence in the home will blame them for their child's violence because they have failed to control the child. One view others may have is that victimized parents do not experience serious levels of violence and are overreacting when they call the police. While it is true that parents usually don't experience the more serious levels of physical violence that adult victims of domestic violence do, the fear and anxiety that is created by a punch in the face, a hole in the wall, or a threat to kill is debilitating to healthy family relations. As a result, parents often keep the violence in their home a secret from anyone. Many parents are very reluctant to get help from anyone, and when they finally call the police, parents often report to us that the calls were "the most difficult decision of my life."

## Denial

Parents themselves don't want to admit their children are being abusive and violent and they justify or deny what their children are doing to them. To acknowledge your own child is abusing you is very difficult for a parent. Two researchers who were the first to write about parent abuse wrote, "Children abusing their parents is so counter normative that it is extremely difficult for parents to admit that they are being victimized by one of their children" (Gelles & Cornell, 1985). Parents often search for different ways to explain their teen's behavior. For instance, some use mental health diagnoses to explain and, in some cases, justify their children's behavior. Other parents refer to abuse in their child's past to explain their behavior. Parents understandably try to explain what their children are doing without having to admit they are inflicting serious harm on them or other family members.

## Social Attitudes That Limit Support to Abused Parents

Parents find their situation is often misunderstood when they reach out for help. Some practitioners point to their parenting as the problem. Parents are given the message that if only they had been better parents their children would never have been abusive and violent. Many parents feel they are seen as the source of the problem by professionals who are supposed to help them. Social attitudes and beliefs about parenting and the role the family plays in our lives define the way we perceive and interpret problems like adolescent violence in the home and have been one of the major hurdles to forging practical solutions. Often, such long-held, universally accepted beliefs are taken for granted. A deeper look at these attitudes and beliefs will help us understand the challenges parents face when they seek help for their families.

## Beliefs About the Family

For societies throughout the world, the family is the bedrock of emotional, social, and economic support for individuals from birth to death (Levesque, 2001). It serves as a protector, nurturer, moral guide, and motivator. The unique status that the family holds is embodied in phrases describing the family as a "haven in a heartless world" since it offers unparalleled comfort and protection like no other place in our lives. For some of us, it defines who we are and it is the foundation of our social and political outlook. We are not always aware of all the ways we are influenced by our families, but most adults know many of their values and morals were formed in their family relationships (Lakoff, 2002). So it is no wonder that the family is idealized throughout the world.

While the family may represent all that is good and right in our lives, it is also the location of some of the most inhuman acts we experience. Three leading researchers come to some stunning conclusions about violence in the family: ". . . the American family and the American home are perhaps as or more violent than any other single American institution or setting (with the exception of the military, and then only in time of war). Americans run the greatest risk of assault, physical injury, and even murder in their own homes by members of their own families" (Straus, Gelles & Steinmetz, 1980, p. 4). Acts of violence perpetrated by family members against one another from childhood to old-age are well documented (Asay, DeFrain, Metzger & Moyer, 2013). The brutality that takes place in families from rape to forced imprisonment to murder is breathtaking. As Roger Levesque states, "The study of violence reveals the general rule that families constitute a pervasive source of violence and contribute to victimization not usually associated with families" (2001, p. 3).

However, this violence is obscured from full view. These acts of violence remain "hidden" in part due to the widespread beliefs that adorn, protect, and idealize the family across all cultures (Levesque, 2001; Charles, 1986). For instance, beliefs about the right to privacy that shield the family from unwanted "expert opinion" or an intrusive government bureaucrat may at times be beneficial; the very same beliefs may also shield victimization of family members. So while the family's special status is based on historic beliefs that rightly protect it, these beliefs also make it difficult to help its victims.

## Beliefs About Parental Control

One researcher has identified beliefs about parents that are common to all cultures. One of these universally held beliefs is that "parents should, can and do control their children" (Levesque, 2001). The power that parents have in the family allows them to shape and direct their children's development, but the same belief protects parents when they use practices that are potentially harmful to children. For instance, policy makers legislate the right to use corporal punishment in the United States because they believe parents should be able to decide how to discipline their children, in spite of evidence of the long-term, harmful effects of spanking.

However, the belief that parents should control their children not only affects how parents are perceived when they use their power in the interests of their children, but it also affects how parents are perceived when power is reversed and directed against them. The power parents have over their children is so universally accepted throughout the world that any deviation from it is incomprehensible. When parents in large numbers report abuse and violence from their children, the dissonance in most people's minds leads them to conclude that such parents must be the root of the problem.

One stereotype held by professionals is that adolescent to parent violence usually takes place in a chaotic home environment where parents do not set limits with their children, have few expectations, have no control, and resort to violence to restore order. For some people, simply the report of violence on the part of a teenager towards a parent is an indication of chaos in the home. In other cases, the characterization of a chaotic home environment is based on a few bits of information that are shaped by a foregone conclusion about chaos in the home. To illustrate, we will use an example:

Daniel is a 15-year-old boy who was arrested for assaulting his mother, Marla. A single mother with two other younger children, Marla was not employed outside the home. During an interview with a court worker, she reported incidents when she pushed, grabbed, and hit Daniel. Daniel confirmed his mother's reported use of harsh language, angry responses, and sometimes physically aggressive behavior towards him. The interviewer concluded in his report to us that Daniel had a mother who had poor parenting skills, had difficulty controlling her emotions, and set few boundaries with her children. The home was described as a typically chaotic home where the youth's behavior was learned from the parent and Daniel's assault of his mother was his way of coping with a difficult parent.

After our interviews, we drew different conclusions. Daniel's father was physically violent and emotionally abusive with Marla and the children, especially Daniel. She was hospitalized after one attack and was eventually diagnosed with PTSD. The father also severely hurt Daniel. After his father left, Daniel vowed never to be like him. Marla was disappointed when Daniel as a teenager began to use foul language towards her. Daniel's behavior escalated over time, particularly when Marla set limits with him. She was now physically afraid of him.

During one incident, Marla warned Daniel a number of times that he needed to get ready for a doctor's appointment, but he ignored her and continued to play his computer game. Finally, she turned off the computer. Marla was shocked and infuriated to hear Daniel verbally attack her using the same vile words and degrading language his father used. Her immediate response was to slap him. On the way to the doctor, when she tried to stop him from breaking the car windshield, he hit her. Marla reported she had pushed, grabbed, and even hit Daniel to stop him from hurting her and his two younger siblings who were very afraid of him. Marla was frustrated because efforts to enlist Daniel's support of her expectations and guidelines for him were only met with resistance and escalating abuse.

Two researchers encourage observers to recognize the context of violent behavior. "More meaning can be conveyed by observing the relationships between characters in a movie than by viewing a series of still photographs. The character's actions, viewed in temporal order, allow us to make causal inferences and thereby increase our understanding" (Gano-Phillips & Fincham, 1995, p. 219). In our interview with Daniel, he acknowledged his mother was simply trying to stop him from hurting anyone or destroying any more property and she was not abusing him.

## Beliefs About Parental Permissiveness

Another belief limiting the support these parents receive is that they are overly permissive. Most people define "permissive" as being too indulgent, too easy going, and too tolerant of children's behavior. This belief holds that parents give their children too much freedom and not enough responsibility. Parents who are permissive see their children as their friends and try to please their children too much. They don't set firm boundaries and clear lines of authority. People who use the permissive parenting label assert that if these parents established their authority more firmly, their children would never have used violence and abuse towards them. If these parents had nipped the problem in the bud with swift and sure discipline at an earlier age, the abuse would never have started.

Permissiveness is seen by many people as a prime characteristic of one of the two competing narratives regarding parenting in America. In the more traditional style of parenting that has been identified by George Lakoff (2002) as the "strict father figure" style, children learn the unambiguous difference between right and wrong that demands strict obedience to parents through the method of reward and punishment. This style of parenting grew out of an earlier era in the early nineteenth century when family roles were more instrumental, lines of authority were more hierarchical, and the father held the reins of power in the family (Skolnick & Skolnick, 1999). The modern style of parenting that Lakoff calls the "nurturant" style is based on the moral code of respect and compassion that places a high value on emotional closeness, warmth, and intimacy in family relations (Larsen & Richards, 1994). This style of parenting, which allows children to freely explore the world and focuses on their individual needs, is synonymous in some people's minds with permissiveness. When children rightly or wrongly fall outside acceptable social norms, permissiveness becomes a readily available explanation.

After interviewing hundreds of abused parents and working with them for months at a time, the permissive parent jacket doesn't fit abused parents. It is used to label parents who are struggling with extremely difficult circumstances and sheds little light on their situation. It conjures up an image of a person who hasn't fully accepted the role of a parent and is trying to find a way around the more difficult decisions that parents must make if they are to be effective parents. Permissive parenting is an easy tag to use against abused parents that resolves the uncomfortable feelings when faced with an unusual problem like parent abuse. Unfortunately, the permissive parenting label has become part of conventional wisdom for all sorts of problems, but especially when youth are violent in the home.

The permissive parenting label is used by some researchers who have written about adolescent violence in the home. Parents are described as "permissive" (Omer, 2000), "abdicating" their authority (Harbin and Maddin, 1979), as "overly indulgent" (Charles, 1986), or as either "permissive or indulgent" (Gallagher, 2004). Finally, other researchers simply accept permissive parenting as a matter of fact in their discussion of this issue (Wilson, 1996; Pagani, Larocque, Vitaro & Tremblay, 2003; Evans & Warren-Sohlberg, 1988; Hong, Kral, Espelage & Allen-Meares, 2011; Laurent & Derry, 1999).

Like many labels and stereotypes, the permissive parent has a kernel of truth. Parents respond to abusive teens in different ways. In instances where a parent gives in to a teen's demand, allows a teen more freedom than he or she seems capable of handling, or doesn't set clear consequences after an abusive incident, parents appear indecisive, inconsistent, and spineless. Service providers are continually frustrated as they watch parents simply give in to their teen's demands. Researchers are satisfied these parent's responses easily fit into the permissive category. After observing parents respond to their teens in these ways, observers conclude they are the causes of the abuse and violence.

Without longitudinal data, Gelles believes researchers may "attribute causal status to variables which may have occurred or arisen after the violence or abusive act" (Gelles, 1979a, pp. 171–172) and sees a "need to nail down cause and effect relations by tracing families over time" (Gelles, 1979b, p. 27). In fact, he describes these observations as a very common form of "fallacious reasoning" among professionals. With this same line of reasoning, we might conclude that "paranoia is the cause of speeding tickets because people who receive tickets tend to act paranoid when the police officer approaches them" (Gelles, 1979a, p. 171).

One important lesson we have learned in our work with families affected by violence is that parents and children are involved in a complex, dynamic, and constantly changing relationship. Parents who are automatically labeled by some as permissive or living in chaos actually face unique challenges that are confusing and often misunderstood. Children are not blank slates; they bring mood, temperament, intellectual capabilities, and genetic predispositions into a relationship with a parent. Parents in turn use a variety of parenting styles and practices that reflect their child's changing temperament and mood and the severity of the problem at hand. So while some types of parenting can obviously contribute to a child's delinquent behavior, a child's problem behavior also impacts parenting practices (Huh, Tristan, Wade & Stice, 2006; Grusec & Goodnow, 1994).

Mothers who are most often victims of teen violence in the home face the additional social stigma of mother blaming. Mother blaming is a cultural narrative that is described as a "serious and pervasive problem" (Caplan & Hall-McCorquodale, 1985). Mothers are held responsible for their children's behavior, health, and overall development in ways that fathers are not, and a woman's role as a mother is more highly scrutinized than a father's when their children exhibit signs of maladjustment. Virtually every modern theory of child development is centered on the mother's relationship with her child and as a result, most psychopathologies, high-risk behaviors of adolescents, and even some childhood traumas like sexual abuse and incest are attributed to mothers. Mothers are particularly vulnerable to condescending, patronizing, and contemptuous responses from professionals when they do not fit the society's model of motherhood: white, middle class, and married (Jackson & Mannix, 2004). Since single mothers are most often victims, they face additional challenges when seeking help.

## Explaining Family Relationships

The effects of youth violence in the home are significant. The most immediate effect on parents is the inability to fulfill their leadership role in the family. Parents try to find ways of assisting their children through the adolescent years, especially with school and peer relationships, so they can succeed as adults. Socialization in the family provides the foundation for the teen's independence. The social health of an adolescent can be to a large degree measured by how well he or she can fulfill the role of son or daughter and brother or sister. A relationship between teens and parents supports independence for the teen when parents take a leadership role in the family so they can maintain a healthy environment. Violence in the home challenges the ability of parents to help their teens navigate a path towards independence.

Family systems theory and attachment theory are two invaluable tools to help understand the debilitating processes at work when a teen is violent with family members. Successfully parenting an adolescent requires interplay between establishing and enforcing guidelines, limits, and expectations and providing a warm, caring, and sensitive environment. These two theories explain the processes at work that undermine the family's capacity to meet these goals. They also provide a bridge to understanding how to help these families.

## Family Systems Theory

Family systems theory views family relationships as the foundation for psychological health and focuses on the interaction between family members as individuals and as members of subsystems within the family. Individuals within family systems have roles to play, and when everyone plays their role, the stability and integrity of the family system is maintained. Family systems theory developed in part as a reaction to the dominant trend in psychology that centers on the individual and instead, looks at individuals within the context of their family.

Family systems theory (Broderick, 1993) describes two processes that are particularly relevant to teen violence towards parents: boundaries and hierarchy. Boundaries are a set of invisible rules that define and organize the way a family functions. A boundary is like a psychological membrane that separates one person or subsystem from another. Boundaries shape the type and amount of communication between the family system and the outside world and communication within the family. Just imagine the enormous difference in the way two parents communicate with each other about their children as opposed to the way they directly communicate with their children. Boundaries define the difference between the two. In general, clear and flexible boundaries support healthy family relationships and inflexible and opaque boundaries promote dysfunction within the family. However, the degree of flexibility and permeability of a boundary evolves with changing circumstances inside and outside the family.

Hierarchy is also related to healthy family relationships. Different subsystems within a family have different degrees of control over decision-making power. Family systems theory puts the parental subsystem at the foundation of functional family relationships. It is responsible for creating and maintaining boundaries. As the family changes, grows, and faces difficult challenges, parents take the initiative in defining new boundaries and ensuring family members respect them. The transition from childhood to adolescence is a prime example of a normative challenge that requires new boundaries.

Adolescent violence in the home destroys healthy family boundaries and undermines the appropriate hierarchy between parents and children. Acts of violence and abuse themselves are a direct violation of boundaries and hierarchy and serve to make sound communication between individual family members and between the parent-child subsystems difficult and at times impossible. These violations also make it unlikely that the everyday family challenges will be discussed and resolved. The anxiety and fear that accompany abuse force parents to interact with their children outside of the customary healthy family boundaries that are a part of functional family interactions. After a teen's violent behavior puts family boundaries and hierarchy in jeopardy, parents have a very difficult time restoring a healthy system.

## Adolescent Attachment Theory

Attachment is the emotional bond between children and parents or caregivers that gives the children a protective safe haven to begin exploring the world around them and a safe base to come back to when they feel threatened (Bowlby, 1988). Although not synonymous with love and affection, attachment is referred to as an "affectional tie" because it is a primary emotional process that supports a person's survival and growth (Ainsworth, 1985). Attachment influences how people view themselves and others in interpersonal relationships and has a major impact on every aspect of personal development.

The influence of attachment continues beyond childhood. Adolescence is a period of rapid neurological, social, and cognitive change that presents new challenges to a child-parent relationship. A secure attachment with a parent is as important for an adolescent's healthy transition to adulthood as it is for a child's successful transition to middle childhood and beyond. Attachment security in adolescence protects against virtually every problem associated with this age group and is a foundation for social, cognitive, and emotional competence (Moretti & Peled, 2004).

While parents hold the primary responsibility for creating a secure base for their children's development, adolescents play a much greater role in their attachment relationship with their parent by taking an active part in creating a safe base. Two measures of healthy attachment in adolescence that are particularly relevant to adolescent violence in the home are de-idealization of parents and maintaining a good relationship with parents even while disagreeing with them. When adolescents de-idealize their parents, the way they think about their parents changes from a child's black and white view to a more mature, nuanced view that allows them to assess their parents' strengths and weaknesses realistically. A de-idealized perspective is not a rejection of or disengagement from parents, but is an important step towards autonomy and independence while still relying on support from a parent's secure base.

A healthy parent-teen attachment is also demonstrated when they can maintain the overall integrity of their relationship even while disagreeing on particular issues. The stress created by disagreement between a youth and parent is analogous to the stress created by a strange situation for an infant. Infants who have a secure base for support can explore uncharted, "strange" situations in their environment (Ainsworth & Bell, 1970); adolescents are also exploring new territory when they assert their own perspectives in disagreements that clash with their parent's perspectives. Infants can tolerate and learn from "strange" new situations due to the secure emotional ties with their parents, and in the same way, adolescents can feel secure disagreeing with their parents, knowing their relationship is not in jeopardy.

Adolescent violence and abuse damage parent-adolescent emotional bonds and undermine the parent-teen relationship as a secure base and safe haven. Violence breeds fear, anxiety, and a lack of trust. Parents are now in the position of feeling insecure in their relationship with their child. Instead of an evolution towards a de-idealized view of the parent, teens attack their parents' value and integrity, and healthy disagreements escalate into emotional attacks and sometimes physical violence. The attachment bond between the parent and the adolescent is damaged and unhealthy.

Family boundaries and attachment bonds reinforce and support each other. Boundaries feel natural and second nature when relationships are safe and secure. A safe and secure parent-teen bond in turn is maintained by boundaries that protect and safeguard family members' roles and status.

An unhealthy teen-parent bond and the lack of secure boundaries impair a family's ability to confront the stresses that are a part of a changing family system. Families and family members have varying capacities and resources to devote to stresses that arise through the normal course of change in family relationships (Hill, 1958; Weber, 2011). Youth in particular have a limited capacity to address the stresses that accompany their transition from childhood to adolescence and rely on parents to make a smooth transition. Healthy family boundaries and attachment bonds allow parents and teens to work together to meet the challenges of both everyday problems and long-term goals. However, adolescent violence stretches the family's resources and capacity far beyond its ability meet these challenges.

## Summary

The single most important challenge facing abused parents is the loss of authority with their children. Parenting any child carries immeasurable moral and legal responsibilities. In order to carry out these responsibilities, parents must be able to set limits and boundaries that provide a framework for children to grow and develop. As children enter their adolescent years, they are beginning a new period of learning that will take them into the beginnings of adulthood. In the adolescent years, parents balance responsibility and freedom so that their children can begin to make some of their own decisions within their parents' rules and guidelines. In order for teens to balance freedom and responsibility, their parents must be able to support them with respectful authority. Without parental leadership a parent-teen relationship collapses.

## References

Ainsworth, M.D.S. (1985). Attachments across the lifespan. *Bulletin of the New York Academy of Medicine*, 61, 792–812.

Ainsworth, M.D.S., & Bell, S. M. (1970). Attachment, exploration, and separation: illustrated by the behavior of one year olds in strange situations. *Child Development*, 41, 47–61.

Agnew, R., & Huguley, S. (1989). Adolescent violence toward parents. *Journal of Marriage and the Family*, 51, 699–711.

Asay, S. M., DeFrain, J., Metzger, M., & Moyer, B. (2013). *Family violence from a global perspective*. Thousand Oaks, CA: Sage.

Baumrind, D. (1971). Current patterns of parental authority. *Developmental Psychology Monographs*, 4 (1, Pt2).

Boss, P. (1987). Family stress. In M. B. Sussman & S. K. Steinmetz (Eds.), *Handbook of marriage and the family* (pp. 675–723), New York: Plenum.

Bowlby, J. (1969). *Attachment and loss*. Vol. 1, *Attachment*. New York: Basic Books.

Bowlby, J. (1988). *A secure base: parent-child attachment and healthy human development*. New York: Basic Books.

Broderick, C. B. (1993). *Understanding family process: basics of family systems theory*. Thousand Oaks, CA: Sage.

Caplan, P., & Hall-McCorquodale, I. (1985). The scapegoating of mothers: a call for change. *American Journal of Orthopsychiatry*, 55, 610–613.

Charles, A. V. (1986). Physically abused parents. *Journal of Family Violence*, 1(4), 343–355.

Cohen, R., Hsueh, Y., Russell, K. M., & Ray, G. E. (2006). Beyond the individual: a consideration for the development of aggression. *Aggression and Violent Behavior*, 11, 341–351.

Condry, R., & Miles, C. (2013). Adolescent to parent violence: framing and mapping a hidden problem. *Criminology and Criminal Justice*. Retrieved from http://crj.sagepub.com/content/early/2013/09/03/1748895813500155

Cottrell, B., & Monk, P. (2004). Adolescent-to-parent abuse. *Journal of Family Issues*, 25(8), 1072–1095.

Edenborough, M., Jackson, D., Mannix, J., & Wilkes, L. M. (2008). Living in the red zone: the experience of child-to-mother violence. *Child and Family Social Work*, 13, 464–473.

Evans, E. D., & Warren-Sohlberg, L. (1988). A pattern of analysis of adolescent abusive behavior toward parents. *Journal of Adolescent Research*, 3(2), 201–216.

Gallagher, E. D. (2004). Parents victimized by their children. *Australian and New Zealand Journal of Family Therapy*, 25(1), 1–12.

Gano-Phillips, S., & Fincham, F. D. (1995). Family conflict, divorce, and children's adjustment. In M. A. Fitzpatrick & A. L. Vangelisti (Eds.), *Explaining family interactions* (pp. 206–231), Newbury Park, CA: Sage.

Gelles, R. J. (1979a). *Family violence*. Beverly Hills, CA: Sage.

Gelles, R. J. (1979b). Determinants of violence in the family: toward a theoretical integration. In W. Burr, R. Hill, F. I. Nye & I. L. Reiss (Eds.), *Contemporary theories about the family*. Vol. 1, *Research-based theories* (pp. 549–581), New York: Free Press.

Gelles, R. J., & Cornell, C. P. (1985). *Intimate violence in families*. Beverly Hills: Sage.

Grusec, J. E., & Goodnow, J. J. (1994). Impact of parental discipline methods on the child's internalization of values: a reconceptualization of current points of view. *Developmental Psychology* 30(1), 4–19.

Harbin, H. T., & Maddin, D. J. (1979). Battered parents: a new syndrome. *American Journal of Psychiatry*, 136, 1288–1291.

Haw, A. (2010). Parenting over violence, understanding and empowering mothers affected by adolescent violence in the home. Retrieved from http://patgilescentre.org.au/about-pgc/reports/parenting-over-violence-final-report.pdf

Hill, R. (1958). Generic features of families under stress. *Social Casework*, 49, 139–150.

Hong, J. S., Kral, M. J., Espelage, D. L., & Allen-Meares, P. (2011). The social ecology of adolescent initiated parent abuse: a review of the literature. *Child Psychiatry and Human Development*, 43, 431–454.

Huh, D., Tristan, J., Wade, E., & Stice, E. (2006). Does problem behavior elicit poor parenting? A prospective study of adolescent girls. *Journal of Adolescent Research*, 21 (2), 185–204.

Ibabe, I., & Jaureguizar, J. (2010). Child-to-parent violence: profile of abusive adolescents and their families. *Journal of Criminal Justice*, 38, 616–624.

Jackson, D., & Mannix, J. (2004). Giving voice to the burden of blame: a feminist study of mothers' experiences of mother blaming. *International Journal of Nursing Practice*, 10, 150–158.

Lakoff, G. (2002). *Moral politics, how liberals and conservatives think*. Chicago: University of Chicago Press.

Larson, R. L., & Richards, M. H. (1994). *Divergent realities*. New York: Basic Books.

Laurent, A., & Derry, A. (1999). Violence of French adolescents toward their parents: characteristics and contexts. *Journal of Adolescent Health*, 25, 21–26.

Levesque, R.J.R. (2001). *Culture and family violence*. Washington, DC: American Psychological Association.

McCloskey, L. A., & Lichter, E. L. (2003). The contribution of marital violence to adolescent aggression across different relationships. *Journal of Interpersonal Violence*, 18(4), 390–412.

Markiewicz, D., Lawford, H., Doyle, A. B., & Haggart, N. (2006). Developmental differences in adolescents' and young adults' use of mothers, fathers, best friends, and romantic partners to fulfill attachment needs. *Journal of Youth & Adolescence*, 35(1), 121–134.

Moretti, M. M., & Peled, M. (2004). Adolescent-parent attachment: bonds that support healthy development. *Paediatrics and Child Development*, 9(8), 551–555.

Nixon, J. (2012). Practitioner's constructions of parent abuse. *Social Policy & Society*, 11 (2), 229–239.

Omer, H. (2000). *Parental presence*. Phoenix, AZ: Zeig, Tucker.

Pagani, L., Larocque, D., Vitaro, F., & Tremblay, R. E. (2003). Verbal and physical abuse towards mothers: the role of family configuration, and coping strategies. *Journal of Youth and Adolescence*, 32(2), 215–222.

Patterson, G. R. (1980). *Mothers: unacknowledged victims*. Chicago: University of Chicago Press.

Paulson, M. J., Coombs, R. H., & Landsverk, J. (1990). Youth who physically assault their parents. *Journal of Family Violence*, 5(2), 121–133.

Peek, C. W., Fischer, J. L., & Kidwell, J. S. (1985). Teenage violence toward parents: a neglected dimension of family violence. *Journal of Marriage and the Family*, 47(4), 1051–1058.

Routt, G. B., & Anderson, E. A. (2011). Adolescent violence towards parents. *Journal of Abuse, Maltreatment, and Trauma*, 20, 1–19.

Skolnick, A. S., & Skolnick, J. H. (1999). *Family in transition*. New York: Addison-Wesley Educational Publishers.

Straus, M. A., Gelles, R. J., & Steinmetz, S. K. (1980). *Behind closed doors: violence in the American family*. Garden City, NY: Anchor Press/Doubleday.

Weber, J. G. (2011). Individual and family stress and crises. Thousand Oaks, CA: Sage.

Wilson, J. (1996). Physical abuse of parents by adolescent children. In D. Busby (Ed.), *The impact of violence on the family* (101–122), Boston: Allyn & Bacon.

# five
# **Understanding Teens**

I hit my mom when I had a bunch of clothes in my hand. She came into my room yelling at me about cleaning my room just as I was starting to pick up my clothes off of the floor. I didn't really hit her though; I just wanted her to get out of my room. I got so mad I didn't know what to do. So I tried to push her out the door, and I kind of hit her in the head by mistake. Earlier this week, she took my cell phone away because I hadn't cleaned my room. She has no idea how much I need my phone. I really wanted it back.

Any abusive behavior can be confusing regardless of who uses it. People naturally look for reasons loved ones hurt each other so they can begin to understand it. The search for an explanation can be painful and frustrating. Rarely are parents satisfied that they truly understand why their child hurts them. Violence towards parents can be confusing to teens as well. When children use abuse or violence against a family member, it's reasonable to assume they are responding to some abuse by a parent, an older brother or sister, or someone who is bigger and stronger than they are. But that isn't always the case. There isn't a simple connection between being hit and hitting someone else. In fact, as we shall see, often when children are hurt emotionally or physically and they later strike out at someone who is an easy target, it is often not the one who originally hurt them.

## Facts About Teens

The variety of teens that we have seen in group sessions is astounding. Some are excellent students and college bound. Others struggle to get passing grades and have behavioral problems in school. Some participate in team sports like football, soccer, or baseball, and others play an instrument in their school band or sing in the choir. Some youth have a difficult time making friends and have few peer relationships. We have had gay and transgender youth. Some have parents born in other countries. They cross all ethnic, racial, and socioeconomic class lines.

The majority of youth violence in the home is committed by boys. Some research shows girls and boys using violence in equal numbers (Walsh & Krienert, 2007; Hong, Kral, Espelage & Allen-Meares, 2012). In King County, Washington, the juvenile court prosecutor's office documents that 65 percent of the offenders against parents and other family members are male (Routt & Anderson, 2011). Our referrals from community mental health agencies confirm boys as the primary perpetrators of violence at home. Given the number of adult males who are arrested for interpersonal violence, the number of boys who use violence in the home is not surprising. Many family violence practitioners are, however, surprised that the rate of offending girls is as high as it is.

None of the research on girls' aggression includes violence initiated by girls against family members. If youth violence at home is rarely discussed, girls who hurt family members are given even less attention. The one report that gives passing reference to it doesn't consider the real damage it causes family members (Chesney-Lind & Belknap, 2004). Most research traditionally describes girls' aggression as relational aggression that does not include physical violence and defines it as "the purposeful intent to inflict harm on another through a social relationship." This includes behaviors such as spreading rumors, gossiping, or excluding the target person from social activities (Bowie, 2007, p. 107). However, research demonstrates that boys who use physical violence also engage in relational aggression (Lansford et al., 2012), and physical violence in general is increasing among girls (Snethen & Van Puymbroeck, 2008). Our data show the number of girls who are violent in the home has remained constant since 1995 (Routt & Anderson, 2011). Girls use violence almost exclusively against their mothers, and as with boys, often these mothers are survivors of adult domestic violence.

Youth of all ethnic groups assault their parents. Some evidence from the United States shows white youth are more likely to assault their parents than African American youth (Agnew & Huguley, 1989), and gender differences for offenders exist among ethnic groups (Walsh & Krienert, 2007). Immigrant families face challenges that are different from native-born families. Youth in immigrant families often have a better understanding of English and mainstream culture than their parents, and as a result, they hold positions of greater power than their parents. Parents' lack of knowledge is used against them and can lead to abusive behavior from the teen. Additionally, the clash of cultural values from the parent's country of origin and North American mainstream culture can create considerable conflict that is an added stress on the parent-teen relationship.

When parents are asked when their teen first used violence, the most common response is the middle school years or somewhere between the ages of 12 and 14. For teens to challenge parental authority during these years is normal and even healthy, but violence and abuse are not. In earlier chapters, we described how parents are physically and emotionally abused by their adolescent children. We learned how parents cope with this abuse and how they react to it. Parents have their own explanations for their children's behavior. Sometimes they refer to previous traumatic experiences like witnessing domestic violence to explain their child's behavior. Other parents look to a mental health diagnosis, like bipolar disorder or attention deficit disorder as an explanation. Still others have seen aggressive behaviors in their children at an early age, and in spite of many hours in counseling and professional help, these behaviors have gotten worse throughout childhood into adolescence. Since aggression towards parents has no single cause, no simple explanations exist.

## Explaining Violent Behavior

Trying to explain why someone uses abuse and violence is like trying to explain why someone has any chronic health problem, like heart disease (Dodge & Pettit, 2003). Neither heart disease nor the use of violence has a single cause. Heart disease is explained by a collection of risk factors that implicate multiple routes to the disease. Poor diet, lack of exercise, excess weight, and smoking all are contributors to heart disease, but by themselves, none causes a heart attack. In addition, these same unhealthy practices that lead to a heart attack also contribute to other chronic diseases, such as cancer and strokes. Not all heart attacks are the same, so each type has a variation that differentiates it from the next one. Some of the risks are general and apply to all types of heart attacks while other risks are specific to a particular type of heart attack. This same discussion applies to violent and abusive behavior. Clusters of risk factors, varying pathways, and different kinds of violence complicate the picture. However, both heart disease and aggressive behavior share a developmental process that includes biological predispositions, psychological mechanisms, and social contexts.

There are few studies that focus exclusively on adolescents who have used violent behavior towards other people, and the few studies that have been done vary widely because they rely on very different sources (juvenile justice, community, psychiatric hospitals) that make generalization difficult (Borduin & Schaeffer, 1997). In addition, work on aggressive youth is embedded in studies of "antisocial" or "conduct disordered" youth who exhibit a much wider variety of problem behaviors, such as substance use, stealing, truancy, vandalism, etc. While violence towards parents is an antisocial behavior and undoubtedly, some antisocial youth are violent towards their parents, the literature rarely mentions it among the problem behaviors of antisocial youth. Since studies on youth aggression don't include violence in the home, we must speculate on how adolescents develop aggression towards family members. Fortunately, we can draw upon our many conversations with youth and parents in interviews and group sessions.

## Biological Factors

Biological factors that put youth at risk for using violence are very indirect and diffuse (Dodge & Pettit, 2003; Seguin, Sylvers & Lilienfield, 2007) and they fall into two categories: genetic influence and the prenatal environment. Genetic influence on violent behavior is complicated. Genetics influences some factors, such as impulsivity, attention deficits, emotional style, and temperament, all of which contribute to the potential for using violence, but these same factors can also contribute to a myriad of other antisocial behavioral problems (Eisenberg & Fabes, 1992). Researchers have different theories about how genes impact behavior, with some focused on the way groups of genes interact to influence behavior while others study the additive effects of genes on behavior.

Exposure to toxic prenatal substances, such as opiates, alcohol, marijuana, cigarettes, or lead, can predispose children to behavior problems (Dodge & Pettit, 2003). Prenatal malnutrition and stressful conditions during pregnancy are linked to behavior problems. Some of these in utero influences can lead to difficulty in attending to social cues, autonomic hyper reactivity, underactive inhibition response, negative temperament, or delay of gratification. Both genetic and in utero challenges make it more difficult for children to meet developmental goals, and this added stress alone can put them at risk for behavior problems like aggression. Children's biological predispositions should not be minimized, but they will not find expression in violence unless they are linked with psychological and social factors that have a more immediate impact on individual children.

### Cultural and Social Context

The cultural and social context that supports violence, like biological dispositions, has an indirect effect on violent behavior. This context can include a wide range of elements, such as socioeconomic status, neighborhood violence rates, school and classroom environment, peer group, and cultural attitudes towards violence. However, little is known about how many of these elements impact adolescent violence in the home because much of the existing research is contradictory or nonexistent. For instance, virtually no evidence exists that the peer group or school environment directly supports teen violence in the home, and in our experience, peer groups do not support violence against family members. Nonetheless, we have chosen two elements that deserve some brief discussion: electronic media and support for aggressive values in North American culture.

## Gender

The fact that the majority of aggressors are boys and the majority of victims, mothers, demonstrates that gender plays a key role in understanding adolescent violence in the home. Much of our understanding of adult domestic violence is based on feminist analysis of patriarchy, which argues that boys are socialized to think of themselves as superior to girls and even their mothers. In addition, adult male perpetrators of domestic violence can have a particularly powerful impact on boys who are witnesses to violence against their mothers by giving them the message that it is acceptable for men to control and dominate women.

Power, control, and domination are defined by some cultural narratives as core features of masculine identity, and boys to some degree adopt this aggressive form of masculinity as their own (Connell, 1995). Entitlement, another core feature of an aggressive style of masculinity, prevents boys from having a fully developed sense of compassion and empathy, especially towards their mothers who may remind them of their vulnerability. Violence may displace feelings of humiliation and the shame of not living up to the cultural demands of being a "real man" (Jakupcak, Lisak & Roemer, 2002; Kimmel, 2008).

Nonetheless, we cannot forget that a significant number of girls use violence against family members. If boys are socialized to identify with power and aggression, girls are pressured to maintain harmonious relationships by remaining calm and compliant (Smith & Thomas, 2000). Even the expression of anger is considered by some as an unfeminine trait. Public discussion about violence against women and girls has led to the image of girls more often being viewed as victims, not perpetrators. However, recent evidence shows many girls no longer identify with values they associate with submissiveness, and some are becoming more aggressive in response to the societal expectation that they embrace passivity (Wolfe, 1994; Smith & Thomas, 2000). While hurt and sadness were once typical ways girls reacted to difficult situations, for some girls anger, destructive aggression, and violence are becoming more common, especially when these feelings are part of a history of victimization. As we said above, discussions about aggression shown by girls usually center on relational aggression, a hidden form of peer bullying originally thought to be used primarily by girls (Maccoby, 2005). Relational aggression doesn't appear to have relevance to violence in the home; however, one of the places girls convey their vulnerable feelings described above is through violence against siblings and parents in the home.

## Violent Media

"The emergence of the mass media as a fundamental element of most children's socialization experiences has been one of the most dramatic changes in child rearing that has occurred in the past 100 years" (Huesmann, 2010). Exposure to media violence increases the risk of using violence, just like exposure to cigarette smoke or lead-based paint increases the risk of health problems. The way children learn aggression and violence from the media is based on empirical research and well-established psychological theory (Huesmann, 2010; Gentile & Anderson, 2006). While children who have grown up in a violent family or a violent neighborhood are particularly vulnerable to the influence of media violence, even those children who have no previous life experience with abuse and violence are vulnerable. Social learning theory demonstrates that exposure to violent media desensitizes youth to the harmful effects of interpersonal violence and provides psychological scripts that model how youth can use violent behavior in difficult social situations (Bandura, 1973). One example of desensitization and modeling is a study of the negative impact of violent song lyrics, which reports an increase in aggressive thoughts and feelings of hostility that can have long-term effects (Anderson, Carnagey & Eubanks, 2003). Cultivation theory indicates that long-term viewers of violent television adopt a more generalized perception of a hostile world that is divided into powerful perpetrators and powerless victims (Signorielli, 2006). Media violence certainly contributes to a youth's aggressive outlook.

Video games are more pernicious than older, more passive types of visual media like television or film because the viewer is actively involved, emotionally and cognitively, in enacting aggression. Currently, players participate in a three-dimensional game environment through the eyes of a "shooter" who fights and kills with highly sophisticated hyperrealistic computer graphics. A typical scene might include a close-range view of an arm being ripped from a socket, exposing bone and sinew with blood rushing from the wound (Gentile & Anderson, 2006). The audience for media violence is changing. For decades, violence has been modeled by males on television and in video games that are integral to boys' socialization. More recently, girls have been targeted by video game producers, and aggressive female characters are included in the pantheon of violent video game and film heroes and heroines (Moise & Huesmann, 1996; Dill, 2010). While girls spend less time with electronic media than boys, exposure is a problem for both boys and girls.

## Exposure to Domestic Violence

Biological predispositions and cultural influences interact with life events to put an individual at risk for using aggressive behavior. Especially when a youth experiences adverse life events in the family, his or her behavior can be profoundly affected. Based on our interviews with teens and parents, over half of the youth were exposed to or witnessed domestic violence in which fathers used physical violence against mothers, and almost 40 percent were also physically abused by their father or male caretaker (Routt & Anderson, 2011). Research demonstrates that about a third of the teens who witness domestic violence are also physically abused, and so while the effects of either of these experiences alone is detrimental, the effects of both are potentially much more severe for these youth (Hughes, Parkinson & Vargo, 1989).

Witnessing domestic violence and experiencing physical abuse have similar effects. Both child witnesses and victims of physical abuse are at risk for depression and anxiety that can increase the risk of aggression and behavioral problems at home, at school, and with peers. Both witnessing violence and being abused at home can lead to a greater willingness to use violence as an appropriate way to solve problems (Jaffe, Hurley & Wolfe, 1990; Jaffe, Wolfe, Wilson & Zak, 1986).

We know that children who witness domestic violence are at risk for even more difficulties (Rossman, 2001). In homes where there is violence between the parents, for example, children are more likely to experience physical, sexual, and emotional abuse (Edelson, 2001). Children are also more likely to be exposed to other forms of family violence and experience violence in the community when they live in a home with domestic violence. Finally, children who live in homes with domestic violence receive less emotional support and attention, which can have negative developmental consequences (Margolin, 1998).

## Harsh Parenting

Apart from the physical abuse of a child, poor parenting practices can have grave negative effects on a child's development. Many parents, especially domestic violence perpetrators, may not meet the legal standard of child abuse in their parenting practices, but are treating their children abusively. Harsh parenting, described by researchers as parenting that is overreactive, emotionally negative, coercive, and authoritarian, includes a variety of behaviors: yelling, name-calling, physical threats, some physical aggression, and frequent negative commands. Harsh parenting has a twofold negative effect on a child. First, as with witnessing domestic violence or experiencing physical abuse, it models abusive behavior as a way to resolve social conflict. Secondly, harsh parenting legitimizes an expression of anger that is threatening and hateful. Harsh parenting couples an aggressive act with an aggressive emotional expression that has serious long-term effects (Chang, Schwartz, Dodge & McBride-Chang, 2003).

Extensive research links inconsistent and negative parenting practices with antisocial and conduct-disordered youth. Some of these youth are physically aggressive, but not all. Gerald Patterson and other researchers at the Oregon Social Learning Center developed coercion theory from their observations of aversive interactions between parents and children (Patterson, 1982). They concluded that antisocial behavior in children originated from parents' unsuccessful efforts to obtain compliance from their child. However, coercion theory has limited applicability to adolescent violence against parents. Many youth who are violent against parents do not fit into the antisocial category that includes a broad range of behaviors that violate social norms. In addition, these studies draw conclusions about parenting without distinguishing the practices of the two parents, when there are two parents. In our experience, the parent who is most aggressive is the least likely to be the target of abuse from the youth, while the parent who is often not using aggressive parenting practices is the most likely target.

## Trauma

As we have described above, children are victims of many forms of abuse—from physical and emotional abuse to bullying and neglect. The variety of child maltreatment is enormous. Each one of these is a traumatic stressor, and when a child experiences more than one, he or she has the potential for having a variety of trauma symptoms. After a child has experienced one type of violence, he or she is at greater risk for experiencing other types of violence (Finkelhor, Turner, Hamby & Ormod, 2011). A small number of children who have traumatic stress meet the standards of post-traumatic stress disorder; most children who have traumatic stress do not. Researchers have discovered that when young people are victimized multiple times in a variety of ways, they can experience many symptoms across a range of disorders. Some of the symptoms serve as precursors to aggressive behavior: explosive anger, negative affect, emotional dysregulation, hypersensitivity, misinterpretation of emotions, impulsivity, distorted attributions, disrupted attachment, poor social skills, and interpersonal conflict (D'Andrea, Stolbach, Ford, Spinazzola & Van der Kolk, 2012).

## Substance Use

Substance use is a risk factor for violence towards family members. Alcohol affects cognitive, emotional, and physical functioning, resulting in reduced self-regulation and reduced capacity to negotiate and resolve conflicts nonviolently. Research also indicates that alcohol in some circumstances even causes aggression (Room, Babor & Rehm, 2005). In addition, the socially accepted belief that alcohol and drug use cause violence can encourage violent behavior by excusing the violence (Field, Caetano & Nelson, 2004). While little research exists on the effects of substances other than alcohol on domestic violence (Kretschmar & Flannery, 2007), there is evidence that the use of at least one illegal substance increases the possibility of domestic violence (Moore & Stuart, 2004). These conclusions are likely to hold true for teens who use violence against parents.

## Clinical Diagnoses

Our data show that mental health issues such as attention deficit hyperactivity disorder, bipolar disorder, and depression are risk factors for violence in the home (Routt & Anderson, 2011). Hyperactivity is a known risk factor for aggression (Taylor, Chadwick, Heptinstall & Danckaerts, 1996), and research indicates the same genes that influence ADHD also influence aggression and violence (Lilienfeld & Waldman, 1990). Bipolar disorder, characterized by impulsivity and poor judgment, is associated with violence (Moeller, Barratt, Dougherty, Schmitz & Swann, 2001). Depression as a type of negative emotionality frequently coexists with aggression (Lahey & Waldman, 2003).

Next we'll examine theories that show the relationship between emotion and cognition. In our work we have found them helpful in explaining how a youth's early life experience and later abusive behavior are related.

## Reactive Versus Proactive Aggression

The role of emotion and cognition in aggression has been the subject of many years of debate. Early on, James Averill (1982) came to an important conclusion: all aggression is not the result of anger and all anger does not result in aggression. Much of the research over the last 30 years has been a variation on Averill's theme. Currently, some researchers believe youth are either proactively or reactively aggressive. Proactive aggression is purposeful, emotionally cold, and focused on material gain or social dominance. Reactive aggression rides on a wave of anger, is retaliatory, and is a response to a real or perceived threat. Research to date fails to show that youth fall neatly into one category or the other, and some researchers think the proactive-reactive debate is no longer relevant. (Hubbard, Morrow, Romano & McAuliffe, 2010; Bushman & Anderson, 2001). Although specific incidents of aggression do seem to be the result of either proactive aggression or reactive aggression, individual youth who aggress use a mix of both reactive and proactive styles. While none of the research on reactive and proactive aggression includes adolescent violence in the home, our experience confirms that youth use both styles, with a tendency towards one or the other from incident to incident.

## Social Cognitive Theory

Social cognitive theory, which explains the impact of cognitions and emotions on decision making, focuses on the underlying patterns of thinking and feeling that lead to abuse and violence and suggests how abusive patterns can be changed. These patterns operate on two levels: one is active and live while the other is more latent and hidden. Social learning theory and social information processing theory describe active, everyday learning and problem solving. Cognitive schema and script theory contain information accumulated from a person's past that interacts with these active processes, but is more hidden from everyday life.

## Social Learning Theory

Albert Bandura pioneered the study of youth violence and aggression by using a social learning approach that eventually led to a more expansive social cognitive theory (Huesmann & Reynolds, 2001). He asserted that all behaviors, including aggression, are acquired through similar learning processes (Bandura, 1973). While direct experience and reinforcement were traditionally seen as the main avenues for learning new behaviors, Bandura showed that observational learning, learning from others, is an equally important learning experience. Behavior that is modeled teaches general lessons in addition to the specific behavior being observed. Tactics and strategies can be extracted that go beyond the immediate observation and features can be molded into new, unexpected patterns of behavior that evolve into new forms of behavior.

However, learning is not a simple, cold, cognitive observation. The learner's emotional attachment to the person modeling the behavior is decisive. Bandura demonstrated that observational learning is especially potent when the observer is viewing someone with whom they have a close relationship, such as a family member or other respected person. The observer also develops personal rules and guidelines about how and when to use the new behaviors based on feedback from the person modeling the behavior. Both direct experience and observational learning are particularly important, since our data on youth reveal a large percentage of them observed violence in their homes and many were exposed to abusive or harsh parenting.

In his exploration of aggressive behavior, Bandura decided that people will not necessarily use a behavior simply because they learned it. Bandura rejected the mechanistic notion that people are simply externally conditioned by reinforcement, like automatons, through rewards and punishments. People regulate or control their behavior by applying moral standards to the choices they make. Moral self-evaluation plays an important role in choosing an aggressive response over a nonaggressive one. A choice of aggressive and nonaggressive behaviors depends on whether individual interests override consideration for the welfare of others. When people engage in conduct that intends to hurt another person, especially family members, their actions often conflict with their moral beliefs and how they think of themselves. They must convince themselves they are right and justify the decision to themselves. Bandura called the cognitive process when someone chooses to be aggressive "moral disengagement." It is particularly important in situations where family members are concerned (Bandura, 1999).

Youth morally disengage in a variety of ways. Sometimes they decide their abusive actions are morally justified and use euphemistic language to obscure the real consequences of their actions. In other cases, they put the responsibility for their actions on the targeted family member by blaming him or her. They also minimize, distort, and disregard the consequences of their aggression. Finally, they dehumanize or degrade a family member. In our work with youth, moral disengagement is pervasive with family members. When we interview parents for the first time, they routinely talk about the denial, blame, and degrading comments directed at them by their teens.

## Social Information Processing Theory

Another social cognitive model that explains aggressive behavior is social information processing theory. This theory uses the computer as a metaphor for
understanding human cognitive and emotional processes in social interactions
(Huesmann, 1998). Some researchers use computer simulation to model human
thought processes and even incorporate computer language like "encoding" and
"database" to describe human thinking. People obviously do not think in the same
way computers process information, but the computer analogy has proven to be a
useful way to understand how attention, perception, and memory are combined
in problem solving. Social information processing theory enables us to break
down the complex internal thought processes and emotional reactions that drive
external behaviors.

This theory focuses on the way youth process information cognitively and
emotionally when they interact with others, especially when problems arise in
their social interactions. Researchers found that aggressive children process information differently from children who are not aggressive (Crick & Dodge, 1994).
In our interaction with youth and parents, these differences are readily apparent
and so this theory is particularly useful. In order to understand the aggressive
versus nonaggressive responses, researchers looked at information processing
by breaking down the progression of a social interaction into five steps. These
steps operate very quickly below the level of everyday consciousness, and so a teen
would not actually be aware he or she is moving from step to step in real time.
Each of the steps leads to aggressive social strategies that value power over people
in social interaction.

In the first step, teens perceive social cues during an interaction and incorporate
the cues into their working memory, which is filled with mental representations
of past experiences. In the second step, they interpret the cues. The perception
and interpretation of an aggressive youth differs from a nonaggressive youth in a
number of ways. Aggressive youth identify fewer cues and more often misinterpret the cues they do identify as threatening. Their negative affect narrows their
perspective. They focus on the hostile cues, ignore others, and very quickly make
negative interpretations and aggressive attributions about the motivations of others in the situation. They are less able to take the perspective of the other person.
For instance, a frustrated parent asking firm questions about failing grades can
trigger a teen's hostile attributions about his or her parent's intent. A teen who is
hypersensitive and impulsive might misinterpret a parent's curiosity about his or
her school day and react with hostility.

In the third step the youth clarifies the goals for this situation. As in the first
two steps, goal selection for the aggressive youth is more limited and narrow than
for the nonaggressive youth. Aggressive youth generate fewer goals, their goals are
more hostile, and they more often seek personal gain than mutual goals. Emotions

and emotional intensity play a role in goal selection too. A happy and contented teen more often maintains a positive emotional state and works towards a mutually agreed upon solution. An angry teen is more likely to want to satisfy his or her personal needs by making demands of the other person in the situation. Intense negative emotions can interfere with a number of the essential ingredients of problem solving: blocking empathy, making it more difficult to assess another's emotions, discounting the multiple perspectives inherent in difficult discussions, disregarding the context of the problem, and inhibiting a cooperative, flexible approach. In general, the youth's goal selection is more rigid and intransigent when his or her emotions are running high.

In the fourth, fifth, and sixth steps, youth generate possible responses to the situation, measure the responses against the goals selected in step three, and then enact the response. Aggressive youth feel more comfortable and competent with an aggressive response. They also see more benefits from aggressive than non-aggressive solutions. The youth's outlook and choices are not simply cognitive processes but also rely on his or her mood. A youth who moves through the first three steps with an angry, hostile outlook will likely choose an aggressive response during steps four and five. A youth's high emotional intensity short-circuits consideration of a broader array of possible responses and usually results in a more self-centered approach that ignores the perspectives of other people. Furthermore, the strength of the emotional ties between the youth and the other parties involved in the situation also influences the kind of responses exhibited. When teens have weak emotional ties to their parents, they are even less motivated to engage in solving a problem.

Unfortunately, no social information processing research has been done with youth who are violent in the home, but the findings we have described above fit with our experience in working with these youth.

## Schemas and Scripts

Both social learning theory and social information processing theory highlight the role of active processes in the everyday life of a teen. However, a person's memory contains representations of past experiences that can have significant influence on these active processes. Social schemas and scripts, which are well established in psychological theory, describe how past experiences are stored in memory and impact everyday life. Jean Piaget made schemas a central component of his theory of child development, and John Bowlby created the idea of working models of social relationships in his attachment theory, which has similarities to Piaget's schemas. Much of our current understanding of aggression and violent behavior has relied on schema and script theory.

Schemas are mental representations or frames of reference that explain how thoughts and emotions are organized in memory and are the building blocks for understanding internal psychological processes. Schemas help filter and organize the overwhelming amount of information available to us in our daily encounters. They influence the way we interact with other people, experience our emotions, and interpret our reactions. Decision making, reasoning, and moral judgments are governed by schemas. Scripts, well-rehearsed sets of behavior, are types of schemas that guide our actions, and as in a theatrical play, direct behavior in certain types of social situations.

Schemas are often activated automatically without conscious awareness and are beyond most people's ability to verbally articulate. For instance, one family member can, with a gesture, tone of voice, or word, evoke a strong emotional response in another family member in a specific context. These emotional responses often come as a surprise to an outside observer who doesn't have these same past experiences that are now stored in family schemas. Even family members themselves can be surprised by their own intense emotional responses and have a difficult time putting them into words. Automatic processing that is made possible by schemas is described as unintentional, effortless, and seemingly involuntary (Narvaez & Bock, 2002).

Many different relational schemas inform a youth's interactions with family members (Baldwin, 1992). However, some that represent insecure attachment patterns provide one example of the way childhood challenges are linked to aggressive behavior. Children experiencing some form of maltreatment are at risk for developing an insecure attachment pattern. Secure attachment is a strong relationship between an infant and a caregiver that satisfies the child's need for safety, security, and protection. When a sensitive and responsive caregiver forms a secure attachment, a child can explore his or her environment with confidence, knowing they can always return to a safe base. A child with a secure attachment to a caregiver would develop a schema that represents an internal model for a healthy relationship based on trust and reciprocity.

When infants are not securely attached to a caregiver, they can be disruptive and oppositional, and with time, they may develop pervasive patterns of mistrust, hostility, and anger towards others, especially family members, as a coping mechanism. When they find themselves in new circumstances, for instance, hostility becomes an effective way of maintaining distance and feeling powerful. Some researchers found insecurely attached children also coped with negative feelings by acting out aggressively to compel their mothers to attend to them (Speltz, Greenberg & DeKlyen, 1990). In social interactions, the insecurely attached child is likely to routinely face anger and hostility from peers in reaction to his aggression, and that would buttress the aggressive child's behavior. An insecurely attached child's expectation of a hostile world becomes a foundation for an aggressive schema and a script that directs him or her not to rely on others. Instead, he or she creates distance with oppositional behavior.

Schemas and scripts are accessed during the information processing steps described above. They become so entrenched that a hostile response feels automatic and instinctive to the person enacting it. Teens read benign cues with a hypervigilance and react in their own words "without thinking," with an emotionally charged response. We have seen youth who are surprised at their own aggressive responses after they have made a commitment to change. For instance, a parent who is simply asking a teen where he or she had been the previous night and what time he or she had come home may become the target of a verbal attack because the teen perceives (or misperceives) his or her parent's questions as a provocation. Even after a youth has made a decision to stop reacting with hostility, the script may still govern the youth's responses until he or she has repeatedly used a new nonaggressive response.

Social cognitive theory tells a developmental story about violent and aggressive behavior in young people. Biological predispositions, sociocultural contexts, peer group interaction, and family relationships contribute to cognitive and emotional processes, the knowledge structures that lead to generalized conduct problems. However, this developmental story is about youth who use violence pervasively, across many different domains in their lives that reach beyond violence towards family members. The research at this time does not include youth whose aggressive behavior is primarily directed at family members.

## Empathy

According to social information processing theory, another difference between aggressive and nonaggressive youth is that nonaggressive youth are more effective, competent, and proficient communicators. They are more attentive to the emotions expressed by the other person in the social interaction. They are more likely to include the other person's perspective in their analysis of the situation. They possess the personal self-regulation skills to engage in a difficult and possibly demanding social exchange. They often propose a range of mutually satisfying solutions and cooperate with the other person in enacting the solution. All of these skills indicate more than just an accomplished communicator. Taken together, these skills are also part of an empathetic response.

Empathy is an antidote to violent and aggressive behavior. The use of aggressive and violent behavior at home is due not simply to a breakdown in processing social information; it is a moral transgression that threatens to undermine the integrity of healthy family relationships. Empathy is a relationship based on reciprocity, affection, caring, and mutual understanding. Violence is associated with a lack of empathy, both in the more cognitive aspect of taking the perspective of another person, and especially in the more affective aspect of sharing an emotional state with another person. Empathy is preeminent among a group of self-conscious moral emotions that include sympathy, guilt, and shame; it, along with moral reasoning, plays an important role in regulating hostile emotions and limiting aggressive behavior. Empathy precedes the sympathetic helping behavior that assists a person in need or distress.

Even though empathy is in part an involuntary, physiological response to another person's distress, many of the risk factors we have described above lead to reduced empathy that makes hostility and aggression more likely. For example, we observe youth who in high conflict situations become entirely self-focused, disregarding the other person's needs. The intensity of their reactions prevents them from thinking through and weighing the issues at hand. It also prevents them from recognizing the emotional cues the other person is expressing. Finally, their tendency to attribute hostility to others in a conflict leads to a distorted perception of others' perspectives.

## Summary

Youth who are violent towards their parents come from all economic classes, ethnic groups, and religious backgrounds, and do not fit any psychological profile. Youth violence against parents has no single cause and is not easily explained. However, many of these youth have had negative life experiences, such as being the recipient of physical abuse, witnessing domestic violence, and suffering other forms of trauma that has affected them emotionally and cognitively. These experiences make it more likely that they will try to resolve conflicts with their parents with abuse and violence than would be true for most teens.

## References

Agnew, R., & Huguley, S. (1989). Adolescent violence towards parents. *Journal of Marriage and the Family*, 51, 699–711.

Anderson, C. A., Carnagey, N. L., & Eubanks, J. (2003). Exposure to violent media: the effects of songs with violent lyrics on aggressive thoughts and feelings. *Journal of Personality and Social Psychology*, 84(6), 960–971.

Averill, J. R. (1982). *Anger and aggression: an essay on emotion*. New York: Springer-Verlag.

Baldwin, M. W. (1992). Relational schemas and the processing of social information. *Psychological Bulletin*, 112(3), 461–484.

Bandura, A. (1973). *Aggression: a social learning analysis*. Englewood Cliffs, NJ: Prentice-Hall.

Bandura, A. (1999). Moral disengagement in the perpetration of inhumanities. *Personality and Social Psychology Review*, 3(3), 193–209.

Borduin, C. M., & Schaeffer, C. M. (1997). Violent offending in adolescence: epidemiology, correlates, outcomes, and treatment. In T. P. Gullota, G. R. Adams, & R. Montemayor (Eds.), *Delinquent violent youth: theory and interventions* (pp. 144–174), Thousand Oaks, CA: Sage.

Bowie, B. H. (2007). Relational aggression, gender, and the developmental process. *Journal of Child and Adolescent Psychiatric Nursing*, 20(2), 107–115.

Bushman, B. J., & Anderson, C. A. (2001). Is it time to pull the plug on the hostile versus instrumental aggression dichotomy? *Psychological Review*, 108, 273–279.

Bushman, B. J., & Anderson, C. A. (2002). Violent video games and hostile expectations: a test of the general aggression model. *Personality and Social Psychology Bulletin*, 28(12), 1679–1686.

Chang, L., Schwartz, D., Dodge, K. A., & McBride-Chang, C. (2003). Harsh parenting in relation to child emotion regulation and aggression. *Journal of Family Psychology*, 17(4), 598–606.

Chesney-Lind, M., & Belknap, J. (2004). Trends in delinquent girls' aggression and violent behavior: a review of the evidence. In M. Putzllaz & K. L. Bierman (Eds.), *Aggression, antisocial behavior, and violence among girls: a developmental perspective* (pp. 203–221), New York: Guilford Press.

Connell, R. W. (1995). *Masculinities*. Berkeley: University of California Press.

Crick, N. R., & Dodge, K. A. (1994). A review and reformulation of social information processing mechanisms in children's social adjustment. *Psychological Bulletin*, 115, 74–101.

D'Andrea, W., Stolbach, B., Ford, J., Spinazzola, J., & Van der Kolk, B. A. (2012). Understanding interpersonal trauma in children: why we need a developmentally appropriate trauma diagnosis. *American Journal of Orthopsychiatry*, 82(2), 187–200.

Dill, K. E. (2010). Girl power? the modern violent media heroine. *How fantasy becomes reality* (blog), August 10. Retrieved from http://www.psychologytoday.com/blog/how-fantasy-becomes-reality/201008/girl-power-the-modern-violent-media-heroine.

Dodge, K., & Pettit, G. S. (2003). A biopsychosocial model of the development of chronic conduct problems in adolescence. *Developmental Psychology*, 39(2), 349–371.

Edleson, J. L. (2001). Studying the co-occurrence of child maltreatment and domestic violence in the lives of children. In S. A. Graham-Bermann & J. L. Edleson (Eds.), *Domestic violence in the lives of children* (pp. 91–110), Washington, DC: American Psychological Association.

Eisenberg, N., & Fabes, R. A. (1992). Emotion regulation and the development of social competence. In M. S. Clark (Ed.), *Review of personality and social psychology*. Vol. 14, *Emotion and social behavior* (pp. 117–150), Newbury Park, CA: Sage.

Field, C. A., Caetano, R., & Nelson, S. (2004). Alcohol and violence related cognitive risk factors associated with perpetration of intimate partner violence. *Journal of Family Violence*, 19, 249–253.

Finkelhor, D., Turner, H., Hamby, S., & Ormrod, R. (2011). Poly-victimization: children's exposure to multiple types of violence, crime, and abuse. *Juvenile Justice Bulletin*, October.

Gentile, D. A., & Anderson, C. A. (2006). Violent video games: effects on youth and public policy perspectives. In N. E. Dowd, D. G. Singer, & R. F. Wilson (Eds.), *Handbook of children, culture, and violence* (225–246), Thousand Oaks, CA: Sage.

Hong, J. S., Kral, M. J., Espelage, D. L., & Allen-Meares, P. (2012). The social ecology of adolescent-initiated parent abuse: a review of the literature. *Child Psychiatry and Human Development*, 43, 431–454.

Hubbard, J. A., Morrow, M. T., Romano, L. J., & McAuliffe, M. D. (2010). The role of anger in children's reactive versus proactive aggression: review of findings, issues of measurement, and implications for intervention. In W. F. Arsenio & E. A. Lemerise (Eds.), *Emotions, aggression, and morality in children* (pp. 201–218), Washington, DC: American Psychological Association.

Huesmann, L. R. (1998). The role of information processing and cognitive schema in the acquisition and maintenance of habitual aggressive behavior. In R. G. Geen & E. Donnerstein (Eds.), *Human aggression: theories, research, and implications for social policy* (pp. 73–110), New York: Academic Press.

Huesmann, L. R. (2010). Nailing the coffin shut on doubts that violent video games stimulate aggression: comment on Anderson et al. (2010). *Psychological Bulletin*, 136 (2), 179–181.

Huesmann, L. R., & Reynolds, M. A. (2001). Cognitive processes and the development of aggression. In A. C. Bohart & D. J. Stipek (Eds.), *Constructive and destructive behavior* (pp. 249–269), Washington, DC: American Psychological Association.

Hughes, H. M., Parkinson, D., & Vargo, M. (1989). Witnessing spouse abuse and experiencing physical abuse: a "double whammy"? *Journal of Family Violence*, 4, 197–209.

Jaffe, P. G., Hurley, D. J., & Wolfe, D. (1990). Children's observations of violence: I. Critical issues in child development and intervention planning. *Canadian Journal of Psychiatry*, 35, 466–70.

Jaffe, P. G., Wolfe, D., Wilson, S., & Zak, L. (1986). Similarities in behavioral and social maladjustment among child victims and witnesses to family violence. *American Journal of Orthopsychiatry*, 56(1), 142–5.

Jakupcak, M., Lisak, D., & Roemer, L. (2002). The role of masculine ideology and masculine gender role stress in men's perpetration of relationship violence. *Psychology of Men and Masculinity*, 3(2), 97–106.

Kimmel, M. (2008). *Guyland, the perilous world where boys become men*. New York: Harper Collins.

Kretschmar, J. M., & Flannery, D. J. (2007). Substance use and violent behavior. In D. J. Flannery, A. T. Vazsonyi, & I. D. Waldman (Eds.), *The Cambridge handbook of violent behavior and aggression* (pp. 647–663), New York: Cambridge University Press.

Lahey, B. B., & Waldman, I. D. (2003). A developmental propensity model of the origins of conduct problems during childhood and adolescence. In B. B. Lahey, T. E. Moffitt, & A. Caspi (Eds.), *The causes of conduct disorder and serious juvenile delinquency* (pp. 76–117). New York: Guilford Press.

Lansford, J. E., Skinner, A. T., Sorbring, E., Di Giunta, L., Deater-Deckard, K., Dodge, K. A., Malone, P. S., Oburu, P., Pastorelli, C., Sombat, T., Uribe Tirado, L. M., Zelli, A., Al-Hassan, S. M., Pena Alampay, L., Baccini, D., Bombi, A. S., Bornstein, M. H., & Chang, L. (2012). Boys' and girls' relational and physical aggression in nine countries. *Aggressive Behavior*, 38, 203–222.

Lilienfeld, S. O., & Waldman, I. D. (1990). The relation between childhood attention-deficit hyperactivity disorder and adult antisocial behavior reexamined: the problem of heterogeneity. *Clinical Psychology Review*, 10, 699–725.

Maccoby, E. E. (2005). Aggression in the context of gender. In M. Putullaz & K. L. Bierman (Eds.). *Aggression, antisocial behavior and violence among girls* (pp. 3–22), New York: The Guilford Press.

Margolin, G. (1998). The effects of domestic violence on children. In P. K. Trickett & C. Schellenbach (Eds.), *Violence against children in the family and the community* (pp. 57–102), Washington, DC: American Psychological Association.

Moeller, F. G., Barratt, E. S., Dougherty, D. M., Schmitz, J. M., & Swann, A. C. (2001). Psychiatric aspects of impulsivity. *American Journal of Psychiatry*, 158, 1783–1793.

Moise, J. F., & Huesmann, L. R. (1996). Television violence viewing and aggression in females. *Annals of the New York Academy of Sciences*, 794, 380–383.

Moore, T. M., & Stuart, G. L. (2004). Illicit substance use and intimate partner violence among men in batterer's intervention. *Psychology of Addictive Behaviors*, 18, 385–389.

Narvaez, D., & Bock, T. (2002). Moral schemas and tacit judgment or how the defining issues test is supported by cognitive sciences. *Journal of Moral Education*, 31(3), 297–314.

Patterson, G. R. (1982). *Coercive family process*. Eugene, OR: Castalia.

Room, R., Babor, T., & Rehm, J. (2005). Alcohol and public health. *Lancet*, 365, 519–530.

Rossman, B.B.R. (2001). Longer term effects of children's exposure to domestic violence. In S. A. Graham-Bermann & J. L. Edleson (Eds.), *Domestic violence in the lives of children* (pp. 35–66), Washington, DC: American Psychological Association.

Routt, G. B., & Anderson, E. A. (2011). Adolescent violence towards parents. *Journal of Abuse, Maltreatment, and Trauma*, 20, 1–19.

Seguin, J. R., Sylvers, P., & Lilienfield, S. O. (2007). The neuropsychology of violence. In D. J. Flannery, A. T. Vazsonyi, & I. D. Waldman (Eds.), *The Cambridge handbook of violent behavior and aggression* (pp. 187–214), New York: Cambridge University Press.

Signorielli, N. (2006). A preliminary demography of television violence. In N. E. Dowd, D. G. Singer, & R. F. Wilson (Eds.), *Handbook of children, culture, and violence* (pp. 149–161), Thousand Oaks, CA: Sage.

Smith, S. L., & Thomas, S. P. (2000). Violence and nonviolent girls: contrasting perceptions of anger experiences, school, and relationships. *Issues in Mental Health Nursing*, 21, 547–575.

Snethen, G., & Van Puymbroeck, M. (2008). Girls and physical aggression: causes, trends, and intervention guided by social learning theory. *Aggression and Violent Behavior*, 13, 346–354.

Speltz, M. L., Greenberg, M. T., & DeKlyen, M. (1990). Attachment in preschoolers with disruptive behavior: a comparison of clinic-referred and nonproblem children. *Development and Psychopathology*, 2, 31–46.

Taylor, E., Chadwick, O., Heptinstall, E., & Danckaerts, M. (1996). Hyperactivity and conduct problems as risk factors for adolescent development. *Journal of the American Academy of Child and Adolescent Psychiatry*, 35, 1213–1226.

Walsh, J. A., & Krienert, J. L. (2007). Child-parent violence: an empirical analysis of offender, victim, and event characteristics in a national sample of reported incidents. *Journal of Family Violence*, 22(5), 563–574.

Wolfe, L. R. (1994). "Girl stabs boy at school": girls and the cycle of violence. *Women's Health Issues*, 4(2), 109–116.

## six
# An Intervention Model for Youth Violence in the Home

We were in family counseling for a long time, but there wasn't much talk about my daughter's violence. It just got worse.

I think his therapist didn't believe he was that violent or scary. He can be really charming and sweet. No one sees him when he's abusive except me. She helped him with a lot of other things, but I still can't say no to him without a firestorm.

He has been in individual counseling, family therapy, and even anger management classes. Nothing has worked to stop the violence.

The treatment of teen to parent violence poses unique challenges. Practitioners are particularly challenged, on the one hand, by parents who feel shame because they believe they are inept as parents, and on the other hand, by youth who have harmed the people closest to them. Stopping violent behavior must be the focus of any practice that deals with these families. For real change to take place, parental leadership must be reestablished, respectful family relationships built, and lines of communication in place.

Unfortunately, traditional forms of family and individual therapy have been unable to fully address this problem. Many parents who we have interviewed expressed frustration that they could not find counseling that stopped their teen's violence. They felt the violence was not taken seriously, and their own experience was not understood by helping professionals. Parents tell us they felt judged, which led only to self-blame, shame, and ultimately, self-imposed silence. Parents reported that their teens seldom disclosed their abusive behavior during individual counseling sessions. When teens did disclose it, they either minimized the violence or blamed it on their parents' overreaction and exaggeration. Furthermore, in family counseling, parents stated the focus was often on parenting, sidestepping the teens' violence. And most unfortunately, during family counseling sessions parents were often afraid to reveal the violence for fear of reprisal by their youth. Clearly, the treatment of teen to parent violence demands new approaches.

## An Overview of the Model

In this chapter, we present an overview of an intervention model designed specifically to address youth violence in the home. The model is practiced in a group setting with parents and youth working together with other families to learn skills for respectful family relationships. Both joint and separate sessions for parents and teens are used. Separate sessions for parents offer support and teach skills that enable parents to reestablish leadership. Separate sessions for teens provide them the opportunity to learn personal skills without their parents. Components of this intervention can also be practiced in a combination of family and individual sessions, if group practice is not an option.

The model takes a restorative practice approach and emphasizes family safety and accountability for violent behavior. Cognitive-behavioral and skills-based practices are used to help youth make specific behavioral changes to prevent violence and abuse. A structured therapeutic approach that involves time with parents and teens together in an environment with clear boundaries creates a safe psychological space for everyone. A reliable, transparent milieu that is positive and encouraging ensures parents that the violence will be addressed and youth will feel supported in making change.

While most of the practices in this intervention model are not new, their combination is unique and unusual. When we began this work, there were no treatment models to guide us or research on interventions with youth who are violent towards family members. We stepped into this work with ideas, concepts, and frameworks from our past experiences with other family violence interventions but did not know how they would apply to youth violence in the home.

## Methods

We adopted methods, used by practitioners in a variety of fields, which have been studied and shown to be effective. The difference is the way they are combined and structured into a framework that weaves together domestic violence treatment, restorative practice, cognitive-behavioral therapy, anger management, solution-focused brief therapy, and family relationship skill building, practiced in a group setting with parents and teens.

Some of the practices that inform our work include the following:

- Cognitive-behavioral learning and skills-based approaches that have become the mainstay of programs that teach nonviolence to children and adults (Crick & Dodge, 1994; Bandura, 1973; Lochman, Powell, Boxmeyer, Deming & Young, 2007; Andrews & Bonta, 2003).
- Motivational interviewing techniques that foster engagement of youth in the change process (Miller & Rollnick, 2002).
- Strengths-based, solution-focused practices that promote change by accentuating the youth and family's existing strengths and positive qualities (Clark, 1998).
- Restorative practice which engages youth in developing empathy and teaches them to take responsibility for harmful behavior (Wachtel, 2013).
- Anger management, relaxation, and self-calming techniques that are effective in promoting the regulation of emotions (Kassinove & Tafrate, 2002).
- Modeling positive behaviors, and giving feedback on performance (Cullen, 2002).
- A Duluth Model (Mederos, 2002) tool for accountability; the Power and Control and Equality Wheels are adapted for adolescent behaviors within the family and relabeled the Abuse/Disrespect and Mutual Respect Wheels.

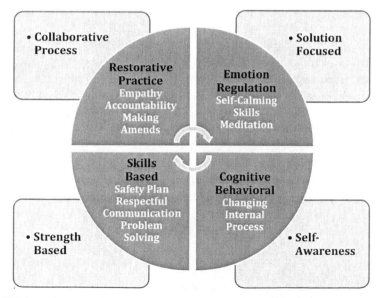

FIGURE 6.1. Building Safe and Respectful Family Relationships

Our learning has also come from trial and error. The parents and teens have been our teachers as we have learned what works and what does not. Listening to families and observing their weekly progress towards nonviolence and respect has guided the evolution of this intervention. We continue to learn from every parent and teen we work with and encourage all practitioners in this field to do the same.

## Respect as an Underlying Principle

Respect, the heart of this intervention, has universal appeal. Respect is a mode of behavior, an attitude, a feeling, a principle, a duty, and a moral virtue valued by all age groups, cultures, and classes. Its broad appeal is demonstrated, on the one hand, by world leaders who invoke respect when they are negotiating international treaties, and on the other, by intimate couples as an essential ingredient of successful, long-term relationships (Gottman, 1995).

The eighteenth-century philosopher, Immanuel Kant, gave respect a simple definition that remains the cornerstone of our current understanding: all persons should be treated "never simply as a means but always at the same time as an end" (Kant, [1785] 1998). To treat people only as a means to an end is to diminish, degrade, and show contempt for them. For Kant, a person's intrinsic worth was unconditional. For Jean Piaget, respect was the recognition and understanding of other people's points of view. In his model of child development, the ability to show respect marked a major developmental milestone away from egocentrism towards "decentration," which is a person's capacity for perspective taking (Piaget, 1932).

Respect between family members and a respectful home where every person feels valued is the primary goal of this intervention. Respect serves as a moral compass for decision making among family members and is the standard by which all family interactions are evaluated. Respect also breeds respect. When children and parents show respect for each other as well as receive respect from each other, not only is their mutuality strengthened, but their personal confidence and self-esteem are bolstered. A culture of respect inoculates the family against hostility and aggression (Mayseless & Scharff, 2011). Helping families learn and integrate a respect template for relating to each other gives them new options for expressing themselves and responding to others in safe and respectful ways.

Our Abuse/Disrespect and Mutual Respect Wheels (Figure 6.2), adapted from the Duluth Model, define respect in terms of actual, lived behaviors. The wheels are practical yet powerful tools for parents and youth to use together to move towards a respectful relationship. Seeing the two wheels together puts abuse and respect in stark relief and clarifies the difference between them. Parents who see them for the first time have an immediate positive reaction since they can see abusive behaviors are part of a pattern that they have experienced in their home and recognize mutually respectful behaviors as realistic, achievable goals. Youth appreciate their direct and deliberate approach.

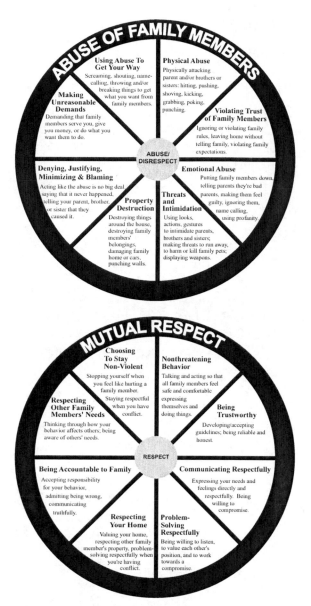

**FIGURE 6.2.** Abuse and Respect Wheels

Source: Domestic Abuse Intervention Project, 202 East Superior Street, Duluth, MN 55802
Phone: 218-722-2781; http://www.theduluthmodel.org/

The Power and Control Wheel was developed in Duluth by battered women who were attending education groups sponsored by the local women's shelter. The wheel is used in our Creating a Process of Change for Men Who Batter curriculum, and in groups of women who are battered, to name and inspire dialogue about tactics of abuse. While we recognize that there are women who use violence against men, and that there are men and women in same-sex relationships who use violence, this wheel is meant specifically to illustrate men's abusive behaviors toward women. The Equality Wheel was developed for use with the same groups.

## Key Components of the Model

### Safety of Family Members

Safety in the home is a preeminent concern when a youth has been violent towards family members. Safety includes practices for ongoing assessment and monitoring of risk level, safety planning, and ensuring a safe therapeutic environment. Stopping the violence and keeping a finger on the pulse of family safety are goals that shape our strategies and are always priorities when working with any family where there is violence.

### Restorative Practice

Restorative practice is a particularly useful way to address the different needs of youth and parents when youth have been violent in the home. Restorative practice has grown to be a major part of our work as we have observed its potent effect on the youth-parent relationship. Restorative practice offers a paradigm that we have found to be particularly effective. It sheds light on the impact of one's behavior on others and on oneself, engages empathy and personal responsibility, and develops competency. Restorative practice principles are embedded in the overall framework of the intervention.

### Respectful Communication

The notion of talking about difficult feelings or needs and working through disagreements while staying respectful is foreign for many people who have experienced violence in their families. For some people there are only two options. One option is to express feelings or views of difficult issues in a highly emotional, blaming, and aggressive way, and the other option is to avoid them altogether. Respectful communication skills are learned and practiced with the parent and teen together, where they can role-play how to talk respectfully even when angry, express feelings and needs, and solve problems while valuing each other's perspectives.

### Understanding Cognitive, Emotive, Behavioral Process

Understanding the relationship between thoughts, feelings, and behavior, and taking charge of all three through self-awareness, empowers youth to change behavior. By recognizing and understanding the feelings beneath their anger, youth learn to move from rage to a place where they can acknowledge difficult feelings and think about how to express feelings and needs in a safe and respectful way.

### Self-Calming and Emotion Regulation

Most teens and parents who come to our program have lived day-to-day with tension between them, enduring cycles of blowups, remorse, and attempts to get along until another outburst sends them back to tension and high emotion. Both teens and parents often lack the ability to calm themselves and manage emotions in the heat of conflict as well as during day-to-day challenges. Once teens and parents learn the skill of disengaging from conflict, they then learn to self-sooth and calm the physical arousal and feelings of anger, frustration, and anxiety they are often left with as they sit in their room or walk around the block. Self-calming techniques are helpful tools to use during a difficult conversation to prevent escalation.

## Support and Skills for Parents

Parents come to counseling feeling they have lost all authority and influence with their teenager, and can no longer address issues of concern with their teen without the disruption of abuse or violence. Parents are supported in reestablishing leadership in the home by learning to safely address behavioral issues with their teen. Parents receive support from other parents and learn skills specific to parenting an adolescent who is violent towards family members.

## Implementing the Model

## Multi-Family Groups

This intervention model is most successful when parents and teens work together in a multi-family group and also participate in separate parent and teen groups. We have primarily delivered the intervention in a group format because the results have been more positive than that of family and individual work with these families.

Some research supports the effectiveness of group sessions over individual sessions (Lochman, Powell, Boxmeyer, Deming & Young, 2007). The reasons we have found group work to be particularly effective include the following:

- The group becomes a community of support for the teen and parent, reducing isolation and the feeling they are the only family dealing with this problem.
- The restorative process is enhanced by occurring in a community of other families, often referred to as a *restorative circle*, where there is accountability to and support from a group of peers in a collaborative and inclusive process.
- Feedback and support from peers helps teens feel engaged, included, and competent.
- The group offers participants the opportunity to observe other parents and teens interact, sometimes having a mirror effect. A teen stated at her last session as she answered questions about what she learned, "I saw other teens acting like I do with their parents, and it made me realize what it really looks like—stupid." A parent reflected, "I watched another mother beginning to lecture her daughter the way I do, and I saw how

her daughter just glazed over and stopped listening. That really made me think. I remember that now when I want to go into lecture mode."

- Conversely, observing respectful interactions between parents and teens provides role modeling and encouragement to newcomers. New parents in the group will say, "It gave me hope to see the relationships between parents and teens who had been in the group for a while."
- As parents and teens get to know each other, following each teen's progress week to week, they begin to work together to help those who are struggling by offering advice, empathy, encouragement, and even by spontaneously clapping when a teen who has been struggling begins to make progress. The teen feels energized by the encouragement of the group, further motivating him or her to "keep it up."
- Skill practice in a group reinforces learning as group members observe each parent and teen role-play the skill, giving feedback and support.
- Skill learning is enhanced in a group, where group brainstorming and discussion is a valuable part of the learning process.
- Parent group is both a support and education group, where parents share their experiences and wisdom with each other and learn new skills together. Parent group is invaluable to those who have been isolated and ashamed, feeling they are alone with this issue.

## Family and Individual Sessions

A group format has many advantages; however, it may not be an option for everyone. The practices we will describe can be implemented in sessions with one or both parents and the teen together or in separate parent and teen sessions. There are some advantages to family and individual sessions:

- Family and individual sessions can devote more time to a family's unique situation, including more time for skill practice and discussion of the barriers or challenges for the parent or teen;
- Individual sessions with the parent and teen provide more privacy and confidentiality for the youth or parent to share personal issues they may not feel comfortable sharing in a group;
- Therapists can spend more time with issues such as school problems, substance use, or mental health issues. Therapists can balance their work on these issues with the work on ending abuse and violence.

A combination of group work along with some family and individual sessions offers the most comprehensive approach, depending upon the needs of the families served. Family sessions can be offered as needed for group members when the family has a crisis or other issues for which the group cannot allow time. Whether parents and youth attend family sessions or group sessions, youth demonstrate better outcomes when parent training is involved (Tolan, Guerra & Kendall, 1995; Kazdin & Weisz, 1998).

## Structure of Group Sessions

Our sessions begin with the parents and teens together for the restorative process of "check-in," to be described in detail in Chapter 8. Skill learning follows check-in, either in separate parent and teen groups or in joint sessions, depending upon the topic. Safety, respectful communication, problem solving, and restorative sessions include both parents and teens. It may be helpful for the parents to be included in some of the teen sessions, as they gain from the learning as well, and can support their youth's efforts to use the skills at home. Teens should not be included in parenting sessions, because it is important to have clear boundaries between teens and parents when it comes to parenting issues. Boundaries are already compromised for many of the families, with teens behaving in a parental role with parent and siblings, and correcting Mom and Dad's parenting.

## Assessment of Youth and Families

Families experiencing youth violence do not fit a specific profile. Youth who are violent in the home have a variety of risk and protective factors, life experiences, and needs. A wide array of influences impacts their behavior. The common factor is that they are hurting and frightening the people in their family. Parents have diverse backgrounds and parenting styles. In spite of their differences, many families have responded well to this model. However, it may not be the appropriate treatment approach for every family, particularly those with complex needs. Accurate assessment determines whether a family is the right fit for the intervention.

During the assessment we collect information from youth and parents about their current situation and family history. Subjects that are particularly important in our assessment include the following:

- current parent/youth relationship
- childhood behavior
- family violence and trauma history
- parenting practices
- behavior issues at school
- youth's interests, strengths
- physical and mental health issues
- drug/alcohol issues
- youth's history of violence in the home

In the following section, we will discuss assessment of youth and families, factors to consider when determining whether a teen and parent are appropriate for this model, and assessment of violence in the home.

## Tips for Interviewing Potential Clients

### Conduct Individual Interviews

Separate youth and parent interviews are particularly important when conducting an assessment for youth violence in the home. Interviewing each person separately allows everyone to be heard. Family members feel safer if they can disclose information without fear of retaliation. Discussions with family members about violence are difficult and sensitive. A parent who is being victimized by a partner may not feel safe talking about domestic violence with the partner in the room. In the same way, parents often don't feel safe talking about their youth's violence in front of the youth. Youth are not comfortable sharing abuse towards them. When there is family violence of any kind, individuals may not feel safe sharing information in the presence of others in the family.

### Pay Careful Attention to Safety Issues

It is essential to this work that the safety of family members is the first priority. Assessment of the severity of the violence and safety concerns of the family are a critical part of the interview. Some parents initially give the impression that they are not afraid of their youth. As they become more comfortable talking to the interviewer, they reveal concerns about their own or other family member's safety. The end of the interview is the best time to clarify, using direct questions, the parents' safety concerns. Ongoing assessment of safety risks throughout the intervention will be discussed in the following chapter.

### Listen to the Whole Story

Parents and teens often relay very different stories in their assessment interviews. Listening to each family member's perspective and getting the whole picture before coming to conclusions is particularly important.

For example, Mary and her 15-year-old son, Leon, came for an intake interview. Over the course of the interview with Leon, he described his mother as "acting crazy sometimes." He said, "The other day she threw a dish at the wall and was screaming at me for no reason. I don't know what's wrong with her." He denied any physical abuse towards her, but said that he sometimes yells and has put "a few holes" in the wall.

During Mary's interview she shared how Leon has been violent with her several times, including pushing her, punching her on the arm, and kicking her. She stated, "The worst part is the verbal abuse. He goes on and on, calling me a bitch and other awful swear words. It can go on and on for hours. I try to ignore him, or leave. But the other day he wouldn't let me leave. I just lost it. I picked up a plate and threw it. I was screaming at him to just stop and leave me alone. I'm at the end of my rope. I can't control him, and he knows it. I find myself just crying and screaming at him."

Differences between parent and teen stories are common. After talking with Leon, a therapist might decide that Leon's violence is a reaction to his mother's behavior and that she might have mental health issues. Once Mary is interviewed, however, the assessment changes, and her behavior makes more sense.

During the assessment each family member relays different viewpoints and experiences, and some will be conflicting. The assessment interview is just a beginning, and the practitioner will gather more information along the way by working with the family. However, before a family begins this intervention, the practitioner must decide whether the family is a suitable fit. This is not always clear after the initial interview. Families and situations where violence occurs are often complex. We hope the following information will help with the challenging task of assessing families to determine their suitability for this intervention.

## Prerequisites for This Intervention Model

In order for a teen to be a candidate for this intervention, the assessment must show that the following are true:

- The youth is the primary perpetrator of violence in the family.
- The youth's violence is not a response to abuse.
- The youth is not currently being abused.
- The youth has not been abused by the targeted parent or parents.
- If either the youth or parents have mental health issues, they are receiving appropriate treatment for this, are able to engage appropriately in group sessions, comprehend the concepts, and learn new skills.
- If either the youth or parents have substance addictions issues, they are receiving recommended treatment and are not currently using any addictive substances.

## Youth as Primary Aggressor in the Family

This intervention is designed for youth who have initiated a pattern of violence against parents or other family members and who have been identified as the primary perpetrator of violence in the home. Youth who are currently being victimized by a parent and are using violence to protect themselves from being hurt by a parent do not fit this definition, and in these cases, professionals are required to follow their mandated child abuse reporting laws.

Sometimes it is unclear who is initiating the violence. For instance, parents may use violence against their youth in order to protect themselves or other family members. Parents who have been enduring abuse for some time may respond by slapping, pushing, grabbing, or hitting in the midst of the teen's physical attack. Or, a father may intervene to protect the mother, and hold the son down or push him up against the wall to restrain him. In these cases, it is important to assess the risk level for harm to both parent and teen and the immediate safety issues.

## Parents Who Contribute to Their Youth's Violence

One parent might support abusive behavior by the youth towards the other parent. For example, a teen who visits with his father, who had been abusive towards his mother in the past, might be given messages that validate or justify the youth's violent behavior, such as, the mother is crazy or the father understands why the youth is abusive with her because she is so difficult. Some mothers report that after visits with the father the teen's abusive behavior becomes worse. These cases are particularly difficult because it is challenging for a teen to change behavior that is being supported by one of the parents.

Another way that parents contribute to their youth's violence is by responding to the abuse with physical responses. Living daily with a teen's name-calling and swearing makes it challenging to stay calm. Sometimes parents slap their teens or push them away. These are parents who regret their highly emotional reactions and want to find other ways of responding; they know they are making the situation worse and not helping their teen.

In other cases, parents use violence to teach or discipline their youth. Parents, especially fathers, want their youth to understand that if the youth uses violence, he or she will receive violence in return. In these cases, the parent's violence is not protective but is being used to stop their youth's violence by overpowering the youth, and in some cases, inflicting physical harm. In our experience, most of these cases result in an escalation of violence in the home, and a pattern of violence between parents and youth develops. These cases are carefully assessed and may require a report to child protection services.

Some parents have used harsh parenting behaviors in the past, but are no longer doing so. This may include using a belt, yelling, put-downs, or slapping. In these cases, and in those described above, the most important consideration is whether the parent can acknowledge the behavior is harmful, feels remorse, and is committed to no longer using such behaviors. In order for parents to regain leadership and respect, nonviolence must be a family standard that everyone follows, and anyone who has used violence or abuse must take responsibility for their behavior. When parents take responsibility for their violence, they are modeling accountability for their youth and setting a standard for their family.

Marion and her daughter, Sasha, are an example of this. Sasha was referred to us after an incident where she threatened her mother with a knife. At the intake Sasha reported that her mother used to spank her with a belt when she was younger and sometimes slap her. Marion said that now she grounds Sasha, takes away her phone, and sometimes yells at her.

Sasha admitted to pushing and hitting her mother at times, and that she kicked a hole in the front screen door and threw her mother's laptop at her. She described most of the conflicts to be about her staying out too late or not going to school. Sasha described the incident of pulling a knife on her mother. "I was going to go out, over to my friend's house, and my mom said I couldn't go because I was grounded for not coming home all night last weekend. I said I was going anyway, and I tried to leave. So she got in front of the door to block me. I ran to the kitchen to get out the back door, and she came after me and said if I go out, I would lose my phone for a month. We were yelling, and then I just grabbed a knife off of the counter and held it and said she better let me leave. Then I ran out the door, and she called the police. I just wanted to leave and didn't want her to stop me. I wouldn't have used the knife. I just wanted to scare her."

Marion told a similar story during her intake, but included incidents where Sasha would "... get in my face and scream at me, calling me a worthless bitch and fat and stupid. It was so hard not to slap her, like I used to do. But I don't want to do that anymore. I am trying to not react and stay calm, but it's really hard. I used to yell at her and slap her sometimes. I know that's not good. I used to let my temper get a hold of me, and I see the same thing in her. It's probably my fault she's like this. I used to spank her with a belt, like my mom did with me. I don't know, I told her I won't do that anymore hoping it will help her not be so violent. She gets in rages and throws things at me and pushes me. I don't know what is the right thing to do. I feel like I shouldn't let her get away with it, and just fight her back. But it makes it worse. When she pulled that knife, it scared me and I didn't know what else to do except call the police for help."

Throughout the interview with Marion it was evident that she felt remorse about her own parenting behaviors and was motivated to change. Because Marion was already working hard on her own to make changes, we determined that she and Sasha were a good fit for the program. Marion's accountability also helped Sasha take responsibility for her own behaviors.

The key questions when assessing parenting behavior include the following:

- Is the parent intentionally hurting the teen as a form of punishment?
- To what extent has the behavior occurred?
- Has it been an occasional response, and the parent feels remorse and wants to avoid repeating the behavior, or is it an ongoing, patterned response?
- Is the behavior only in response to the teen's abuse or violence, or does it occur at other times?
- Has the parent been physically or emotionally abusive to the youth in the past, prior to the youth becoming aggressive?

If the parent who is the target of the youth's abuse has been physically or emotionally abusive to the youth in the past, careful consideration must be given. The restorative process in this intervention model focuses on helping youth take responsibility for their behavior, develop empathy, and make amends. If the person a youth is abusing has not acknowledged and taken responsibility for his or her own abusive behavior, it would be unbalanced and unfair to expect the youth to do this.

However, if the parent is accountable with feelings of remorse, the restorative steps can be an effective way to engage parent and teen together in a mutual process of accountability and restoring a respectful relationship. The restorative process, as we will discuss, often ignites personal responsibility for one's own behavior. When parents can acknowledge their behavior, and show their teen they are working on change as well, it helps the young person change. If both are willing to stay respectful towards each other, this treatment model offers the skills and support to help them succeed.

## When There Is Domestic Violence Between Parents

Assessment of domestic violence, current and past, is essential with these families because many youth who use violence in the home have been exposed to domestic violence in the past. Individual interviews are important for safety reasons and will provide the most accurate information. If there is current domestic violence, the first step is to assess the safety of the victim and family and refer them to community resources for help. If there is domestic violence in the home where the youth is living, we do not recommend this group intervention. Portions of the intervention can be used in individual and family sessions with the youth and the nonabusive parent, combining counseling to address the youth's violence, and help with the challenges of living with domestic violence.

Of the families we serve who have experienced domestic violence, most are single or remarried mothers who have left an abusive partner. From our experience, the youth's violence usually begins after the abusive father is no longer in the home.

It is important to know there may be domestic violence between parents that was not identified in the initial interview. Practitioners should be aware of indicators such as disrespectful communication or controlling behaviors. Speak confidentially to each parent separately about your concern. Explain to parents that if there is abuse in the parent's relationship, the best way to help their teen is for the abusive parent to get help and change their behavior. The offending parent should be referred to a domestic violence offender treatment program, and domestic violence survivor support resources should be offered to the victimized parent.

## Substance Abuse

Youth and parents should both be screened for chemical dependency issues. If youth are using substances more than occasionally, it may interfere with their ability to engage in the change process. Likewise, if a parent has alcohol or substance addiction issues, he or she is unlikely to be able to participate in a helpful way. Referral to services for help with these issues comes first.

## Mental Health Issues

About half of the youth we serve have a mental health diagnosis and are receiving mental health treatment in addition to this intervention. If the teen is able to participate appropriately in the group or session, he or she is a good fit for this intervention. It may be unclear at the assessment whether or not this model is appropriate for the youth. We have found that we don't always know at the assessment interview if the young person is an appropriate fit, so we have them start group sessions to see how it goes. We have been surprised by some teens about whom we had reservations, but who turned out to do exceptionally well. We have learned to give it a try, unless it is clear the youth is not ready for this type of intervention.

If the youth presents mental health symptoms, and has not had an evaluation or a treatment provider, we refer them for a mental health evaluation and tell them to follow the recommendations of the mental health provider before beginning this intervention.

## Collaboration with Other Providers

Communication with all other treatment providers involved with the youth is critical in this work. Shared therapeutic goals for family safety and nonviolence provide the young person with a consistent message along with support by all in the change process. Working together as a team empowers everyone's work.

## Assessment of Abuse and Violence

The Behavior Checklist (Table 6.1), administered to the teen and parent pre- and post-treatment, identifies the teen's abusive and violent behaviors and their frequency of use. It is both an assessment tool for level and severity of violence and abuse, and a pre- and post-measure of behavior change. It can also be used during treatment to measure progress, serving as a motivator for behavior change. The Behavior Checklist gives a more accurate view of what is really going on and facilitates real change by providing a way to measure that change.

The following is a Behavior Checklist that parents fill out at the intake interview and again at the end of the program. Teens fill out the same checklist about themselves.

Talking to parents and youth about violence in their home can be difficult. Both parents and youth bring a strong sense of shame, for very different reasons, to an interview and may not feel comfortable talking with anyone about violence and abuse.

Helping professionals may feel uncomfortable talking about abuse and violence with families. We have developed a simple tool (Boxes 6.1 and 6.2) that can assist professionals when they interview parents and youth about violence in their

**TABLE 6.1** Behavior Checklist

| Behaviors done in the last six months | Never | Rarely (Once) | Occasionally (Once a Month) | Frequently (Once a Week) | Almost Every Day |
|---|---|---|---|---|---|
| 1. Called you names. | 1 | 2 | 3 | 4 | 5 |
| 2. Tried to get you to do something by intimidating you. | 1 | 2 | 3 | 4 | 5 |
| 3. Gave you angry looks or stares. | 1 | 2 | 3 | 4 | 5 |
| 4. Screamed or yelled at you. | 1 | 2 | 3 | 4 | 5 |
| 5. Threatened to hit or throw something at you. | 1 | 2 | 3 | 4 | 5 |
| 6. Pushed, grabbed, or shoved you. | 1 | 2 | 3 | 4 | 5 |
| 7. Put you or other family members down. | 1 | 2 | 3 | 4 | 5 |
| 8. Threatened and/or hit brothers or sisters. | 1 | 2 | 3 | 4 | 5 |
| 9. Demanded that you or other family members do what you want. | 1 | 2 | 3 | 4 | 5 |
| 10. Said things to scare you. | 1 | 2 | 3 | 4 | 5 |
| 11. Slapped, hit, or punched you. | 1 | 2 | 3 | 4 | 5 |
| 12. Told you that you were a bad parent. | 1 | 2 | 3 | 4 | 5 |
| 13. Threw, hit, kicked, or smashed something during an argument. | 1 | 2 | 3 | 4 | 5 |
| 14. Kicked you. | 1 | 2 | 3 | 4 | 5 |

home. It identifies behaviors that are grouped into different abuse categories, the people in the family who are targeted by the behavior, how often the behaviors are used, and the time period that the youth used the behaviors. We ask parents and teens these questions in their separate interviews.

To put people at ease, we begin the discussion by simply saying, "Most families who come to us are struggling with violence in their home. We help families who have experienced violence and we want to learn about your family and how to best help, and so I will be asking you questions about violence in your family. We are asking you about violence in your home so we can understand how we can best help you."

---

### Box 6.1 — Violence Interview Form, Part 1, History

Please tell me which of these things your child (if a parent is being interviewed) or you (if a teen is being interviewed) has done when they are fighting with family members. Tell me how often each behavior was used on a scale of zero to five. Zero means it never happens and five means it happens every day.

| Physical abuse | To Whom | Frequency | Time Period |
|---|---|---|---|
| Slap | | | |
| Push | | | |
| Grab | | | |
| Punch | | | |
| Kick | | | |
| Choke | | | |
| Use a knife or other weapon | | | |
| Other | | | |

| Threats | To Whom | Frequency | Time Period |
|---|---|---|---|
| Threats to hurt | | | |
| Threats to kill | | | |
| Threats to report to CPS or police | | | |

| Intimidation | To Whom | Frequency | Time Period |
|---|---|---|---|
| Smashing, throwing, breaking things | | | |
| Hitting, punching doors/walls | | | |

| Verbal /Emotional Abuse | To Whom | Frequency | Time Period |
|---|---|---|---|
| Screaming/yelling | | | |
| Profanity towards person | | | |
| Name-calling | | | |
| Degrading/humiliating words | | | |

While understanding specific behaviors is important, a context for violent behavior in the home is another valuable source of information. To understand more of the context and assess the risk level for further violence by the youth and the safety concerns of the parent, we use the following assessment tool.

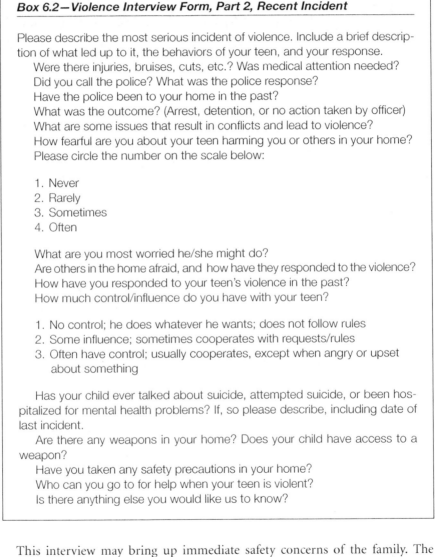

### Box 6.2—Violence Interview Form, Part 2, Recent Incident

Please describe the most serious incident of violence. Include a brief description of what led up to it, the behaviors of your teen, and your response.

Were there injuries, bruises, cuts, etc.? Was medical attention needed?
Did you call the police? What was the police response?
Have the police been to your home in the past?
What was the outcome? (Arrest, detention, or no action taken by officer)
What are some issues that result in conflicts and lead to violence?
How fearful are you about your teen harming you or others in your home?
Please circle the number on the scale below:

1. Never
2. Rarely
3. Sometimes
4. Often

What are you most worried he/she might do?
Are others in the home afraid, and how have they responded to the violence?
How have you responded to your teen's violence in the past?
How much control/influence do you have with your teen?

1. No control; he does whatever he wants; does not follow rules
2. Some influence; sometimes cooperates with requests/rules
3. Often have control; usually cooperates, except when angry or upset about something

Has your child ever talked about suicide, attempted suicide, or been hospitalized for mental health problems? If, so please describe, including date of last incident.

Are there any weapons in your home? Does your child have access to a weapon?

Have you taken any safety precautions in your home?
Who can you go to for help when your teen is violent?
Is there anything else you would like us to know?

This interview may bring up immediate safety concerns of the family. The interviewer should be prepared to address the immediate risk of harm and provide assistance to the family. This may include: facilitating a safety plan with the youth and parent before they leave the office, or safety planning with the parent alone (see Chapter 7, "Safety Plan and Safety Planning with Parents"); calling on other resources to assist the family, such as with temporary placement of the youth outside of the home; or if there is imminent danger and there has been a recent violent episode, law enforcement response may be needed.

## The Role of the Juvenile Justice System

One of the greatest challenges for parents and professionals in this work is engaging youth who refuse counseling. Many youth are unwilling to attend counseling, and parents have limited influence with a teen who is violent towards them. When there is physical violence by a teen in the home and he or she refuses help, the juvenile justice system can be a vital source of support for the family. It may be the only way to engage the young person in changing violent behavior.

In addition, when there is court system involvement it sends an important message to the teen: violence in the family is not acceptable. When youth are continually violent towards family members without police or court response, they are learning that violence is not a crime and is acceptable, as long as it is within the family. Violence in most schools is swiftly responded to, with no tolerance policies clearly put forth to all students. Unfortunately, violence is taken less seriously when it is directed towards family members.

It helps youth to experience a response to their violence from the larger community, not just from their parents. They benefit from recognizing it is not just their parents who are worried; the larger community is concerned about their behavior and the safety of their family members. It helps parents feel backed when others, such as a police officer or judge, tell their teen that their behavior is not safe and it is worthy of attention from the court and helping professionals. It is important to find out how your court system handles these cases so you can provide accurate information to families. When the court has options for youth to prevent charges by attending counseling, parents feel more comfortable with court intervention.

From our experience, many teens regard their court experience as helpful to them, often citing their arrest or a few days in detention as a motivator for them to change. We have found that accountability to the court can be a "kick start" in the therapeutic process to motivate teens to engage in counseling. It also helps them "stick with it" during the change process. Once they start to experience the benefits of their behavior change, such as getting along better with their parents and a calmer home, they become internally motivated to continue doing so. The skill learning in the intervention helps them sustain their nonviolence. When there are relapses of violence the restorative process offers a constructive way to address it and get back on track.

## A Coordinated Community Response

The intervention we described in this chapter is more effective if it is part of a community-wide effort to end violence in the home. The Duluth Model pioneered a community response to domestic violence when they created a coherent philosophical approach that prioritized victim safety, developed best practice policies for intervention agencies, reduced fragmentation in the court system's response, built a system of monitoring offenders, raised awareness of the harm domestic violence does to children, and fostered a supportive community infrastructure (Mederos, 2002). From our experience, when law enforcement, juvenile court, and community agencies work together towards common goals, family safety is enhanced. For instance, when we first started our work, police who responded to emergency calls were frustrated because juvenile detention sometimes refused to detain teens due to department protocols. Parents were very frustrated because some cases involved injury and threats with weapons. After meetings that included police and detention staff, the protocols were changed and teens were detained in appropriate circumstances. Another example of coordinating efforts is when we worked with our local sheriff's department to produce a training video for police officers because in some situations officers were unsure about how they were supposed to respond. The sheriff enthusiastically participated in filming the video.

## Summary

This intervention model centers on restoring safe and respectful family relationships. Restorative practice engages empathy and accountability as teens' recognize the impact of their behavior on others. They learn how their thinking and feelings lead to hurtful behavior and how to change unhelpful thought patterns. Respectful communication skills give teens a new way to talk about feelings and resolve conflicts. And self-calming skills provide a way for teens to handle themselves when they are angry and escalated to prevent violence and abuse.

Success depends on careful assessment of families to ensure they are the right fit for this model, along with assessment of the severity of violence and the safety concerns of family members. The juvenile justice system can be a valuable source of support for parents, and motivate youth to engage in the change process.

## References

Andrews, D. A., & Bonta, J. (2003). *The psychology of criminal conduct.* 3rd ed. Cincinnati, OH: Anderson.

Bandura, A. (1973). *Aggression: a social learning analysis.* Englewood Cliffs, NJ: Prentice-Hall.

Clark, M. D. (1998). Strengths-based practice: the ABC's of working with adolescents who don't want to work with you. *Federal Probation Quarterly,* 62(1), 46–53.

Crick, N., & Dodge, K. (1994). A review and reformulation of social information processing mechanisms in children's social adjustments. *Psychological Bulletin,* 115, 75–104.

Cullen, F. T. (2002). Rehabilitation and treatment programs. In J. Q. Wilson and J. Petersilia (eds.), *Crime: public policy for crime control* (2nd ed.), pp. 253–289. Oakland, CA: ICS Press.

Gottman, J. (1995). *Why marriages succeed or fail.* New York: Simon & Schuster.

Kant, I. (1998). *Groundwork of the metaphysics of morals.* Translated by M. Gregor. New York: Cambridge University Press. First published 1785.

Kassinove, H., & Tafrate, R. C. (2002). *Anger management: the complete treatment guidebook for practitioners.* Atascadero, CA: Impact.

Kazdin, A. E., & Weisz, J. R. (1998). Identifying and developing empirically supported child and adolescent treatments. *Journal of Consulting and Clinical Psychology,* 66, 19–36.

Lochman, J., Powell, N., Boxmeyer, C., Deming, A. M., & Young, L. (2007). Cognitive-behavior group therapy for angry and aggressive youth. In R. W. Christner, J. Stewart, & P. A. Freeman (Eds.), *Handbook of cognitive-behavioral group therapy with children and adolescents* (pp. 333–348), New York: Routledge.

McClennan, J. (2010). *Social work and family violence theories, assessment and intervention.* New York: Springer.

Mayseless, O., & Scharff, M. (2011). Respecting others and being respected can reduce aggression in parent-child relations and in schools. In P. R. Shaver & M. Mikulincer (Eds.), *Human aggression and violence: causes, manifestations, and consequences* (pp. 277–294), Washington, DC: American Psychological Association.

Mederos, F. (2002). Changing our visions of intervention—the evolution of programs for physically abusive men. In E. Aldarondo & F. Mederos (Eds.), *Programs for men who batter* (pp. 1–23), Kingston, NJ: Civic Research Institute.

Miller, W. R., & Rollnick, S. (2002). *Motivational interviewing.* 2nd ed. New York: Guilford Press.

Pence, E., & Paymar, M. (1993). *Education groups for men who batter: the Duluth model.* New York: Springer.

Piaget, J. (1932). *The moral development of the child.* Oxford, England: Harcourt, Brace.

Tolan, P. H., Guerra, N. G., & Kendall, O. H. (1995). A developmental-ecological perspective on antisocial behavior in children and adolescents: towards a unified risk and intervention framework. *Journal of Consulting and Clinical Psychology,* 63, 577–584.

Wachtel, T. (2013). Defining restorative. The International Institute for Restorative Practices. Retrieved from http://www.iirp.edu/pdf/Defining-Restorative.pdf

# seven
# **Foundation for Change**

## A Safe Environment

*What is home? "A safe place," a place where one is free from attack, a place where one experiences secure relationships and affirmation. It's a place where people share and understand each other. Its relationships are nurturing. The people in it do not need to be perfect; instead, they need to be honest, loving, supportive, recognizing a common humanity that makes all of us vulnerable.*

—Gladys Hunt, Honey for a Child's Heart: The
Imaginative Use of Books in Family Life

## It's All About Safety

When parents living with a violent teen seek help, their first concern is restoring a climate of safety in their home. Helping families build respectful family relationships begins with family safety as a priority. A safe environment provides a platform for honest communication, conflict resolution, and problem solving that is necessary for a teen-parent relationship as they navigate the road towards the young person's independence. When parents don't feel safe with their adolescent they avoid setting boundaries, following through on consequences, and addressing problems. Teens do not receive the guidance and accountability they need during these important years of developing personal responsibility and independence. When a parent is unable to provide guidance because of fear of a violent outburst, not only is the teen's healthy development thwarted, but a lesson is continually reinforced: *aggression is an effective way to achieve my aims.*

The resounding phrase throughout this intervention is "being safe with each other." Acting safe and feeling safe are essential to restore trust and a healthy relationship. When a relationship loses a sense of safety, replaced by fear of being hurt physically or emotionally, the sense of connection based on trust and security is destabilized. As we know, this happens all too often in families. When children fear physical or emotional harm from their parents or caretakers, when there is domestic violence between parents or sexual abuse, the home is no longer a place of safety. We have encountered youth and parents who have never known a complete sense of safety in their home. When we talk with families about having a home where everyone feels protected from harm and respected, some are unfamiliar with what this feels like. Most young people agree that it is important to feel safe in their own home, particularly those who have not felt safe at some point in their lives. They know the feeling of fear and uncertainty around a family member, and understand that feeling safe in their own family is important and desirable. Discussion of this topic and how each family member plays a role in making the home a safer place for everyone can be the first step in engaging youth in the change process.

## Lessons Learned from Our Own Experience

We have learned from experience how easy it can be to mistakenly empower teens to become more abusive. We have noticed how teens misinterpret parenting suggestions, changing the message to, "She's a bad parent; it's her fault I'm like this." They have also misread our compassion for their difficulties and frustrations as justifying their abusive behavior. We have learned the importance of balancing compassion for their feelings with accountability for their abusive actions and discussing parenting in a separate parent's group only.

We have learned to pay close attention to how we impact family safety. Each week, we check in with families, using the Abuse and Respect Wheels, to learn how the strategies we teach play out at home and to gauge the increase or decrease in violence and abuse. (Check-in will be discussed further in Chapter 8.) We also invite parents to notify us immediately when they feel the intervention is increasing the abuse or violence. Remembering our goal is safety in the home and keeping a finger on the safety pulse keep our practice safe for the families.

## Lessons Learned from Adult Domestic Violence Programs

When our treatment team began planning this intervention, the first concern was to assure that the practice approach would not compromise the safety of family members. From our experience in the field of adult domestic violence we knew that some approaches are not recommended due to the risk of increasing the violence. Family counseling is strongly discouraged in these cases because of safety risks for the victimized person. Most people do not feel safe being open in a session with someone who abuses them. In addition, offenders sometimes use the counselor's suggestions as another way to control and further abuse their partner. Individual therapy with offenders is not advised because of the tendency for practitioners to collude with offenders in a one-on-one relationship, without other perspectives or the victim's account. Offenders often minimize their violence and blame their victims, diverting attention away from their own accountability.

For all of these reasons, the recommended practice model for treating domestic violence with adult offenders is behavior change group work, along with therapist contact with the victim, if she chooses, to obtain information about the violence history, safety concerns, and any further abuse or violence while the offender is in treatment. Victims are referred to separate agencies for counseling and support.

In planning our practice approach, we drew from the safety practices of adult domestic violence treatment programs. The wisdom of those who have worked in the field of adult domestic violence over many years has been acquired through the lessons learned from numerous tragic outcomes. Violence between family members can be lethal, and while teen to parent violence has resulted in far fewer deaths, attention to the risk is critical. Parents report to us that they fear for their lives all too often. Teen to parent violence is newer in the family violence treatment field, and while different from adult domestic violence in many respects, there are similar safety concerns for a great number of the families.

## Safety on All Levels

When working with youth who are violent in the home, the practitioner must examine safety on three levels. We do this by asking ourselves a series of questions.

### Safety in the Practice Model

The following questions relate to the structure of the overall practice model.

- Have I assessed the violence level and risk of harm thoroughly at intake?
- Does each parent feel safe talking about the violence in sessions with his or her teen?
- Am I attentive to the risk level for violence on an ongoing basis?
- Is my practice increasing the risk of violence?
- Am I offering lines of communication to parents to allow them to speak openly without fear of reprisal from the teen?
- Am I inadvertently justifying the youth's behavior with him or her?
- Am I structuring my sessions so the leadership role of the parent is enhanced?
- Am I setting boundaries between parent and youth by providing times and opportunities to address parenting issues alone with the parent?

## Safety in Group Sessions

The next set of questions addresses how the practitioner anticipates and handles safety during group sessions.

- Are there clear boundaries and expectations for respectful communication during sessions?
- Do I have a communication contract in place between all participants?
- Do I immediately intervene to stop disrespectful words used in session?
- Do I have a clear plan for how to respond to verbal abuse or violence during sessions?
- Does every participant have a safety plan in place before starting sessions?
- Do I continually monitor the verbal and nonverbal reactions of group participants to gauge whether everyone feels safe during and after group sessions?

## Safety in the Home

The final set of questions addresses safety in the home, after participants leave the session.

- Does every youth have a safety plan in place?
- Is there a check-in at the start of every session to monitor safety in the home, addressing violent or abusive behaviors during the prior week?
- If there was violence during the prior week, is there a plan in place before they go home, such as reviewing and revising the safety plan?
- Does the parent have a plan for how to respond to further violence from their youth so they feel safe?
- Am I keeping a focus on teaching skills for safety and nonviolence on an ongoing basis?

## Safety in the Practice Model

My son and I went to counseling together about his violence. Right after we left the office he would go off on me for what I had said. I'd have to pay for it all week. He used things the counselor said as a way to abuse me more, like parenting advice. He interpreted it as all being my problem and would put me down for being a bad parent or not doing what the counselor said I should do. He thought her suggestion that I listen more meant I had to stay there and listen to him as he yelled and called me names. I don't think she understood what it is really like with him. It gave him more power to abuse me. I didn't know what to do. I finally stopped going.

> He has been in individual therapy for a while, and I don't know what he is working on. He refused to sign a disclosure form and doesn't want me to talk to his counselor. I'm left out of it while he continues to abuse me. He just blames me all the more. The violence has gotten worse, and I don't think his counselor has any idea.

Parents often say that individual and family therapy increased their teen's violence and abuse. Skilled and well-meaning practitioners may inadvertently increase risk of harm using strategies that work well with most families, but may increase risk of violence with a teen who is abusive. We have learned this through our experience working with these families.

## Teens and Parents Together in Joint Sessions

One of our first important decisions was whether to include parents and teens in a group together. Initially, we were concerned that parents would not feel safe discussing the abuse in the presence of their youth for fear of retaliation, and that violence might increase because of the parents' disclosures. We decided to begin with separate parent and teen groups and learn from them as we moved forward. After several weeks, however, parents began asking, "Why are we in separate groups? We live with our teens every day. We want to learn with them, so we can work together on this. I know I have things to change, too, and I'd like to learn what he is learning, too."

In addition, with separate parent and teen groups, it was challenging when the teen had a completely different story at check-in from what the parent described. Teens would often say everything was fine during the week, while their parents would talk about holes in walls, screaming, and profanity towards them. We soon realized that holding separate groups was not a helpful approach for either the teens or the parents.

Before adjusting the treatment framework to include sessions with parents and teens together, we spent time learning more from parents about how safe they felt talking about the violence in the presence of their teen. We found that some parents felt more comfortable talking openly about their teen's behavior, while others had reservations.

One parent told us, "I'm talking to him about it all week, with no support. I'd actually feel safer if I can talk about it with your help." Other parents were more hesitant, expressing concerns such as, "I do worry a little about what he'll say to me when we get out to the car; it could be a rough car ride home."

Some parents acknowledged risk for retaliation, but felt learning how to talk about it together is the only way towards changing things. These patients expressed sentiments such as, "If we can't talk about it, how will it ever stop?"

We concluded that working with parents and teens together for part of the time was essential, with safety precautions in place. We began having parent-teen groups in addition to separate parent and teen groups. We found that joint sessions actually increased safety by providing a safe and respectful environment where families were supported in learning safety skills together.

To ensure participant safety, we put the following into place before we held any joint sessions:

- Clear guidelines for maintaining a safe, respectful environment during group sessions.
- A communication contract, which each group participant needed to sign prior to attending.
- A safety plan for the youth, with weekly goals for safety.
- Weekly safety monitoring through the check-in process.
- Incorporation of teaching and practice of safe, respectful communication skills.

The following checklist summarizes the safety precautions for working with parents and youth in joint sessions.

- Assess violence level and parent's safety concerns before beginning group or family session (see "Assessing Level of Violence," in Chapter 6).
- Conduct separate parent and teen assessment interviews.
- Assess whether parents feel safe participating in sessions with their teens.
- Discuss parents' safety concerns about disclosing their teens' behavior in the group or family session and communicate regularly with them about ongoing safety concerns.
- Keep your attention on violence and abuse level every week. Monitor safety concerns through a weekly check-in.
- Avoid parenting suggestions or advice in the presence of the teen. Provide parent education in parent group/session only.
- Facilitate a written safety plan with the teen and parent before beginning each group session, or at the first group session.
- Maintain a climate of safety and respect during sessions, with clear expectations that all language and behavior must be on the Respect Wheel.

## Safety in Group Sessions

### Setting the Stage

A climate of safety and respect must be in place for engagement in the change process to succeed. Clear boundaries and expectations for communication during sessions set the stage for families to feel safe and comfortable. Within a group, community building can begin with setting ground rules that promote respect for all. When participants are involved in establishing ground rules, they take ownership and are more dedicated to following those rules. Rules about respectful behavior should be explicit and reviewed regularly. We post a list of respectful group behaviors on the wall for easy reference when boundaries are crossed. We also post the Respect Wheel as a reference for behavior during group sessions. And finally, we use a communication contract to invite agreement between everyone to remain safe and respectful with each other at all times.

The communication contract (Box 7.1) promotes respectful communication between each person in the group. It is an agreement between participants to use respectful language and behavior, and is an early task during a first session or orientation for new group members. It is meant not only to be a set of guidelines for communication with the others in a session, but at home with family members as well. The communication contract can also be used as a teaching tool, describing what respectful communication looks and sounds like and how to do it. Each of the statements in the contract can be a point of discussion about respect versus disrespect. Participants are asked to commit to following the contract and sign a document with all the essential points listed on it. This is the beginning of understanding respect and practicing respectful relationships.

---

### Box 7.1—Communication Contract

## Communication Contract

- Speak respectfully.
- Speak without blaming, criticizing, yelling, swearing, or put-downs.
- Think before speaking.
- Take a moment to think about how you can say it in respectful words.
- Speak in a nonthreatening way.
- Pay attention to your voice level, tone, words, and body movements so that others feel at ease with you.
- Use "I" statements to express your feelings or perspective.
- Say how it is for you, "I feel _____, when you _____," without blaming the other person.
- Listen to each other.
- Let go of your own thoughts while you listen. Try not to think about how you are going to respond.
- Try to understand each other's feelings and opinions, even when you disagree.
- Put yourself in the other person's shoes while you listen. Imagine how you would feel if you were that person. Think about how it is from the other person's perspective, even if you think he or she is totally wrong.
- Wait until the other person has stopped talking before you respond.
- Do not interrupt; interrupting is a bad habit that is difficult to break. Pay attention to what the other person is saying rather than responding to it.

_____    _____

Signature                                    Date

---

Facilitators interject the following messages during discussion about the communication contract:

- Our group needs to be a place where everyone feels safe and respected at all times.
- Every group member has a right to speak up if they feel unsafe or disrespected.
- We are modeling a safe, caring, and supportive community in our group where relationships can be healed and restored.
- Anytime a group member feels unable to follow the communication contract, he or she will take a break from group. Ask for help, and one of the facilitators will step outside with the participant to offer support.

## Handling Disrespect and Abuse in Group Sessions

Abusive or disrespectful behavior during a session provides a learning opportunity for everyone. Addressing it immediately after it begins prevents further escalation and models how to stop an interaction the minute it becomes abusive. This practice helps group participants in several ways:

- Group members learn there is a no-tolerance policy for abuse or disrespect.
- They learn how to stop an interaction as soon as disrespect begins to prevent escalation.
- They observe how it is possible to catch a behavior, change it, and get back to the conversation without a huge blowup.
- They have a model for doing this at home.

For many families, this is a whole new experience. A supportive and encouraging manner by the facilitator helps the teen feel more willing to stop and cooperate with trying it another way, modeling for parents how to do this at home. What follows is an example of a typical parent-teen interaction during check-in where the teen becomes disrespectful.

Jaylen raises her voice and says to her mother, "I told you I needed a ride home! How do you expect me home on time when you're too lazy to . . ." The facilitator immediately breaks in and says, "Jaylen, hold up a minute. Look at the communication contract. Can you say that again, following the communication contract?" Jaylen stops, is quiet for a moment, and then says in a calm voice, "Mom, I remember telling you I needed a ride home, and then you didn't pick me up, and you got mad at me for not being home on time. But I had to take the bus. I thought you were going to pick me up." The conversation continues on to reveal that Jaylen's mother did not get the message about picking Jaylen up, and they were able to find a solution for next time.

When confronted with a situation such as the one described above, the facilitator needs to think and respond quickly. Because it's essential that the facilitator model respectful behavior in the moment, it helps to have a repertoire of statements that can be used to respectfully intervene and redirect. Below you will find a list of such statements.

---

**Box 7.2—Group Facilitator's Response to Abusive or Disrespectful Behavior**

Facilitator's Response to Abusive or Disrespectful Behavior:

- Can you restate that message staying on the Respect Wheel? Or, how about saying that on the Respect Wheel?
- How might you communicate your opinion, feelings, and thoughts in a respectful way?
- Try using one of the skills you have learned to rephrase that. How about using an 'I' statement for that message?
- This would be a good opportunity to use your assertive communication skills.
- It sounds like you're angry about this, and you are being verbally abusive to your mother right now. Talk about how you feel using your skills from the feelings session. Remember how we talked about the feelings below anger? Think for a moment about what your feelings are, and try communicating them to your mother in a respectful way.
- Let's look at the communication contract for a moment, and see where you are with it. What can you do to get back on track?

When Behavior Escalates to Physical Violence or Threats:

- Let's have you use your safety plan. Step outside into the hallway and take a break. Use your self-calming skills, think about what you want to say in a respectful way, and then come back when you are ready.
- (To the teen) Let's stop talking now. We'll have you go home for the night. I'd like you both to agree not to talk about this on the way home. (To the parent) If you feel uncomfortable going home with your son (or daughter), we'll call a family member or friend to pick up your son (or daughter) to take him (or her) home. We'll call you tomorrow to discuss what we should do next.

---

If physically abusive or threatening behavior occurred, you may need to call the emergency services number (911 in the United States and Canada). Also, the youth should not return to group until the following week, provided the group feels safe having the youth back. This needs to be discussed with the group and assessed by the facilitators.

When the youth returns to group, process the incident with the entire group by asking the youth to answer the restorative inquiry questions (See the section titled, "Taking Responsibility for My Abusive Behavior," in Chapter 8). This provides an opportunity for the youth to hear how the behavior impacted the other members of the group.

Using the disrespectful and abusive behavior that arises during group as a learning opportunity enables parents to practice, in a real situation, how to respectfully interrupt such behavior. When a teen derails the discussion with aggressive behavior, the facilitator can model for the parent how to redirect the teen to using their skills and then to commend the teen on the choice to do so. Teens begin to feel a sense of self-control knowing there are options and another path. In the past, the pattern would have been to continue on as their parent tries to stop the teen, inviting more resistance. As the interaction escalates, it feels as though there is no way out. Both parent and teen feel they cannot lose the battle. Given the opportunity to practice interacting with each other in the group and to experience the outcome of letting go of the battle, separating, and calming down, the next time this happens at home they have a new script to follow.

## Safety at Home

An important skill learned during this intervention is how to use a personal safety plan at home. When parents and teens are asked upon completion of this intervention what helped the most, the common answer is "the safety plan." As one teen put it, "I never knew how to back out of it once I got started up. It felt like there wasn't a way out and I just kept it up. Now I have something I can do to stop it. It really works."

We named this strategy a safety plan because it is most helpful when we frame the problem as an issue of safety, putting attention on how abusive behavior impacts others. When we reframe the problem with a focus on its effects—i.e., people don't feel safe when someone is screaming and throwing things and the home needs to be a place everyone feels safe and secure—it changes the teens' understanding. Few young people would argue against the importance of feeling safe in their own home.

Many teens have never recognized their violent behavior as unsafe. As one teen said, "I was just trying to get my point across." Another teen remarked, "I just wanted her to stop telling me what to do and leave me alone. So I pushed her." They view their actions by the intent, feeling they were not trying to be hurtful. Some teens seem surprised to hear their little brother or sister is afraid of them. To further illustrate a teen's lack of awareness of how his behavior affects others, the following conversation between a mother and son unfolded during group check-in.

Riley and his mother were talking about an incident during the previous week where Riley had started yelling and swearing at her. She had reminded him of his weekly goal of not swearing at her, and he calmed down, muttering under his breath as he left the room. Riley's mother said his six-year-old sister, Amy, ran out the back door when Riley had started yelling. She found her in the backyard hiding and crying.

When Riley heard this, his first reaction was, "She's not afraid of me. She's never been scared of me. I would never hurt her." He seemed genuinely surprised. He was quiet. His mother said, "Riley, ever since that time when you were threatening me and you punched that wall, she gets really afraid when she hears your voice rise. She usually runs to her room. She is scared of you. She doesn't know what is going to happen when you start to get mad."

Riley seemed impacted by this. He had tears in his eyes. It was clear he did not want his little sister to be afraid of him. This conversation helped him understand for the first time how much his behavior scares others, and he became more open to working on change. Teens usually don't realize what their behavior looks like when they are aggressive. They are focused on themselves and their own feelings, and unaware of others' reactions.

When we talk about behavior as an issue of safety, there is usually less dispute about the need to change behavior. Holding attention to this theme throughout the process helps teens view the need to change in a less accusatory way, relaxing their defenses and opening them to engage in the change process.

## The Safety Plan

The safety plan is a step-by-step plan, created by a teen, explaining what he or she will do to prevent hurtful behavior when an interaction begins to escalate. The goal is for teens to recognize early warning signs, or what we call "red flags." A red flag signals that the teen is heading towards hurtful behavior and warns the teen to separate from the person or situation before hurtful language or behavior occurs. Anytime a teen is becoming too angry or upset to continue talking respectfully, it is time to use the safety plan.

The safety plan consists of the following five steps:

1.   Notice your red flags, and make the decision to separate.
2.   Tell the other person you are using your safety plan and separate from the person.
3.   Go to a place where you can be alone and use your self-calming skills (discussed further in Chapter 9).
4.   Once you are calm, think about how you can respectfully communicate your feelings, needs, or opinion to the other person. Think about skills you can use to work out the conflict, such as problem solving.

5.  Once you are calm enough to be safe and respectful to others, go back to the person and make a plan about what to do next, such as:
    - Finishing the discussion, staying on the Respect Wheel
    - Planning a time to talk about it later
    - Just letting go of the feelings and doing nothing, if the parent agrees

Both teens and parents can initiate the separation. Parents can use the safety plan and separate from their teen when the teen refuses to do so, or if the parent recognizes she or he is becoming angry and needs time to take a break. However, if the parent always initiates the separation, the teen does not have the opportunity to learn how to use this important skill. The goal is for the teen to learn to recognize when it is time to separate, and to follow the safety plan on his or her own initiative. They may need reminders from their parent in the beginning, and if reminders trigger further escalation (which is not unusual at first), the parent can then say, "I am going to use the safety plan right now," and separate from the teen.

For both teens and parents, the use of the safety plan is a challenging skill. Separating from a situation in the middle of a heated argument is not easy. The more escalated the teen is, the more challenging it is to stop midway, turn around, and walk away. For parents, there is a feeling of giving in if they disengage, accompanied by a fear of losing authority and feeding the misbehavior. Teens don't want to let go until they have accomplished their mission, which is usually to change their parent's mind about something. Both feel an overwhelming need to get their point across.

Once the ability to stop oneself midstream and separate from an escalated argument is mastered, a substantial part of the work towards becoming nonviolent in relationships is accomplished. Most violence is the result of an inability, or unwillingness, to stop and step away from heated conflict. Most of the problem in any highly emotional argument is a power struggle where both are hooked and don't want to let go. The win-lose aspect becomes the focus, and walking away feels like losing. The ability to override this drive to win, stop oneself midway, and separate is a large step in the change process for teens. For some adolescents it is extremely challenging to back off and let go of a power struggle. Parents can help with this by doing it themselves, and modeling it in a calm and respectful way. Another way that parents can support youth with this challenge is to have a family rule that the moment disrespect begins, everyone stops and separates to go calm down. By including siblings and other family members, teens feel they are not singled out in needing to follow this rule.

Once acquired, this is a skill that transfers to all parts of an adolescent's life—school, peers, work, and in the future, with partners and children. This competency is the most important part of this work. It takes practice, time, and weekly support from the practitioner for families to become competent using this skill.

*Box 7.3—Safety Plan*
_____

The Safety Plan

**I agree to the following plan to prevent abuse or violence:**

1. I will separate from my family member(s) when:

    - I start to feel angry or upset and might become hurtful.
    - I start to use any hurtful behaviors including the following:

        Yelling
        Put-downs
        Name-calling and profanity
        Threats
        Intimidating behaviors
        Property damage
        Unwanted physical contact, such as: hitting, punching, pushing, kicking, slapping, grabbing, choking, or other unwanted contact

2. I will tell the other person I am separating by saying:

    _____

3. I will separate from the person and go to one of the following places:

    _____

4. While I am separated I will do something to calm myself down, such as:

    _____

5. I will stay away from others for _____ minutes, or until I can be respectful to everyone in the house.

**I agree to the following rules:**

- I will not use this plan as an excuse to leave the house, or to get out of chores or other things I'm supposed to do.
- After my separation time I will return and make a plan with the other person about what to do next (for example, finish the discussion, plan a time later to talk about it, or let it go).
- If the other person separates from me I will respect their time alone and not bother them.
- I will stay away from the other person until they are ready to talk again.

**I understand if I am violent the consequences will be:**

_____

---

**I agree to be nonviolent at home.**

Youth Signature: _____

Date: _____

**Parent Agreement:**

I also agree to be nonviolent and to support my youth in following this plan.

Parent Signature: _____

Date: _____

---

## Paying Attention to Red Flags

Teens might not view a raised voice or disrespectful words as a safety issue, and will say, "Why do I need to use my safety plan? I am not hurting anyone. I'm just using words. I'm not doing anything physical." It can be helpful to show teens and parents the progression that typically occurs before physical violence happens. In most cases, it begins with a disagreement and arguing that becomes disrespectful; it progresses to yelling, swearing, or name-calling; and finally it degenerates to a push, shove, or hit.

When disrespect is caught the moment it begins, it is much easier to separate, and the calming down process is faster and easier. In fact, when teens really pay attention to their behavior, they notice it early enough to turn the behavior around without the need to separate and calm down. The very earliest signal is usually a feeling, such as frustration, irritation, or anger.

When teaching teens about their red flags, we ask, "When you are in an argument with your parent, do you know the feeling you have before you start to use disrespectful or abusive language?" There is usually an immediate nod and acknowledgment that they know the feeling well. We then say, "That's your first red flag letting you know you have a choice. You can use your safety plan to take a break and calm down, or you can put attention on keeping your words and behavior respectful even though you are having difficult feelings. It may help to tell your parent how you feel in a respectful way, which reduces the desire to express it in an abusive way."

Abuse or violence is usually used to express difficult feelings. When teens learn how to talk about their feelings they can calm down and feel less of a need to lash out. Learning and practicing communication skills such as "I" statements and assertiveness gives them more options.

To help teens identify their red flags, we ask them to think about a recent experience when they became abusive or violent, and to remember their thoughts, feelings, body sensations, and behaviors before they escalated to abuse or violence. This reflection process helps raise teens' awareness of themselves in a way they have never experienced. Teens have described their feelings in many ways. One teen said, "I feel a rising feeling of anger and irritation, starting in my stomach, and it rushes up to my head." Another teen explained, "I start to feel tension in my forehead, and like I just want to scream at her." Another teen had a difficult time naming the feeling and explained, "I can't really describe it. It feels like I'm being pushed into a corner, and I want to lash out." And yet another teen told us, "I start thinking how stupid my mom is, and that she doesn't get it at all. Then I just feel angry at her and like I want to *make* her get it."

Parents can help their teens become aware of behavior that expresses feelings by sharing their observations when their teens start to escalate. For example, we have heard parents describe this behavior as follows: "I notice you start pacing around," "You get closer to me," "You start pointing your finger at me," and "You start talking faster and your voice gets louder and then the 'F' word . . ."

Noticing red flags makes a difference in how a teen responds to any incident where he or she would normally have reacted instantaneously with abuse or violence. The teen's self-awareness is raised, an important step towards changing the response.

## My Red Flags — Practice Exercise

Each teen is asked to describe a situation in the recent past when he or she was in conflict with a parent and he or she became disrespectful, abusive, or violent. The teen is then asked to identify his or her red flags, which may include negative thoughts or self-talk, difficult feelings, body signs, and specific behaviors. Given an awareness of the red flags, the teen is then asked to identify the earliest point at which he or she could have stopped and separated from the other person.

## Safety Planning with Parents

In the parent group, we help parents develop their own plan for how they will respond to violence by their teen. Parents often tell us this was the most valuable skill that they learned in the program.

## How to Respond When Your Teen Is Violent

When a teen becomes violent in the home, whether it is hitting a parent, punching a hole in the wall, throwing things, or making threats to harm someone, parents react in many different ways. Sometimes a parent will try to stop the behavior, physically or verbally. Other times a parent will try to calm the teen down. Another will leave or call the police. The most effective response depends upon many variables: the teen's reaction to different approaches, past incidents of violence, and the parent's view of the situation. Every teen, parent, and household is different and one situation is different from the next. The most important consideration is the safety of everyone in the home.

The safety plan is the first tool to call upon. However, when teens refuse to follow their safety plan, and their behavior escalates to violence, parents should have a plan in place about how they will respond. Separating from the violent person is the best way to prevent harm and give teens the message that others will not engage with them when they are violent or abusive. When parents stay engaged, it puts them at risk of physical harm. In addition, the parents' own emotions add fuel to the fire. Parents may feel they have to stop the behavior. Failed attempts to calm the teen down, or restrain him or her physically, causes frustration and anger for both the teen and parent. The situation easily spirals into a more out of control, violent situation.

When parents think through how they will respond and make a step-by-step plan, they will be able to remain more calm and focused when the violence occurs, and less likely to react from fear or anger. Teens will de-escalate sooner when their parent responds in a calm way.

## Making a Plan for Responding to Violence and Abuse

When making a plan for responding to violence, two important things to think about are:

1. Safety. What can I do to keep myself and my family safe?
2. What message am I giving my teen? How can I let my teen know that violence is not okay and is not tolerated in our home?

These two goals do not always go hand in hand.

- For example, telling your teen that violence is not tolerated and talking about consequences at the time of the violence can escalate the behavior and compromise your safety.
- Likewise, if you separate from your teen when he or she is violent to keep yourself safe, but do not address the behavior later, the teen gets the message that violence is not a big problem.

How can you stay safe and let your teen know the violence is not tolerated?

We recommend family members physically separate from a teen who is violent or seems to be heading in the direction of hurtful behavior. It is the best response to prevent harm or injury. It also sends an important message to the teen that you will not engage when he or she is aggressive.

The following is a plan we recommend to parents for responding to physical violence.

## How to Respond When Your Teen Becomes Violent

When your teen starts to threaten you, to break things, or to do anything physically violent, accept that you can't stop him or her at this point. The most important thing is to keep yourself and your other children safe.

## Steps to Take When Your Teen Becomes Violent:

1. Do not continue the argument or discussion. Don't argue or yell.
2. Accept that you cannot physically stop your teen's behavior.
3. Separate yourself and your other children from the teen. Go to another room, or if necessary, bring your other children with you and leave the house.
4. Call 911, if appropriate (see "Calling the Police," below).
5. Do what you can to help yourself stay calm (take a walk, call a friend).
6. Don't be around your teen or talk again until he or she is calm.
7. When you do talk to your teen again, give him or her the following messages:

When you are violent I will separate from you. Your behavior is/was not safe. Our home needs to be a safe place for everyone. We will address what happened later and help you make a plan to prevent this from happening again.

Within the next few days, when everyone is calm, the behavior should be addressed. In Chapter 10, "Helping Parents," an intervention plan is described that uses the restorative inquiry process to help teens take responsibility for the violence and make amends for harm caused by their behavior.

## Calling the Police

Calling the police is not easy, particularly when it is about your own child. Parents feel guilty and worried about what will happen. Many are afraid of how their teen will respond, possibly retaliating out of anger and making the violence worse. Most parents do not want to involve their teen in the juvenile justice system and try as many other options as possible first. The police should be called anytime the parent feels a violent incident is escalating and needs to be stopped, or if anyone is in imminent danger. When the violence has occurred multiple times and is continuing in spite of all efforts to stop it, calling law enforcement can be an effective way to help the teen understand that violence towards family members is not tolerated. In spite of how difficult it can be to pick up the phone and dial 911 on your own child, parents often say it was the best decision they made in helping their teen. During parent group, there are frequent discussions about how the violence did not stop until the police were called. Parents encourage and support each other in taking the difficult step of calling the police.

When advising parents about calling the police, it is important to have knowledge about how your local law enforcement responds to this problem. Police response varies widely in different areas, and even within one city. Responding officers may just talk with the young person and give them a stern warning, which may be enough for some teens. Others write a report, which may result in a court date and possible charge, or mandated counseling in order to avoid a charge. Or the teen may be arrested and taken to detention for one or more days. Some follow their state's domestic violence mandated reporting laws. Many courts have options for youth to avoid charges if they attend counseling. It is helpful for parents to know what might happen if they call the police.

Unfortunately, because this problem is often misunderstood, and the violence not regarded seriously, some officers respond by reprimanding parents for calling the police about a "parenting matter." Parents may be blamed by officers, empowering the teens to continue, and possibly escalate, the violence. However, many officers are supportive to parents and genuinely helpful to the situation.

Parents are often deterred from calling the police because they are concerned about their teen being in a detention facility. However, parents of youth who have been to detention frequently talk about how it helped their teens, sometimes saying, "he came home a different kid" or "he finally decided he wanted to learn how to manage his anger." Teens even tell us that detention helped them. We observe the difference in youth before and after they have been arrested, with a change in attitude and increased motivation to engage in the change process after they have been in detention. Teens also tell us that detention helped them want to change. The positive results that parents report at home and the results that we observe in the group are a strong indication that detention can be an important part of instigating change for many youth.

It is important to learn about your local detention facility so that you have information about it to give parents, and for your own knowledge. Take a tour, talk to court staff, and if possible ask youth what it is like. We ask teens that have been in detention what their experience was and how they felt about being in detention. This is important information for parents when they are considering calling the police. If you find your local facility is overcrowded or unsafe, there may be alternatives to detention in your community. Most parents and helping professionals alike do not want to "criminalize" young people, and not all youth need the push from the law to engage in help. However, calling the police is often the only avenue of help for families and can be a significant support for parents who don't know where to turn when nothing else is working.

## Summary

When working with any family where there is violence, responsible practice means assuring the approach does not compromise the safety of victims. The role that a practitioner plays in increasing or decreasing the violence—what we say, suggest, recommend, ask them to delve into, etc.—impacts what happens in families' lives after they leave our office. This is true with all therapy, and it is how we help individuals and families. However, when there is violence and abuse, we may inadvertently increase violence. Competent practice with families experiencing violence means holding awareness of safety at all times, taking steps to assure that our approach is not increasing the risk of violence, and measuring how our strategies impact safety in the home. In the next chapter, we'll discuss ways to help teens change their violent behaviors.

# eight
# A Restorative Practice Approach

Restorative practice offers tools for healing and restoring relationships damaged by hurtful behavior. It creates a framework for honest and respectful dialogue between a parent and teen. The restorative process engages youth in thinking through the impact of their behavior on others and how to take responsibility for harm they have caused. Through reparative acts, teens understand the true meaning of accountability for behavior. They learn skills to build personal competency and make a plan to prevent hurting others again. Restorative practice fosters understanding, compassion, and empathy and moves the parent-teen relationship forward in a new way.

When we began our work with families we knew very little about restorative practice. We were familiar with restorative justice as a way to bring offenders and victims together to help offenders understand the impact of their offense and take responsibility through reparative actions. However, it wasn't until several years into our work that we discovered our most successful approaches were indeed restorative practices. Restorative practice was threaded throughout our intervention. We began learning more about the principles of restorative work, finding it to be especially helpful to the families we served because of the way it balances accountability for hurtful behavior with support for positive change.

Restorative practice addresses a major challenge for practitioners: how to engage youth. The value of restorative practice is embodied in the statement, "People are happier, more productive, and more likely to make positive changes in behavior when those in authority do things *with* them, rather than *to*, or *for* them"

(Wachtel, 2012). When young people feel the process is fair, that all sides are listened to, and every person is valued and respected, they are more willing to engage and take part. Family practitioners have used restorative principles in their work. Ted Wachtel, a leader in restorative practice, states, "The most critical function of restorative practices is restoring and building relationships" (Wachtel, 2013a, p. 4). Restorative work with families focuses on resolving conflict, strengthening family relationships, and making a plan to prevent the recurrence of particular problems. Parents are encouraged by restorative practice because the support and encouragement offered to youth is balanced with clear boundaries and consistent enforcement of behavioral standards.

## What Is Restorative Practice?

Restorative practice evolved out of restorative justice, with the growing recognition that its philosophy and principles apply to areas outside of the justice system. For example, it can be used where there is a need for resolution to wrongdoing and conflict within schools, the workplace, and families. There are now communities, and even cities, that call themselves restorative (Wachtel, 2013b) and use a restorative model of "conferencing" or "circles" to resolve conflicts and prevent recurrence of the problem. Restorative practice also includes processes for prevention by "proactively building relationships and a sense of community to prevent conflict and wrongdoing" (Wachtel, 2013a, p. 1).

Restorative justice practices have a long history in communities all over the world. Aboriginal communities in New Zealand and Australia have used restorative circles to address wrongdoing and resolve conflicts. Native American and First Nation Canadian communities have long used peacemaking circles as a form of community justice (Zehr, 2002). In the criminal justice field in the United States, the concept first emerged in the 1970s out of Mennonite case experiments with victim-offender encounters that became prototypes for programs such as Victim Offender Reconciliation. Restorative justice has since grown to be an adjunct to traditional responses by courts throughout Canada and the United States, as well as in the United Kingdom, Australia, and New Zealand. In 1989, New Zealand made restorative justice a central feature of its juvenile justice system, developing the Family Group Conference model that is now widely used in juvenile justice and child welfare systems in several countries (Zehr, 2002).

Restorative practice is guided by the following principles that help participants engage in the process and feel invested in successful outcomes:

- "Respect for all" proposes that all sides in a conflict must be listened to, and that every person is valued, respected, and has a chance to be heard.
- "Collaborative problem solving" obliges all parties in a conflict to work together to find a solution.

- "Fair process" means all participants feel they are treated fairly. When a person is challenged for doing something wrong, it is in a firm but fair manner. The person's point of view is included in the process. Expectations are clearly explained with input from all who are involved.

A restorative circle, group, or conference is a meeting with all the relevant parties involved, which may be a family, a neighborhood, a classroom, or a department in a company or public agency. When families use restorative practice, the participants in a circle can range from a few family members to an entire extended family and even include family friends and neighbors.

Restorative practice is especially helpful with youth violence that is targeted towards family members, as opposed to youth violence towards peers or community. The restorative process evokes empathy, accountability for harm, and responsibility for restoring family relationships. Youth are more empathetic and remorseful after hurting a family member than they are after hurting a friend or classmate. They usually want to restore relationships with their family, regardless of how challenging those relationships may seem. However, accountability may be more difficult to achieve because of the shame youth feel after they have hurt someone in their family. In some families, youth may feel they are being treated unfairly when other family members who have been violent are not also held accountable. However, the restorative process enables teens to understand and experience accountability as an empowering and healing process.

Howard Zehr, a leading writer and teacher of restorative justice, defines it as "a process to involve, to the extent possible, those who have a stake in a specific offense and to collectively identify and address harms, needs and obligations, in order to heal and put things as right as possible" (Zehr, 2002). Briefly described, restorative justice focuses on the harm done by the offense and helps offenders understand how their actions have affected people so they can take responsibility by repairing the harm done. It is more meaningful to both victims and offenders and possibly transformative for the offender, reducing the likelihood of future offenses. An emphasis on victims' experiences and their resulting needs provides victims with acknowledgment, validation, and support. It gives offenders an opportunity to experience empathy for their victims and insight into the consequences of their actions. A final step in the process is for offenders to address the causes of their behavior and develop competency in order to keep from reoffending.

## The Basics of Restorative Practice

Howard Zehr describes the three pillars of restorative justice: harms and needs, obligations, and engagement (Zehr, 2002). This means the harm done to and related needs of those impacted, *including* the offender; obligations that result from the harm; and engagement in dialogue with everyone involved. Restorative justice implies a concern for the healing of victims, offenders, and communities (Zehr, 2002). Communities may be defined as family, the workplace, a school, or neighborhoods (Rundell, 2007).

How the restorative process actually plays out in the legal system is not always clearly defined and can be controversial, since differences exist on which individuals to involve and how the process is implemented. Some models bring the victim and offender together for facilitated dialogue, a victim-offender conference, where there is an opportunity to talk about what happened and how it has affected the victim. Conferences may include friends, family, and community members impacted by the offense. In other models, the victim and offender do not meet together. Rather, a trained facilitator works with the offender, either with or without victim input. However, without victim input, many do not consider this true restorative justice (Wachtel, 2013a).

Restorative justice practice is strongly discouraged for intimate partner violence for safety reasons. It has been criticized for perpetuating power imbalances between the victim and offender (Stubbs, 2002), often revictimizing the person and creating more fear and increased abuse. This may also occur with youth to parent violence if the intervention is not properly structured. Specific precautions should be established to create a safe environment. The teen must agree to speak respectfully during any meeting with the parent and can be coached prior to the meeting about how to state his or her concerns to the parent in a respectful way. Parents may feel angry and resentful so they should understand the need to speak respectfully as well. Any interaction between a teen and parent should be stopped at the first sign of abuse.

An analysis of restorative youth justice conferences with youth to parent violence in Australia found that the standard, onetime conference model "is poorly equipped and resourced to address the violence" (Daly & Nancarrow, 2008, p. 33). The analysis demonstrated how a restorative justice dialogic process as a stand-alone, 90-minute to 2-hour session, without ongoing therapeutic intervention for both the offender and for the victim, results in poor process and outcomes (Daly & Nancarrow, 2008). These cases showed the need to integrate the restorative process within a longer intervention that makes safety primary and develops skills in respectful communication.

## The Social Discipline Window: How to Help Youth

Because restorative practice draws wrongdoers into a more active role in righting their wrongs, it is well suited to meet the difficult challenge of engaging youth. The Social Discipline Window illustrates four approaches to addressing wrongdoing: a punitive approach that is doing things *to* the person; a neglectful approach that does not respond at all; a permissive approach that does things *for* the person; and a restorative approach that does things *with* the person to facilitate positive

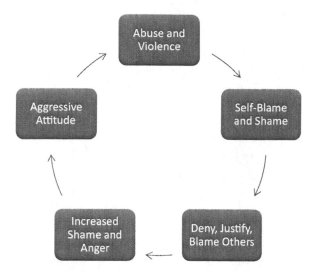

**FIGURE 8.1.**  Shame Cycle

change. The window is supported by two axes, a vertical axis representing the level of "social control" exerted on the person and a horizontal axis representing the level of "support" offered to each person. "Low social control" includes vague or no behavioral standards and rules that lack consequences. "High social control" involves explicit boundaries and expectations regarding behavioral standards, along with consistent responses to violations. The level of support ranges from "high support," in which guidance and assistance are provided, to "low support," where there is minimal help, concern, and encouragement.

The punitive approach is high in control, but low in support, offering less social or emotional incentive for change, leaving fear of punishment done *to* the offender as the only motivator to make change. The permissive approach is high in support, but tends to rescue and protect the offender from consequences. The neglectful pane, with low control and low support, leaves the offender alone, without incentive or support for change. The restorative "with" approach, with high support and high control, provides a balance of what is needed for young people to make change—clear boundaries and behavioral expectations, consequences that help them take responsibility for their behavior when they go off the path, plus support and encouragement to help them feel competent to make change. Briefly said, it is a balance of accountability for behavior and support for making change.

## Guilt and Shame

When people use violence, they morally disengage from the people they hurt and find a reason or justification for their behavior (Bandura et al., 1996). Restorative practice attempts to evoke moral emotions, such as guilt, empathy, sympathy, and compassion. Perpetrators are often unaware of the repercussions on the victim's life and on the lives of others who are impacted by their behavior. When they understand the harm they have caused to another person, feelings are evoked. The ability to feel empathy and take responsibility for the harm done is influenced by whether those feelings are shame or guilt.

There are good ways to feel bad about wrongdoing and ways that are not so good (Tangney & Dearing, 2002). Shame and guilt are two very different emotions and shape a person's perspective of his or her wrongdoing. Put simply, shame is self-focused while guilt is behavior-focused. Shame is a negative evaluation of the self, while guilt is a negative evaluation of behavior. It is the difference between "who I am" and "what I did," or self versus behavior (Tangney & Dearing, 2002, p. 24).

Feelings of shame can interfere with accountability, empathy, and behavior change. Tangney and Dearing (2002) state that shame appears to be the less "moral" emotion, explaining that when people feel ashamed of themselves they are less motivated to take responsibility and make things right. Instead, they deny responsibility, withdraw, and avoid people. They may become hostile and angry at the world. "In short, shamed individuals are inclined to assume a defensive posture, rather than take a constructive, reparative stance in their relationships" (Tangney & Dearing, 2002, p. 180–181). Numerous studies indicate that shame interferes with "other-oriented empathic responses" (Tangney & Dearing, 2002, p. 89), possibly because the personal distress of shame distracts one from the ability to put attention on the other's experience (Hoffman, 2000, p. 238).

Guilt, on the other hand, has a more adaptive function. Tangney and Dearing state, "It may be uncomfortable, but is still adaptive (for ourselves and others) to experience guilt in connection with specific behavioral transgressions. The tension, remorse, and regret of guilt causes us to stop and re-think—and it offers a way out, pressing us to confess, apologize, and make amends" (Tangney & Dearing, 2002, p. 180).

When people feel guilty, they feel bad about what they have *done*, motivating them to change that behavior. When they feel shame, the wrongdoing feels as if it is integrated into who they are, resulting in feeling like a failure and a bad person, which for some turns into depression, hopelessness, anger, and hostility.

Some in the restorative justice field have used the term "shaming" for what they do. However, John Braithwaite, an Australian criminologist and leader in restorative justice, introduced the idea of reintegrative shaming in 1989, and has refined the concept over the years. He describes two kinds of shaming, stigmatizing and reintegrative. Stigmatizing shaming puts forth disapproval with disrespect that humiliates and labels the behavior and person as bad. Reintegrative shaming is respectful and labels the person as good, but the act as bad. This theory is considered to be a key concept of restorative justice. In our view, this is a bit of confusion over terminology. We believe reintegrative shaming, as described by Braithwaite, is not shaming, but rather reduces shame, with the focus on the behavior, not the person (Braithwaite, 1995).

Restorative practice reduces shame for a number of reasons. It works *with* the person in a supportive atmosphere, with a focus on behavior instead of the person. The restorative milieu and dialogue provide an opportunity to express other emotions in addition to shame (Wachtel, 2013a). There is an opportunity to express personal perspective about what happened. It shows respect and honor for the offender as a good person who chose a harmful behavior. It shifts perspective from "I am a bad person and am not capable" to "I am a good person, capable of doing something about the harm I have caused, and can choose a different behavior next time." When it is a matter of choosing behaviors instead of changing who I am as a person, change is more achievable.

When shame is lifted, there is a greater capacity for empathy. Without the oppression of shame, the person is better able to handle the difficult feelings that arise from empathic awareness without being overwhelmed by internal distress. The feelings of guilt that result from recognizing how one's behavior has impacted others promote feelings of accountability, and accountability further reduces shame. We have observed that accountability is a major factor leading to behavior change in the youth who come to our program; these observations are described in the next section.

## Transforming Shame Through Accountability

In our work with teens we often see a pattern of abuse, violence, shame, and blame. Following a violent incident a teen often blames others, justifies the behavior, or denies the severity of it. Many parents tell us, "The worst part is the blaming. If only once he would acknowledge what he did, or even be willing to sit down and talk about it without denying it and blaming me all the time." Parents describe their teen's increasingly irritable behavior, and the feeling that he or she will "go off at the slightest thing." This is when parents feel like they are tiptoeing around, not knowing when there will be another blowup. There may be times of calm, sometimes withdrawal and distance, but eventually tension builds as each episode goes without discussion or resolution. Another violent episode occurs, and the pattern begins again.

When adolescents talk to us about their hurtful behavior, most feel bad about themselves. Many are embarrassed, don't want to talk about it, or find ways to minimize or excuse it. Blaming and justifying is a way to try to make sense of their behavior and convince themselves and others that they are not really bad people. "There was a reason I pushed my mom, I don't just go around hitting my mother." The shame associated with this type of behavior is likely higher than with other teen transgressions as they do love and care about their parents. They make sense of it by finding explanations and causes outside of themselves.

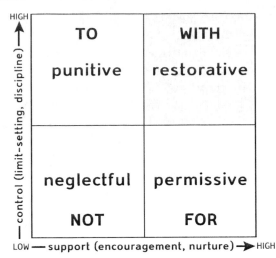

**FIGURE 8.2.** Social Discipline Window

**Source:** Wachtel, T., & McCold, P. (2003). In pursuit of paradigm: a theory of restorative justice. Paper presented at the XIII World Congress of Criminology, August 10-15, 2003, Rio de Janeiro, Brazil. Retrieved from http://www.iirp.edu/article_detail.php?article_id=NDI0

This is a common way of responding to one's own wrongdoing. People want to feel better about themselves by finding an explanation for their behavior. Rachel Condry, in her book, *Families Shamed* (2007, p. 101), states, "Explaining untoward actions—offering explanations, citing reasons, contextualizing—is something we all do and is part of the process of making sense of our lives." Although a teen blames and justifies to cope with shame, it's counterproductive to the teen, parents, and their relationships. It usually increases the frustration and anger of family members, giving the young person more reason to blame them and feel victimized. As the teen walks around holding these difficult feelings, not knowing what to do with them, tension builds and it does not take much to trigger another outburst.

## Accountability Helps Break the Pattern

Accountability helps break the teens' repeating pattern of feeling ashamed and blaming others for their hurtful behavior. It defuses feelings of shame, transforming it to feelings of responsibility and the capability to make change. Taking action to repair the harm they have caused gives teens something they can actively do about what has happened. It lifts the feeling of hopelessness that many young people feel when they realize they have been hurtful once again.

Once teens take the first steps to make amends, such as repairing a hole in the wall or helping their father clean the garage, they gain self-respect and a sense of competence. It releases the tension they have been holding, using unhealthy coping mechanisms to deal with their self-blame and shame, and feeling there was no pathway out. In our experience with youth, we often see a shift occur after they have been accountable and actively made amends. This is usually when the teen takes a step forward in the change process, becoming more engaged and hopeful, and we start to see them smile more. The following example shows this process in the words of a teen girl in our program.

## A Case Example

A 15-year-old girl who recently completed our program described her own process of change during her last session in the group. She answered a series of questions that we posed to reveal what helped her change her behavior.

Melanie and her mother, Susan, came to us at Susan's request after an incident where Melanie had pushed Susan and hit her because Susan had taken away Melanie's phone. Melanie lives with her mother and younger sister. Her parents divorced a few years prior. Susan reported some verbal abuse by Melanie's father. Melanie has no mental health issues or history of physical abuse. She had been exposed to some of her father's verbal abuse of Susan. She is a good student and socially involved in healthy ways.

This was the first time she was physically violent with her mother. She had been increasingly verbally abusive to her mother, yelling and swearing at her, and putting her down. She had thrown and broken things in the past. After she hit her mother, Melanie wanted to leave the house, but Susan told her she could not leave or she would keep her phone longer. Melanie started throwing things, so Susan called the police. The police talked to Melanie and said they would not take her this time, but if it happened again they would arrest her.

The following are quotes from Melanie as she answered questions during group regarding her change process since the incident and completion of our group sessions.

Right after I hit my mom, I just wanted to get away from her. I wanted to leave and she wouldn't let me. I was so angry that I just started throwing things at her. Then she called the police and when they came I told them she had made the whole thing up. I don't know, it was weird. I started to believe my own story. I blamed my mom for everything. I convinced myself that I didn't even do anything, that she was just a liar and a horrible person. When I look back on it I see how I just twisted everything around.

When I came here, I still said she made it all up. I just wanted to hide and be invisible. I didn't want to be here, I didn't want to talk, and I didn't want my mom to speak. You saw how I interrupted her all the time and blamed her for everything. It was like that most of the time. She would try to talk to me, and I thought everything she said was a way to control me. I would call her horrible names and swear at her all the time. I just felt so mad all the time. I thought everyone else was making my life miserable. But it wasn't them at all. But I couldn't see it.

I don't know exactly when or what helped me change, but finally I started listening to people in the group, and I realized I wasn't the only one who does this. Other parents were saying the same things my mom says, and I could hear it better from them, and I saw how they are a lot like us. The other teens could talk about what they did. So, I started talking about it and admitting what I did. Then I started to feel better. It was like—a relief. After that things got better. I realized I could talk about it and it would actually be better, not worse like I thought.

The communication skills we were learning helped us a lot. Before, we didn't really know how to talk about problems without getting mad at each other. We finally really listened to each other. Before, we never really did that. Well, my mom tried to. Then I started to see it from her point of view. I never did that before. It made me feel bad when I realized how I had been. It was bad. I was really mean. She didn't deserve that. I wanted to do something to make up for it.

I started to make amends by actually doing some chores. I hadn't done a chore in years. My mom is so happy. I have mostly made amends by not yelling and screaming and interrupting her like I used to. Talking about what happened was the first part of it all, though. Talking about it helped me stop fighting it.

What I need to keep working on is not going back to the way I was. We still argue sometimes, and I feel myself getting really mad again. It is so easy to just start yelling again. The safety plan helps. I just take a break and go calm down. We do that a lot. And then we talk about feelings. I finally started talking about how mad I was about the divorce and my dad, and we had some good talks. It helped because I learned how to talk about my anger and my feelings without getting aggressive. I don't feel like punching walls anymore. What I learned about myself is that I can change. Once you start to be able to change, it gets easier because you realize it's not that hard.

Melanie's mother, Susan, was present for these questions about the change process and gave her responses as well, confirming Melanie's explanations. Susan noted how Melanie seemed to calm down remarkably after coming to the group for about six weeks. Susan attributed it to exposure to other families experiencing the same struggles, and the breakthrough of being able to talk about what happened.

Melanie is a particularly self-perceptive and verbally skilled adolescent who was able to express her process with more insight than many youth who answer these questions. However, the process she described is similar to that experienced by many other youth who talk about how they changed. She described a textbook picture of shame at the beginning, wanting to hide, be invisible, not talk about it, and when she did, it was with denial and blaming.

The shame began to lift when she listened to others and realized she wasn't the only one who had behaved that way. She shifted her perspective to see it as her behavior, not herself as a person. The reduced shame allowed her to be willing to listen to her mother's perspective and feel empathy, engaging a desire to make amends. She described how admitting what she did and talking about it helped her feel some relief. She had been carrying self-blame that she did not know how to handle and now was able to express it in a productive way and move on to mend the relationship and work on behavior change. Melanie learned communication skills that enabled her to talk to her mother about the divorce and her father and express the feelings underneath much of her anger and aggressive behavior. Melanie's story demonstrates how the interplay of shame, self-blame, anger, accountability, empathy, and the desire for change are part of the restorative process.

## Tools for Restorative Practice

### Restorative Inquiry

A set of questions called "restorative inquiry" are used to guide the person who has exhibited harmful behavior through a process that is the "essence of restorative justice" (Zehr, 2002, p. 38). The questions are designed to engage the person in reflecting about the effects of the harmful behavior on others, experience empathy, and take responsibility for the harm that was caused by making amends.

When a youth has been violent towards a family member during the previous week, we ask him or her to read and respond to the following restorative questions below. As opposed to restorative conferencing where the victim tells the offender how he or she was affected, we ask the teen to take the perspective of the parent. The parent can then describe and clarify his or her experience.

1.  Who was harmed by my behavior? Who else in my family was affected by my behavior?
2.  What was the harm, damage, or loss resulting from the hurtful behavior?
    • How did my behavior affect each person?
    • How did it affect our relationship?
    • How did the behavior cause a problem?

    This helps youth understand the impact of their behavior from other people's perspective and activates empathy. It helps them begin to feel a sense of responsibility for their behavior.

3.   How did it affect me?
     - How do I feel about how I handled the situation?
     - What were the negative consequences for me?

4.   In this situation what could I have done differently?
     - What could I have done differently so that I was not hurtful?
     - What other respectful choices did I have for how to respond? Are there any behaviors on the Respect Wheel that I could have used?
     - What skills could I have used?
     - How could I have expressed my feelings or needs in a respectful way?

This question reminds them that behavior is a choice and that they have other options for responding to anger. This helps them think through and remember the skills they are learning for nonviolent, respectful responses.

5.   How can I make amends?
     - What do I need to do to repair the harm or problems caused?
     - What can I do to address the needs of those harmed and make amends?
     - What do I need to do to begin to repair the relationship?

6.   What is my plan to prevent me from repeating the behavior?
     - What specifically will I do the next time this situation arises?
     - What might get in the way of behaving in a new way and what should I do to prevent that?

## Check-In: Accountability, Behavior Change, and Restoring Relationships

Every group opens with check-in. Teens use the Abuse and Respect Wheels (see wheels in Chapter 6) as they think about their previous week and recall their behaviors. Parents give their perspective, adding respectful or abusive behaviors that they feel are significant and were not reported by the teens. If a teen has been physically violent or has threatened physical violence during the previous week the teen answers the restorative inquiry questions, with input from the parent.

During check-in, teens also report their progress on their behavior change plan, or what we call their "goal for the week." Teens evaluate the extent to which they met the previous week's goal and set a goal for the following week. For example, if they were physically violent during the previous week, their goal would be an action they intend to take to prevent further physical violence. Teens complete a series of questions on a worksheet that helps them think through how they will meet the goal. They identify respectful behaviors that they will substitute for the abusive ones. Goal setting is discussed further in the next chapter.

Check-in serves a number of purposes for teens, parents, and group facilitators. Teens are held accountable to the group for their behavior and for meeting specific personal goals. They're given the opportunity to evaluate their progress towards using more respectful behaviors. And, they're given positive reinforcement from the group as well as their parents for using respectful behaviors at home.

Weekly check-in using the Abuse and Respect Wheels raises teens' awareness of their behavior at home during the week. When teens know they will be reporting to group about their behaviors, it gives them incentive to use more respectful behaviors. Teens tell us that check-in helped them pay attention to their behavior more. Some parents say that they believed check-in was the most influential in helping their youth change.

Parents learn to reframe their perspectives on their teens' hurtful behaviors. Instead of simply responding with anger and criticism, parents learn to evaluate behavior based on whether it was respectful or disrespectful. This allows them to talk about hurtful behavior with their youth in a different way. They learn to notice and acknowledge respectful behavior, reinforcing the use of respect in the home for the entire family.

Check-in provides a way for facilitators to measure teens' progress, identify particular problem behaviors, and tailor specific strategies for each teen. When a teen is having difficulty meeting a weekly goal, the facilitator can invite suggestions from other group members of other ways they might meet their goal. The facilitator can remind parents to praise youth by having parents recall specific times during the week when their teen was respectful. They can model for parents how to talk to teens about abusive behavior, and how to acknowledge positive behaviors. And finally, facilitators can identify specific parent-teen dynamics that might be barriers to progress.

## Making Amends

Making amends is the cornerstone of the restorative process; it is where true accountability is demonstrated and relationship restoration begins. Accountability has two parts: acknowledging that one has hurt another person and repairing the harm done by making amends. Parents who are victims of teen violence and abuse, however, are very apprehensive and skeptical. They've experienced multiple apologies and promises to turn things around, only to see the same behavior again and again. They may have seen their teen make real changes, only to return to abusive behavior. Because of the confusion over what making amends really means, both youth and parents should have a clear vision of what making amends looks like.

We begin by posing questions to elicit teens' and parents' ideas about what it means to make amends before we give them any information. This ask-before-telling process helps teens engage and begin thinking on their own. Our questions include the following:

1.   What kinds of damage or harm can be caused by abuse or violence towards a family member? Include physical, emotional, and relationship damage.

2.    What are some ways to repair harm or fix problems?
   • Repair something that has been damaged or pay to have it fixed.
   • Do chores to help pay for repairing damage.
   • Create a family motto: "If you hurt someone, you help them."
   • Acknowledge your behavior; be willing to sit down and talk about it.
   • Make a plan to prevent being violent or abusive again and share it with the other person.
   • Ask the person what you can do to make amends.

After producing a list of ideas, different scenarios are presented from everyday accidents such as bumping a stranger with your grocery cart and causing him to drop an armload of groceries, purposefully hitting your little brother, or punching a hole in the wall. The group brainstorms all of the ways the person could make amends for the behavior. In most skill development sessions, teens first apply the skill to scenarios with situations involving other people before applying it to their own situations. This helps them feel comfortable sharing their ideas more openly with others.

The session ends by asking teens to think of a recent time when they were abusive or violent to a family member and what they have done or can do to make amends. After writing down their ideas, everyone shares them with the group. This exercise provides group feedback, support, and shared learning.

Important messages that we stress during this session include the following:

■    Making amends is not just saying you are sorry. People sometimes apologize with the purpose of leaving the situation behind, hoping the other person will "forgive and forget." Such apologies are more for oneself than the other person.

■    When you do something to make amends for hurtful behavior, it does not mean that everything goes back to the way it was. The person harmed may feel upset for a while. The purpose of making amends is not to hear the victim say that everything is OK. The purpose is to show you have concern for what happened and to take responsibility for your behavior.

## Responsibility and Empathy Letters

Towards the end of the program, teens write both a responsibility letter and an empathy letter addressed to their parent or family members about an incident when they were violent towards them, usually the incident that brought them to the program. Two aspects of the letter-writing exercise make it a powerful learning experience. First, it is a way they bring together all of their learning and apply it to the situation that brought them to the program. This includes the restorative elements of accountability, empathy, and making amends, as well as their cognitive-behavioral process, safety skills, and respectful communication skills.

Second, they read the letters to their family and group members. Family members who were not a part of group sessions, but were affected by the violence, are invited to attend. Since the teens have practiced accountability during many weekly check-ins and have answered numerous questions over the same weeks regarding the effects of abuse and violence on family members, they are well rehearsed for this final session. Most feel confident as they read their letters.

During a special group session, teens learn about the purpose of the letters, read sample letters, and get feedback from other teens and the facilitator on the practice letter that they write. If writing is difficult, teens can work with the facilitator to compose the letter.

## Responsibility Letter

The responsibility letter challenges them to describe their behavior in a specific incident without blaming other people involved, minimizing its impact on other family members, justifying it as right or reasonable, or denying the harm caused. In addition, the letter provides an opportunity to show they understand the thoughts and feelings that were a part of their decision to use violence, and how they could have handled it differently using the skills they have learned.

In the responsibility letter, teens are asked to address the following questions:

- Describe what happened when you were violent.
- What negative thoughts or self-talk were you having at the time?
- What self-talk would have helped you respond differently?
- What were you feeling?
- How could you have expressed your feelings in a respectful way?
- If you were too angry to talk respectfully, what could you have done to prevent getting abusive or violent?
- What could you have done differently from the beginning to prevent the violence?
- How did your actions affect people in your family?
- How did your behavior affect you?
- How have you taken responsibility for your behavior and made amends?
- What do you need to continue to do?

The teen composes the letter, and gives it to a group facilitator who reads it and gives the teen feedback. The teen makes any necessary changes to the letters and reads them to the entire group.

## Empathy Letter

Teens also write a letter to themselves as if they were the parent or family member who was the target of their violence in the incident. They imagine what their parent or family member may have felt, thought, and experienced during the violent incident. This letter is much more difficult to write than the responsibility letter.

Teens must imagine themselves in the role of a parent who has a violent teen. They must understand the perspective of their parent as a person who is in many ways vastly different from them: their personality, their likes and dislikes, their values. For a teen to imagine being in his or her parent's shoes is very challenging.

Teens are asked to address the following questions in their empathy letter:

- Describe what happened in the violent incident from the point of view of your parent, caretaker, or family member who was hurt by your behavior.
- Describe what you think your parent or family member was feeling during the incident. Include the different feelings the parent or family member may have had and how their feelings may have changed during the course of the incident.
- What were the effects on the person who was the direct target of your behavior?
- What were the effects on other people in the family?

For the family members, listening to the letters being read out loud is an emotional and moving experience. It takes them back to when their home was filled with anger, tension, and tears. It highlights the changes the teen has made, as he or she reflects back on the incident and talks about it with a new perspective after all of his or her learning and personal change. Many parents never imagined they would hear these words from their teen. It allows the teens to recognize their transformation as well.

## Examples of the Responsibility Letter and Empathy Letter

Brian, age 15, came to the program with his mother and stepfather. His stepfather had been in his life since he was three, and he regarded him as his father. Brian also has a nine-year-old sister who lives with them. Brian had been aggressive with periodic episodes of violence since he was in elementary school. He had been in counseling off and on since he was in third grade. Since middle school, his behavior had become more dangerous with increased verbal and emotional abuse towards his mother. His stepfather would often intervene to protect his mother, resulting in his stepfather being hit or kicked by Brian. He was close to his stepfather, for the most part, and often got along better with him than with his mother. He was in individual therapy, but had recently refused to go to therapy any longer. His parents decided to try out a different approach and brought him to our group after an incident where he had assaulted his mother. Brian read the following letters to his mother and stepfather at his last group session. The first letter is his responsibility letter.

Dear Mom,

I'm writing to you about that Sunday when I pushed you down and kicked you, and broke the TV. We were arguing because you wanted me to stop playing Xbox and do my chores. I got mad and I was swearing at you and calling you names. I yelled at you to shut up and get away from me and leave me alone. You kept saying I was over my time limit on the game and had to do my chores. I got up and pushed you and you tripped back and fell, and then I kicked you. Dad came running in and I picked up the game controller and threw it at the TV and it broke the screen. Dad yelled at me to go upstairs, so I ran up to my room. I saw Amy peeking her head out of the bathroom door and then she shut the door and locked it.

My negative thoughts were that you always interrupt me and I hate it. I was thinking how I have to finish my game and you were bothering me. I could have changed my thinking to self-talk that I can save the game and finish it later. It's not worth getting crazy over. My feelings were anger and frustration because you interrupted my game. I wanted you to just leave me alone.

I could have talked respectfully and said I'm almost finished with my game and asked you for ten more minutes. If I knew what I know now, I could have used my safety plan when I started getting mad, and went for a walk or something else to calm myself down. I would have prevented the whole thing if I just remembered the rules about game time when you reminded me, and just got off the TV.

My actions affected the whole family. I really hurt you, Mom. I scared you. You were really upset about it. You had a bruise on your leg from me kicking you. I can't believe I did that. It was really mean. Dad was scared too. He had to hear me yelling at you and come in and didn't know what I did to you. He came up and tried to talk to me after that and I was rude to him and wouldn't talk. Amy was scared. I could tell she heard it and was hiding in the bathroom. She stayed away from me for a while. She was probably worried about Mom.

How my behavior affected me was mostly how much I hate seeing you angry and upset with me, Mom. And Dad. At first I was just trying to find any excuse about how it was your fault, but it wasn't. But, I didn't see that for a while and it feels bad when we don't get along. I finally was able to push past that and let you in and talk about it.

I think the biggest thing I have done to take responsibility was to admit to myself that I was wrong. That made me see I have to stop hurting you and being so mean. I found out I have control about it and don't have to act like that. It actually wasn't that hard once I decided I really wanted to do it. I don't have to go crazy at you and Dad like that. I have changed a lot and it's better now that we aren't fighting all the time.

I have made amends by not being violent anymore. I talk to you more now. I try not to be so rude. I did chores to earn money to get a new TV. I made amends to Amy by spending time with her and telling her my behavior wasn't right. I said I was sorry she had to be afraid of me.

What I need to continue doing is remember how bad it was and how much better it feels when I'm not mean to you and Dad. I need to keep using my safety plan and all the skills I have learned. And remember I have control of myself.

I'm sorry for hurting you. I love you.
Love, Brian

The second letter is Brian's empathy letter.

Dear Brian,
The day you pushed me down and kicked me, and broke the TV, was a bad day. You have done things like that before but this was the worst. We made rules about game time and I just wanted you to follow the rules and stop your game and do your chores. I never thought you would be that violent to me. I felt scared and shocked by how you acted. I hated seeing you like that and it made me worried about you. Afterwards, I was sad and didn't know what to do. You wouldn't talk about it. That made me feel angry and like giving up. I just wanted you to get help with your anger and stop being so mad all the time. When we finally talked about it, and you agreed to get help I was relieved. I'm happy you are not hurting us anymore and you seem happier, too. You have worked hard to change. You are much nicer to be around now and our whole family is getting along better. I love you.
Mom

## Summary

Restorative practice offers valuable components for addressing youth violence in families. It balances accountability for behavior with support and encouragement for change. Adolescents can be difficult to engage in making behavior changes, particularly when we are asking them to be accountable for wrongdoing. Restorative approaches help young people feel more open to looking at their behavior and considering change. Restorative principles of working *with* them, respecting their voices, and collaborating together to solve problems motivates teens to engage.

Restorative inquiry provides an indispensable tool that guides teens through a process of examining their violent behavior. It sheds light for them on the impact of their behavior on others and ignites empathy, leading them to feel a sense of responsibility. This is true accountability coming from within themselves, bringing about a desire to change their behavior.

Most teens and parents want to restore their relationship, but do not know how. The restorative process gives them a framework with stepping-stones to do this. In a safe and supportive environment, parents and teens dialogue about what has happened. Slowly, through accountability, empathy, and making amends, there is forgiveness and a new pathway forward.

# References

Bandura, A., Barbaranelli, C., Caprara, G. V., & Pastorelli, C. (1996). Mechanisms of moral disengagement in the exercise of moral agency. *Journal of Personality and Social Psychology*, 71(2), 364–374.

Braithwaite, J. (1989). *Crime, shame and reintegration.* Cambridge: Cambridge University Press.

Braithwaite, J. (1995). Reintegrative shaming, republicanism, and policy. In H. D. Barlow (Ed.), *Crime and public policy: putting theory to work* (pp. 191–205), Boulder, CO: Westview Press.

Condry, R. (2007). *Families shamed.* London: Willan Publishing.

Daly, K., & Nancarrow, H. (2008). Restorative justice and youth violence toward parents. In J. Ptacek (Ed.), *Feminism, restorative justice, and violence against women* (pp. 150–174), New York: Oxford University Press.

Hoffman, M. (2000). *Empathy and moral development: implications for caring and justice.* Cambridge: Cambridge University Press.

Rundell, F. (2007). 'Re-story-ing' our restorative practices. *Reclaiming Journal*, 16(2), 52–59.

Strang, H. (2004). *Repair or revenge: victims and restorative justice.* Oxford: Oxford University Press.

Stubbs, J. (2002). Domestic violence and women's safety: feminist challenges to restorative justice. In H. Strang & J. Braithwaite (Eds.), *Restorative justice and family violence* (pp. 42–61), Melbourne, Australia: Cambridge University Press.

Tangney, J. P., & Dearing, R. L. (2002). *Shame and guilt.* New York: Guilford Press.

Wachtel, T. (2012). What is restorative practice? Retrieved from http://www.iirp.edu/what-is-restorative-practices.php

Wachtel, T. (2013a). Defining restorative. Retrieved from http://www.iirp.edu/what-is-restorative-practices.php

Wachtel, T. (2013b). *Dreaming of a new reality.* Pipersville, PA: Piper's Press.

Wachtel, T., & McCold, P. (2003). In pursuit of paradigm: A theory of restorative justice, restorative practices. *Restorative Practices eForum*, August 12.

Zehr, H. (2002). *The little book of restorative justice.* Intercourse, PA: Good Books.

# nine
# A Pathway to Nonviolence

## Helping Youth Develop Skills for Success

This chapter summarizes the key skill sets that help adolescents make behavioral changes to prevent violence and abuse towards family members. Changing behaviors that have become patterned responses is not easy, even with a strong desire to change. Learning new behaviors is a first step, but without continual practice, ongoing support, reminders, and feedback, continuing a newly learned behavior is challenging for anyone, particularly teens. Integrating a new behavioral skill set to replace established behaviors takes small steps, time, and a great deal of encouragement and patience.

## Teen Skill Development

The skill development in this model is designed to help teens learn, use, and reinforce new skills throughout the intervention. Teens are supported during weekly check-in to apply skills to situations at home. Teens set weekly goals that break new behaviors into smaller, achievable steps, with application of their new skills. They are accountable to the group to use their skills by reporting their progress with their goals. Teens receive parental support in using skills at home, something we have found to be a key element of success. Parents learn how to support their teens' behavior change in separate parent groups where they learn ways to encourage their teens to use their newly learned skills.

Additionally, the restorative practice milieu offers a format for addressing relapses of violent behavior by reminding teens of the effects of their behavior on others and themselves and giving them a way to get back on track. Setbacks are common, tempting parents and teens to give up because they've been there before and come to feel that nothing works. Group facilitators face this feeling as well when a teen seems unchanging, with continued violence reported every week. We have learned that the process is slow for some teens, and may take several months for change to come about. There have been numerous times when it seemed the intervention was not working for a teen, and just as we were about to refer him or her elsewhere, he or she came to the group beaming after the first full week of staying completely nonviolent.

Youth change at different rates, and so it is best to tailor the time frame for the intervention to the needs of each family. Some teens have been aggressive since they were young while for others it is a more recent behavior. Youth need time to integrate new skills into their daily lives. The full intervention is 20 sessions, and we have found that the majority of teens need this amount of time to fully integrate their new learning and change their behavior patterns.

It is not within the scope of this book to cover the entire 20-session intervention for teens. We have selected the most essential skills for this chapter, providing an overview of how we help teens understand, learn, and practice those skills. The full curriculum is available at an online web page (Routt & Anderson, 2004).

## Learning About Violence and Abuse

While this session is designed primarily for teens, it can be conducted with both teens and parents present.

The ability to define violence and abuse in behavioral terms is an important starting place for teens. On the one hand, many teens do not regard the language and behavior they use at home as abusive. They regard it as just their way of expressing themselves. On the other hand, parents sometimes label any disrespectful or annoying behavior as abusive when it is only difficult teen behavior not intended to be hurtful. Understanding the difference between abuse and disrespect helps families distinguish between the two kinds of behavior and helps them work towards a mutually agreed upon goal of respect.

Equally important is the message that teens and parents must work together to resolve conflicts, prevent violence and abuse, and learn respectful ways to communicate feelings and needs. Collaboration between youth and parents is the most effective way to learn these skills.

### Defining Violence and Abuse

When we introduce a topic during a group session, we begin with questions to invite reflection and conversation, helping participants consider the topic on their own first. We use the Abuse and Respect Wheels as a reference for a better understanding of the difference between abusive and respectful behaviors. Because the wheels are used during the weekly check-in, group members become very familiar with them. The following are questions we ask to engage group discussion about abuse and violence:

- What is physical abuse?
- What is verbal abuse? Emotional abuse?
- Why would someone use violent or abusive behavior?
- Where might they learn it?
- Why do you think a teenager would get violent or abusive to someone in his or her family?

We define abuse as words or behaviors used purposefully to hurt, scare, intimidate, humiliate, overpower, degrade, or distress another person. It is intended hurtful behavior towards another person. We explain that abuse is disrespect, but disrespect is not necessarily abuse. The intention is the distinguishing factor.

## Reasons Teens Use Violence and Abuse

This conversation sets the stage for the youth to begin to reflect on the behavior they use at home. By objectively looking at others' experiences first and by considering abuse simply as a topic for discussion, teens feel more comfortable joining in the conversation and engaging in an honest discussion of how violence affects family members. Group conversation gets teens involved and talking. Most teens become interested once a few of their peers join in. The questions guide them from thinking of others to thinking about themselves. Before they know it, they are *talking* about themselves.

At this point in the discussion we hear explanations from the teens such as, "You do it to have power and make people do what you want, and then it works, and you keep doing it. Even though you know it's not right." Another typical reason for using violence and abuse is, "I do it to get my point across when I feel like no one is listening to me." Others say, "I just blow up. I don't know why. It just happens really fast, when I get mad about something."

We write their ideas on the board as they brainstorm all of the reasons they think a teen might be violent or abusive towards a parent or family member. The reasons we hear most often include the following:

- To have power and get what you want
- Revenge
- To get your parent to leave you alone
- When they won't listen
- When they say "no" about everything you want to do
- Feeling penned in, wanting freedom

- Something at school or with your friends is making you angry and you take it out on everyone at home
- Failing in school and your mom keeps asking about it
- Anger, frustration
- Because it was done to you before
- You saw it in your family
- It seems like nothing else works

After a list is generated, we ask the teens the following questions:

- What are the payoffs for someone who is abusive or violent? What does the abusive person get out of it?
- What are the outcomes or consequences? How does it affect the situation? The person abused? The relationship? The person who used violence? What happens later if they keep it up?
- Do people who use violence or abuse have a choice about how to respond to situations?
- Looking at the list, what other choices do you think teens have for responding instead of violence and abuse?
- What gets in the way of choosing more respectful responses?

These questions acknowledge the power and benefit that abuse and violence can have for a youth. Adults are often reluctant to have a discussion about the rewards of abusive behavior because they think discussing it reinforces the behavior. However, we have found that when a teen admits that abusive behavior has a purpose or meets a need, the teen is, at the same time, acknowledging that there is an unmet need. We can then go on to discuss the cost of using abusive behavior to meet that need, whether the cost outweighs the benefits, and whether the need is truly met by using abusive behavior. This discussion opens the door to exploring nonviolent alternatives.

## Barriers to Respectful Communication

The last question on the list above leads into a discussion about the many barriers to respectful communication. This is a focal question that the teens will hear asked frequently at check-in. "What could you have done differently? And, what got in the way of doing that?" This begins a process of self-reflection about their own behavior: "Why *do* I act like this? What is going on for me?" It also sends them the message that they have knowledge about themselves and we are interested in their perspective. Together, they explore answers to these questions. It becomes a group effort. They begin to feel comfortable talking about the issue and talking about themselves.

Even reluctant teens find themselves joining in the conversation. As one said, "When I first started I thought this was stupid, and I didn't want to talk. But, the conversations were interesting. I liked that we really talked about it. And it's like we were all trying to figure it out together."

We summarize by saying that this is all about learning what they can do instead of being hurtful to others when they are angry, feel powerless, want to get a point across, or any other reasons for violent and abusive behavior. This is about learning other ways to respond that are healthier for them and their relationships.

## Common Threads

Each discussion about abuse and violence is different depending on the particular people who make up the group. We are fascinated by the variety of answers to the questions, the insights from the youth, and the degree of seriousness that each group of teens gives to the topic. As facilitators, we stay mindful of the following messages, common threads that underlie our entire program, which we inject into the discussion:

- You have wisdom and knowledge about yourself and what helps you.
- Violence and abuse is a behavior; it is not who you are. You have the ability to change your behavior, and we will all support each other with this.
- People use violent or abusive behaviors for many different reasons. Regardless of the reason, you can learn new ways of responding that don't hurt people and help you feel better about yourself.

## Learning About Respect

Another session focuses on respect. It consists of a discussion about respect, similar in form to the discussion of abuse and violence, and is followed by the initial training on respectful communication skills. While this session was designed primarily for teens, we frequently conduct it with both teens and parents together.

## Defining Respect

We begin by asking the following questions to invite reflection and conversation about the meaning of "respect":

- What does respect mean to you?
- Think of someone who you feel respects you. How does this person act towards you? How do you know he or she respects you? How do you feel when you are with this person?
- Think of someone you respect. How do you act towards that person? How does that person know you respect him or her?
- What is self-respect? How do you respect yourself? What does self-respect have to do with respect for others?

## Respectful Communication When There Is Conflict

Next, we ask participants to make a Do's and Don'ts list for respectful communication. This discussion helps teens start to see which of their behaviors are
respectful and disrespectful. Identifying these behaviors helps both teens and
parents recognize immediately when a conversation starts to move in the direction of disrespect. Parents say this helps them stop the conversation and say,
"It's getting disrespectful now," or "Let's get on the respect wheel." After learning
this together in the group, teens remember and are more willing to cooperate.
This is not to say it is easy. Such a large behavior change requires small steps and
patience.

After the above exercise, we ask the following questions:

- ·Can you be respectful towards someone, even when you disagree with
  the person? How? What helps you do this?
- Can you be respectful towards someone, even when you feel angry with
  the person? How would you do this?

We discuss how it is difficult to remain respectful when you are angry.

When parents and teens realize everyone struggles with this problem, they
do not feel so alone. The discussion above begins with open-ended questions
about respect and ends with questions asking what specific behaviors they will
use that will allow them to succeed. Making a list of specific behaviors is helpful
and can include some suggestions, such as going to another room to calm down
and talk about it later or paying attention to language and tone of voice. This
introduces teens to a central question we will ask them and explore together
many times in the program: What can you do to prevent becoming abusive or
violent?

## The Respectful Communication Skill Set

The respectful communication skill set has two parts: 1) how to talk respectfully
to someone about a problem and how it affects you, and 2) how to listen fully to
another person's point of view and reflect back what you heard. Listening and
reflecting back what the person said is challenging for many teens and parents,
particularly when they disagree with what was said. The respectful communication skill set is critical to successful problem solving, and for this reason, it is the
first phase of the problem solving process they will learn. We spend one session
where parents and teens learn and role-play this skill set before we move on to
problem solving.

We give special attention to respectful communication because it is where
problem solving gets off track and communication breaks down, possibly
escalating into abuse or violence. Once these skills are acquired, and are used

continually throughout the problem solving process, it proceeds more smoothly and is more likely to be successful. Most problem solving models in communication training are less specific and do not isolate the critical skills of how to talk and listen respectfully to prevent anger escalation and increased conflict. Because these families are at such high risk for abuse and violence, slowing down the process and carefully learning each step before moving on to the next is critical.

## Respectful Communication Skill Practice

In this skill practice, parents and teens use the Guidelines for Respectful Communication (Box 9.1) with each other. Either the parent or teen begins by choosing something that causes conflict between them. Both the speaker, the person presenting the problem, and the listener, the person listening to the problem, pay attention to and follow the Guidelines for Respectful Communication.

---

***Box 9.1—Guidelines for Respectful Communication***

Guidelines for Respectful Communication

**When you are speaking:**
   Keep it brief, just one to three sentences. Talk only about the specific situation, event, or behavior that is difficult for you. Describe how you feel.

Use "I" statements: "When _____ happens, I feel _____."
You may add: "Because _____."

> **Teen example:** "When you tell me you'll do something with me, like take me shopping, and then you don't, I feel disappointed and mad."
> **Parent example:** "When I wake you up in the morning for school and you shout and swear at me, and don't get up, I feel disrespected and worried because I don't know what will happen with school if you keep being late."

**Do not:**

Blame
Criticize
Put the person down
Yell, name-call, swear
Bring up the past or other things that bother you (stick to one behavior or problem)
Talk about the other person's personality, attitude, or motives

---

**When you are listening:**

Listen carefully
Do not interrupt
Listen for the feelings of the other person
Don't think about how you are going to respond
Try to put yourself in the other person's shoes

**When you respond to the speaker:**

Describe what you heard the person say
Say what you believe the other person was feeling

**Do not:**

Correct what the other person said
Argue about what happened
Deny the other person's feelings
Bring up the past or things that the other person does that bother you
Criticize, yell, put-down, blame, or justify your behavior

Each parent and teen practices this exercise while the other families watch and give feedback. At the end, we ask, "What was most challenging about this exercise? What did you like about it?" Most say the hardest part was not interrupting the other person when they didn't agree with what the other person was saying and wanting to defend themselves or point out what the other person does to instigate their behavior. They like being able to express their thoughts and feelings, knowing it won't result in a big fight. Parents often say, "It is good to be able to really say what I feel and not worry he will go off on me, or just walk out the door." Teens say, "I like having my dad really listen to what I'm saying without telling me I shouldn't feel that way or give me advice. He just listened." We find that families appreciate this skill and really use it. They tell us how much it helps in day-to-day interactions. While it seems simple, it is new to many and quite challenging.

The Guidelines for Respectful Communication session is followed by a problem solving session where parents and teens learn a 10-step problem solving process, and practice it with each other using the issues they brought up during this skill practice.

We continue building this communication skill set in other sessions by teaching assertive communication, "I" statements, and how to communicate feelings. It is reinforced during group and check-in, as needed, whenever we ask, "How could you have communicated that using the guidelines for respectful communication?"

## Thinking, Beliefs, and Feelings: How They Work Together to Influence Behavior

Helping teens become aware of how their thoughts, feelings, and beliefs interact with and influence their actions raises self-awareness and insight about what is happening internally for them when they become aggressive. We explore how peoples' perceptions and thinking about a situation impact how they feel and react, and even more importantly, how perceptions and thinking can be inaccurate. Teens learn how changing the way they think about a situation can calm or shift negative feelings so these feelings are less intense. Teaching teens how to slow down and observe their cognitive, emotive, behavioral process leading to hurtful behavior provides information that can help them change their response. Likewise, looking at their cognitive process when they choose nonviolent, respectful responses informs them about their ability to steer their course in a positive direction by thinking and believing in more helpful ways.

This cognitive-behavioral segment of the intervention includes four sessions, Understanding Thinking and Self-Talk, Understanding Beliefs, Understanding Feelings, and Putting It All Together: Changing Hurtful Moves into Helpful Moves. The concepts and learning from these sessions are integrated throughout the entire intervention for reinforcement and for application to current situations in teens' lives.

When a teen makes a positive or negative behavioral choice, we ask the following:

- What were your thoughts, or self-talk, before you made that decision?
- What did you believe about yourself, others, or the situation that helped you make the choice?
- What feelings were you having before, during, and after the situation?

For example, a teen says at check-in, "This week when my dad asked me about my math grade, I was about to yell at him that it was none of his business, like I usually do, but I stopped myself and actually talked to him about it without yelling."

We ask which thoughts or self-talk helped him make that decision. "Well, my first thought was, 'Crap, I forgot to finish that assignment.' Then I just wanted him to leave me alone, and I thought, 'I'm not talking to him about this.' That's when I was about to yell at him that it was none of his fucking business. But, then I realized it would turn into a fight because I would say things I shouldn't and so I thought, if I just talk to him it won't turn into a big blowup this time."

Next we ask what beliefs he held about himself or the situation. "My first belief about me was 'I'll never pass math.' My belief about my dad was that it's not his business, and he should back off. The belief that helped me was that it's not right to blow up at my dad just because I'm doing bad in math, and he does have the right to ask me about school—he's my dad."

Finally we ask the teen about his feelings. "At first, when I realized I forgot to finish the assignment, I was mad at myself because I've been trying to get my grade up, and I can't miss any more assignments if I want to pass. I felt like a screw-up again, a loser. And stressed. Then I was angry at my dad for asking and I didn't want to talk about it. When I decided I should just talk to him, I felt less angry. Once we talked and we both didn't get angry, I felt calmer and less stressed."

The following is a description of the four group sessions that focus on helping teens understand their cognitive emotive process, and help them develop skills for shifting their process towards nonviolent, respectful behaviors.

## Understanding Self-Talk

In this session we explore how thinking impacts feelings and behavior. Self-talk is another word for thinking that is experienced as an inner voice that tells us how things are or why something happened, often judging ourselves or others. It can be thoughts we pressure ourselves with, or messages we have acquired throughout our lives, which may or may not be true. This inner voice narrates a story about what is happening. For example, when a friend isn't texting you back, you think, "She doesn't really like me that much. She must be hanging out with her other friend. She likes her better." Later, you find out her phone was just dead.

Self-talk can be helpful or unhelpful. We can change it, if we give it attention. Most people are unaware of their self-talk, and so the first step for teens is to start listening to their thinking. As they become more aware, they notice more and more. Eventually they realize they have a choice. They can embrace it, ignore it, or challenge it.

We teach helpful self-talk by starting with a discussion that uses real-life scenarios that illustrate how negative self-talk can lead to disrespect and abuse. Changing negative self-talk to helpful self-talk can calm a person's negative emotions, allowing him or her to handle the situation in a more respectful manner.

## Understanding Beliefs

This session explores personal beliefs, how we develop them, and their impact on our feelings and behavior. We discuss how beliefs are different from self-talk in that they are notions we hold about the way things are or should be, sometimes referred to as "core beliefs." They often have to do with values or perspectives acquired from our family, community, or culture. They reflect what we think is important as well as what we think is right or wrong. We also develop beliefs about who we are as persons, our capabilities, self-worth, and personality. Beliefs influence self-talk. For example, if I have a core belief that I am powerless and incompetent, then when faced with a challenge I might say to myself, "I can't do anything about it; it's hopeless, nothing will ever change."

Beliefs support certain behaviors, in positive and negative ways. They influence whether we use abusive behavior or respectful behavior in difficult situations. Using scenarios or real situations that group members have experienced, teens explore what set of beliefs a person might hold when making an abusive or respectful choice and where people learn different sets of beliefs. Teens, just like adults, often have conflicting beliefs and values that come into play in some situations but not others. These discussions clarify how beliefs enter into our decision-making process.

Just as with self-talk, teens can challenge and change beliefs that do not serve them well. We ask the teens to work together to come up with ideas of helpful and unhelpful beliefs and how the unhelpful beliefs can be changed. The session wraps up with the teens writing down some of their own personal beliefs and how they influence their behavior in positive and negative ways. They then think of new, helpful beliefs to replace the unhelpful ones.

## Understanding Feelings

Talking about feelings is new for many families. Parents and teens both partici-pate in this session because both need to learn about feelings and practice how to communicate feelings with each other. Parents can support their teens at home by acknowledging their feelings, and reminding them to talk about feelings instead of acting out with aggression. Participants, especially youth, can benefit from learning about feelings in two ways. First, they can expand their understanding and vocabulary about feelings to communicate more effectively during conflicts. Second, they can more readily separate anger from their behavior. They will be able to feel and express anger without hurting a family member.

### What Is Anger?

When we ask teens what they were feeling when they were aggressive, they usually say "angry" or "mad." When asked what other feelings they experience, most look at us blankly. Many have come to believe that anger is the cause of their behavior. They have been told they have an anger problem or need to control their anger. Because anger is the feeling most commonly associated with violence and abuse, and often used as an excuse for aggression, we take some time to explore it. We invite group discussion by asking what anger is.

Following discussion of their ideas about anger, we explain that anger is one of many feelings we all experience regularly in our lives. Anger is not a bad thing. It is a feeling that lets us know that things are not right for us, something is bother-ing us, or something is amiss. It is a sign that we should stop and figure out what's going on. Feeling angry can mean many different things. The best way to figure it out is by going beneath the anger to other feelings that might be fueling it.

Anytime a person feels angry, there are also other feelings. We explain the iceberg concept of anger, and that anger is like the tip of an iceberg in the ocean, with a larger mass below the surface that is unseen. People often express anger only when they have difficult feelings. But just as a captain must know what lies beneath the water in order to successfully navigate the ship, knowing what lies beneath the anger helps people understand what is really going on. We ask them to think of feelings that, like the mass beneath the iceberg, are submerged beneath the anger. As they brainstorm the different feelings that anger might be masking, they expand their vocabulary for different feelings and enhance their self-awareness.

## Feelings Are Information

Feelings give us important information that helps us understand ourselves and realize that the conflict is *within ourselves*, rather than *with others*. What follows is a story that can be used to illustrate this to the group.

Chris came home Sunday afternoon after a weekend visit at his dad's house. His mom asked him how his weekend was, and Chris replied "Fine" and went to his room. Later she asked him to do his weekly chore of taking out the garbage, but Chris ignored her. After asking several times, he yelled at her, "Get out of my room!" Later at the dinner table his little sister was singing a song, and Chris yelled, "Just shut-up, would you!" Mom said, "Chris, don't yell at your sister or use that word! Your sister has a right to sing songs. What is going on with you? Why are you so angry?"

Chris got up and threw his plate in the sink, shattering it, and went to his room. Later, Chris's mom went to his door and knocked, asking to come in. Chris let her in and she sat on a chair. She said, "I know you're really angry, but you're being mean to us and breaking things. Can you tell me what's going on?" Chris started crying. He said he missed his dad. It was hard for him to leave his dad that day. He wished he could see his dad more, but his dad is always so busy. He felt sad that his dad didn't see him more often. They had planned to be together for the whole evening and go out for dinner, but later Dad said he had to do some work, and so he had to take Chris home. Chris cried and his mom hugged him. He said he was sorry he was so mean to her and his sister.

Chris, like many people, responded to his vulnerable feelings with anger. Anger is like a shield or protection against the difficult feelings, helping a person feel power when he or she feels powerless. It puts a person on the offensive, giving a sense of strength to fight off the vulnerable feelings. For Chris, feeling hurt and disappointed by what he saw as his dad's indifference to him turned into anger, and he responded by directing the anger towards his mom and sister. Once he identified the real feelings and talked about them, he calmed down and was able to recognize his hurtful behavior and feel remorse.

Knowing all of his feelings gives him information about what he is dealing with. He misses his dad. He feels hurt because it seems like his dad doesn't care about him. He feels disappointment because his dad did not spend more time with him. Now he can make a decision about what he wants to do with his real feelings.

After sharing this story, we invite parents and teens to come up with ideas about how the teen can respond to his or her feelings. In our example of Chris, two ways he might respond are as follows:

1. Chris could look at his self-talk and beliefs to figure out whether he perceives the situation accurately. His self-talk may have been, "My dad doesn't care about me." The belief that supports this may be something like, "I'm not worthy of my dad's attention" or "I must have done something wrong." He could change his belief to "I am worthy of my dad's attention, even if I did something wrong," and change his self-talk to "Maybe he is just really busy with his work, and does want to spend more time with me."
2. Check out this perception by talking to his dad about his feelings. Let his dad know he misses him and wants to see him more. He may find out his dad misses him too and feels badly about not seeing Chris more. Then they can talk about what to do.

Next, we ask what are Chris's options if he doesn't feel comfortable talking to his dad in this way, or if his dad is not responsive, and doesn't say anything to indicate he misses him or wants more time with him. How can Chris handle his feelings if his dad continues to let him down?

Some difficult feelings are real and nothing can be done to change them. Recognizing the feelings and talking about them with someone who is supportive helps reduce intensity and anger. Remaining aware that difficult feelings can impact behavior towards others may prevent a teen from targeting a family member, as Chris did. Accepting difficult feelings is not easy, but even when a teen is unable to accept them, he or she may be able to avoid being caught in turmoil with them. Talking about feelings is a first step.

## Why Does Putting Feelings into Words Help?

In a 2007 study at the University of California at Los Angeles (Lieberman, 2007), researchers found that simply identifying negative feelings makes them less intense. The study found that labeling negative feelings activates the right prefrontal cortex, the area of the brain that processes emotions, controls impulses, and calms a person. In addition, labeling feelings diminishes the response of the amygdala, the area of the brain where fight or flight, fear and panic are triggered. The findings suggest that talking about feelings "diminishes emotional reactivity" and helps to "alleviate emotional distress." The same results occur in people who identify feelings in someone else. So, when a parent acknowledges a feeling in his or her teen, the parent calms down.

## Identifying and Talking About Feelings—Skill Practice

We begin this skill practice by asking participants to identify their own feelings, beginning with feelings they had during the past week. Using a feelings chart that lists the entire range of feelings is helpful. We ask each person to recall one feeling he or she experienced during the previous week and to describe the situation that was occurring when he or she had the feeling.

We then ask participants to identify other feelings people have when they are angry. A variety of scenarios are presented where someone is in a situation that would probably make them feel angry. We ask the group to come up with feelings the person might be experiencing in addition to anger.

Finally, we ask them to think of personal situations in which they were angry. They identify the feelings other than anger that they experienced and explain how they could have communicated those feelings in a respectful way. We end by having each participant share his or her situation and feelings with the group.

During discussions about feelings, the facilitator encourages participants to practice the skills that they have learned so far during group sessions, for example:

- If you are too upset to communicate feelings respectfully, separate from the other person to calm down.
- Anytime you are angry, ask yourself what else you are feeling.
- Decide what to do about the feelings: talk about them, just feel them and acknowledge they are there, do a self-calming activity, or look at the situation that triggered the anger and figure out what you should do to solve the problem.

## Putting It All Together: Turning Hurtful Moves into Helpful Moves

Thoughts, beliefs, and feelings are three elements that work together when we make decisions about what to do in difficult situations. In this exercise teens learn how people's decisions about how to respond to different circumstances are impacted by the interplay between these three internal processes and whether their responses are *helpful* or *hurtful*.

Teens learn how the three elements work in a two-step process. In the first step they apply the elements to a situation or scenario that is about someone else, and in the second step, they apply the elements to themselves using a personal situation. We first present a scenario about a teen who has made an unhelpful decision about how to respond to a situation with her mother.

Sara wants her mother's attention, but her mother is helping Sara's little brother with a school project. She keeps pestering her mom to take her to the store, and her mom says, "No, I'm busy with your brother now." Sara shouts,

"All you care about is him!" Sara picks up a vase and throws it against the wall, shattering it.

Teens are prompted with questions such as the following to identify the possible thoughts, feelings, and beliefs that may have informed Sara's decision to respond as she did.

Teens fill out a worksheet similar to the example below as they generate their ideas.

- What would Sara be thinking or what self-talk would she have in this situation that would lead to her shouting and throwing the vase?
- What feelings would she have in this situation?
- And what beliefs might she have that would justify throwing a vase against the wall?

Then teens are asked how Sara's decision-making process would be different if she were to change her thinking and beliefs.

- How could Sara change her unhelpful thinking so she could make a more helpful move?
- What are some realistic thoughts in this situation that would reduce her feelings of anger, and allow her to feel some emotions that would help her respond without aggression?
- What beliefs might Sara have that would help her make a more helpful move?

TABLE 9.1  Hurtful Moves and Helpful Moves

| Hurtful Moves | Helpful Moves |
| --- | --- |
| **I Think/Self-Talk** <br> *"She doesn't care about me."* <br> *"All she cares about is my brother."* | **I Think/Self-Talk** <br> *"My brother is little, he needs more attention."* <br> *It's not that she doesn't care, she's just busy."* |
| **I Feel** <br> *Angry at Mom.* <br> *Abandoned, hurt, alone.* | **I Feel** <br> *Understanding, empathy.* <br> *Still feels disappointed and alone, but less angry.* |
| **Behavior** <br> *Yells at Mom and throws a vase.* | **Behavior** <br> *Asks Mom when she will have time to spend with her.* |
| **I Believe** <br> *"If someone makes me feel bad, I have a right to revenge."* <br> *"I need to make her feel bad too."* | **I Believe** <br> *"I can feel mad and not attack people. It's not okay to hurt people."* <br> *"I can ask for what I want."* |

Following this discussion, teens write their own personal scenario of a situation when they made a hurtful move. They fill out a blank worksheet with their thoughts, feelings, and beliefs that may have led to their decision to respond in a hurtful way. With help from facilitators and other group members, they contemplate how they could have changed their thinking and beliefs to support them in making a more helpful move.

Once teens have learned about their cognitive-behavioral process, practitioners can reference it with teens when they bring up difficult situations by asking about their thoughts, feelings, and beliefs. Teens need a lot of coaching with recognizing their thoughts and beliefs. However, once they comprehend it, they usually realize that they have already been using the strategy of shifting their thinking to cope with challenges, but have not recognized it.

## Self-Calming Techniques to Regulate Emotions

Strong negative emotions such as anger, rage, or anxiety can feel like an uncontrollable, inner storm. Teens tell us one of their biggest challenges is calming down once they escalate; they feel as if they go from irritation to rage instantly. Parents say their teens are moody and irritable much of the time, and are "set off" by small annoyances. Both parents and teens ask for help with how to calm down and be less reactive. Skills for self-calming and regulating emotions help both teens and parents. These skills are interspersed throughout the sessions, with two sessions specifically on these topics, Self-Calming and Understanding Warning Signs. Additionally, we use weekly meditation and relaxation exercises at the beginning of each group session.

Neuroscience research over the last 20 years has dramatically increased our knowledge of the brain and central nervous system. One of the most helpful new insights is our capacity to change our brains to help us function in healthier ways. We can activate parts of our brain, strengthening them over time, and gradually rewire the brain to improve our mood.

We discuss the following simple activities that teens and parents can use to calm themselves and have a more balanced emotional life:

- Focus attention on a healthy activity that you enjoy, such as drawing or playing a musical instrument.
- Write in a journal.
- Say your feelings out loud.
- Let go of negative thinking.
- Engage in physical exercise: run, play basketball, skateboard.
- Breathe by taking slow, deep breaths, with emphasis on a long exhale.
- Go outside and walk, touch the grass, or sit by a tree.
- Be in your body. Feel your feet on the floor, wiggle your toes, feel your heartbeat.

- Ground yourself. Feel your feet on the ground. Connect to the earth, imagining roots growing down from your feet deep into the earth.
- Move your body. Walk, stretch, do yoga, engage in rhythmic movement such as dance or rocking in a rocking chair.
- Squeeze a squishy ball or play dough.
- Walk in nature.
- Relax your pelvic muscles. Breathe into your pelvis and feel the breath expand and relax, or tighten the muscles and then relax them.
- Take a warm bath or shower.
- Drink warm fluids such as tea or hot milk.
- Do healthy relaxing things that you love to do.

We end with each person making a personal self-calming plan, including activities to do when they are escalated in the moment, and ongoing activities to improve overall mood.

## Meditation and Relaxation

Two techniques can be helpful to teens and parents. The first is called mindfulness meditation, which is simply paying attention to the present moment from a stance that is nonjudgmental and nonreactive. This can be done in many different ways. One method is to bring focus to the present moment and put attention on the physical senses—what one sees, hears, smells, or physically feels. This can be done while sitting or walking. Rest in the present moment, let go of thoughts, and simply observe the senses without judgment. When thoughts or feelings arise, observe briefly and let them go.

The second technique is called progressive muscle relaxation. While there are a number of methods, all involve focusing the attention on major muscle groups while alternately contracting and releasing the muscles, thereby releasing tension.

Beginning every session with a relaxation exercise or mindfulness meditation teaches participants a variety of methods and starts each session by helping everyone let go of tension and be more present and relaxed. This gives families a way to become accustomed to this kind of practice and experience the benefits every week.

## Goal Planning and Self-Evaluation

Teens make a specific behavioral goal each week to use their skills at home to prevent violence or abuse towards their family members. When they return to the group the following week, they evaluate their progress by rating themselves on a scale, measuring their progress. When they have not been successful, they identify barriers that prevented them from meeting their goal and how they can overcome those barriers in the coming week. When they successfully meet their goal, teens identify the steps they took that led to their success.

Goal planning is a vehicle for applying newly learned skills in family relationships and integrating them into daily life. The goal planning steps teach teens how to proactively think through their behavior in the coming week, and identify their challenges and barriers to remaining nonviolent and respectful at home. They learn how to make a step-by-step plan for changing a specific behavior. The self-evaluation process gives youth responsibility for monitoring their own progress in making change, with support of and accountability to the group. Box 9.2 contains our goal worksheet, filled in with a typical example written by a teen.

Goal planning in a group setting can be a powerful experience. Group members offer suggestions when a youth seems stuck. When a teen sets a goal with group support, the following week that teen faces the entire group of people who want to

---

### *Box 9.2—Goal for the Week*

## Goal for the Week

**Name:** Max    **Date:** March 3

**The behavior I will work on is:**

*I won't swear at my mom and call her names*

**Steps:**

1. When do you usually use this behavior?

   *When I get home from school and I want to leave and she says I need to get my homework done first.*

2. What is the new behavior you will use? (be specific)

   *When I feel like yelling or swearing at my mom, I'll do my safety plan and calm down.*

3. What can you say to yourself that will help you do this?

   My self-statement is:
   *I don't want to hurt my mom. It's easier to just let it go.*

4. Is there a skill you can use to help you succeed with your goal?

   *Use my self-calming plan.*

**How Did I Do?**

1. Rate yourself on a scale of 1 to 10 (1 = worst, 10 = best): 7
2. If you had some success, how did you do this?

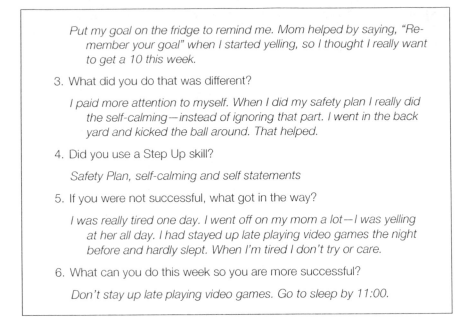

*Put my goal on the fridge to remind me. Mom helped by saying, "Remember your goal" when I started yelling, so I thought I really want to get a 10 this week.*

3. What did you do that was different?

   *I paid more attention to myself. When I did my safety plan I really did the self-calming — instead of ignoring that part. I went in the back yard and kicked the ball around. That helped.*

4. Did you use a Step Up skill?

   *Safety Plan, self-calming and self statements*

5. If you were not successful, what got in the way?

   *I was really tired one day. I went off on my mom a lot — I was yelling at her all day. I had stayed up late playing video games the night before and hardly slept. When I'm tired I don't try or care.*

6. What can you do this week so you are more successful?

   *Don't stay up late playing video games. Go to sleep by 11:00.*

know if the teen was successful. The teen hears questions such as, "Well, how did it go? Did you use your safety plan?" The teen realizes people are paying attention and that they care; group members become emotionally invested in helping each other succeed. If the teen has been successful, the group often claps and the teen beams. It bolsters confidence, fostering even more motivation to continue working on change. If the teen did not do so well, the group helps with new ideas and support to continue trying.

When we ask teens who are completing the program what helped them the most to change their behavior, many cite the goals. One teen, at his last session, said, "I think the goals helped me the most. If I wasn't following my goal I would think about having to tell everyone I didn't do it, and they had all helped me. That would make me try harder to remember to do it. I wanted to show the group I could do it. Now it's easy and I just do it."

## Summary

Teens stop using aggression and violence when they begin to feel confident in their ability to respond in a respectful way. Learning new ways of responding to conflict or difficult feelings gives them a way to stop lashing out at the people they love. As they learn and practice new behaviors such as communicating respectfully when they are angry, talking about their feelings and problem solving with their parent, they begin choosing those behaviors over violence and abuse. Over time, teens integrate new patterns of behavior and feel more confidence in their ability to handle difficult situations and feelings. As one teen said at his last session, "I just look at things differently now. I feel better about myself, so it's easier to be nice to people in my family. I can see how they care about me, and I care about them. I didn't see that before."

## References

Lieberman, M. D. (2007). Putting feelings into words: affect labeling disrupts amygdala activity in response to affective stimuli. *Psychological Science*, 18(5), 421–428.

Routt, G., & Anderson, L. (2004). Step up: a curriculum for teens who are violent at home. Retrieved from www.kingcounty.gov/courts/step-up

# ten
# **Helping Parents Restore Leadership in the Family**

I know I'm supposed to be his parent. But, I'm afraid to do my job. It's hard to admit it, but I'm scared to say no to him. I just don't know what he'll do.

How do you parent a teen whom you fear? How can you set limits and hold your ground when the last time you tried, the kitchen was destroyed? "It's fine as long as I don't say, 'No,'" are words we hear regularly from parents. A 15-year-old boy in our program responded to the question, "Do you think your mother is a good parent?" by saying, "When I let her." This short response sums it up; he decides whether or not to let his mother parent him.

Holding a leadership role with a teen who responds to boundary setting with violence is extremely challenging for parents. Parenting approaches that are effective for most teens don't work with them, and often result in profanity hurled at the parent, holes in walls, or the teen walking out the door. When we began our first parent group we quickly realized we had a lot to learn.

As we noted in the preface, we decided the best way to help parents was to learn from them first. We began by listening to the stories and experiences of the parents in the group as they shared their knowledge and perspective of their children and themselves. Simply allowing time for parents to tell their stories to each other alleviated their feelings of isolation and abandonment. For the first time they could speak with other parents who understood them as they described giving in to their teens out of fear or exhaustion, or hiding out in their rooms.

They were relieved to know they were not the only parents walking on eggshells with their teenager.

Parents validated each other's feelings and experiences in a way no other person would be able to do. They began supporting each other by sharing strategies and coping methods. With a diversity of skill sets and experiences, parents had a lot to offer one another and were a valuable resource to each other.

After learning more about parents' daily challenges and their own view of their needs, we began to understand how to help them. The strategies we share in this chapter have been developed by observing parents' struggles and by working with them in parent groups as they try out different approaches and share their successes and failures.

We offer parents a variety of parenting tools, recognizing there is not one solution for every parent and teen. Many of the parenting skills we teach are designed to enable parents to support their teens in using the new skills that the teens learn in their intervention group. The skills that teens and parents practice together in joint group sessions pave the way for parents to start using their new parenting skills at home. These parenting strategies would not be as effective with a teen who is not participating in the group intervention. Teens learn new skills, with weekly goal plans, in addition to parents and teens learning skills together. For example, if a teen is working on successfully using his safety plan, and his dad has been working on his own skill of disengaging from power struggles, they can work together on each of their parts. At home, when the teen is disrespectful and Dad decides to disengage, he can remind his teen of the plan they made in the group.

Most of the skills we offer parents are not new parenting approaches; they are adapted to the unique challenges of parenting a volatile teen, with attention to safety. In this chapter we focus on parenting strategies specific to parenting teens who are violent and abusive. However, we incorporate other positive parenting skills that are established best practices, and we advise other practitioners working with these families to do the same. The Step Up curriculum includes other parent sessions.

## Strengths, Challenges, and Changes

In our opening session we guide parents through a self-inquiry process about their parenting. They recognize their gifts as a parent and the many ways they parent well. They think through their challenges and what is most difficult for them. The many ways they have tried to help their teens change are considered, evaluating the results of these approaches. Parents reflect on their teen's positive qualities and the strengths in their relationships. And finally, parents identify changes they want to make in their parenting behaviors, choosing one behavior to begin focusing on, and developing a personal behavior change plan.

## Recognizing Parenting Strengths

Parents come in the door feeling like they have really blown it. One of our first goals in working with parents is to help them recognize their strengths as a mother, father, or caregiver. Getting back in touch with what they do well as a parent stops the self-denigration and relieves the hopelessness. Parents make lists and share them with each other. Every parent has competence in some areas. Shedding light on strengths helps them recognize they are not bad parents, as many have come to believe.

We encourage parents to pay attention to their parenting behaviors during the week and add more strengths to their list as they notice themselves parent in ways they feel are effective. This raises awareness of their parenting behaviors and broadens their perspective. As parents become more mindful of their parenting, they also notice behaviors that they don't feel fit on the strengths list. We point out that it helps to recognize the less effective parenting behaviors as well, not for the purpose of disparaging themselves, but for the purpose of learning. We suggest that when they recognize behaviors they feel are less effective, to take a step back and just observe what happened. Regard it as information. Then say to oneself, "Good to know. What did I learn?" And, "How can I use one of my strengths as a parent to do that differently?" Keeping a log at home gives them a tangible way to observe their parenting behaviors. This leads to the next exercise, Identifying Parenting Challenges.

## Identifying Parenting Challenges

Next we help parents explore their challenges as a parent. Because most parents' attention has been focused on "what I *cannot* do," recognizing challenges is usually easier than recognizing strengths. In this exercise parents are asked to consider their own behavior, rather than their teens' behavior. A common response to this question is, "My biggest challenge is my teen's violence." This is a good starting place, but we want them to think about the challenge in terms of their own behavior, for example, "I don't know how to respond to my teen's violence."

We keep the focus on the parents' behavior because their own behavior is all they can control. This opens up a conversation about how one person cannot control another's behavior; one can only control his or her own behavior in an attempt to influence the other. We point out that this does not imply parents are to blame for their teen's challenging behavior. Nor does it mean changing their behavior will necessarily change the teen's behavior, as most parents well know from experience. Because parents cannot make their teens change, the only option is for parents to change their own behavior.

As parents share their challenges with each other, they begin to reflect more deeply on their parenting practices. Through this self-evaluation process, parents begin to recognize the changes they want to make in their own behavior that might influence change in their teens and improve the relationship. The next activity guides them towards identifying one specific behavior they want to change or one skill they want to develop.

## Changing Parents' Behavior

Although parents will be taught a variety of parenting tools in the parent group, we first ask them to identify the changes they want to make in their behavior as parents. This approach honors their knowledge and wisdom about what they need and what is best for their family. Because parents have felt disempowered, increasing their self-efficacy is a key part of our work with them.

Parents answer the following questions to think through changes they want to make and develop a Behavior Change Plan for one behavior to begin working on during the following week.

### Making a Behavior Change Plan

1.  Think of some things you would like to do or change that will help your relationship with your teen. Make a list of ideas.
2.  Pick one behavior from your list that you want to focus on in the next week.
    *Example: I will not engage with my son when he is disrespectful to me.*
3.  What is your reason for choosing this behavior?
    *Example: When I engage with my teen when he is disrespectful, his behavior just gets worse.*
4.  Make the behavior specific. Then make a step-by-step plan.
    *Behavior: The moment my son starts using disrespectful language I will tell him I am separating.*
    *Plan:*
    a. *I will tell my son about my plan to separate any time he starts to yell, put me down, swear at me, or use any other disrespectful language.*
    b. *I will remind myself every day by putting a note on my dresser in my bedroom.*
    c. *When my son starts to speak disrespectfully, I will tell him, "I am separating from you because you are not being respectful. Let's talk later when you are able to talk respectfully to me."*
    d. *Separate and go to another room or leave and take a walk.*
    e. *Later, check in with him to see if he is ready to talk respectfully.*
    f. *Thank him if he talks respectfully.*

As parents begin to learn skills during their group sessions, they identify additional changes they can make in order to use these new skills. The Behavior Change Plan becomes a weekly goal-setting tool, similar to the weekly plan used by the teens. When parents go home with a plan for a specific, achievable, behavioral change, whether it is for their own self-care or to strengthen their relationship with their teens, they feel they have more control in their lives. They also feel hopeful with renewed energy.

## Effects of Raising an Abusive Teen on Parenting

This session invites parents to look at how their parenting behavior has been affected by their teens' abusive behavior. Parenting behaviors are often a reaction to feelings and may not be the most helpful responses to the abusive situation. Through group discussion, parents consider the many feelings that arise while parenting a teenager who becomes aggressive when boundaries are set. Parents come to understand that by feeling responsible for their teen's behavior; their ability to set limits and hold their teens accountable for hurtful behavior is diminished.

We help parents understand how their thoughts affect how they feel and behave. The relationship between thoughts, feelings, and behaviors is explored using scenarios and their real life situations. Identifying automatic thoughts and feelings that are triggered by interactions with their teens helps parents understand their reactions. Parents examine how their own negative thoughts influence their response to their teens' behavior and how they can change their thinking to respond more effectively.

We ask parents the following questions, inviting group discussion:

1.  What are some of the feelings you experience when your teen is violent or abusive?
    *Some of the feelings parents express include fear, anger, powerlessness, exhaustion, helplessness, guilt, responsibility, inadequacy as a parent, and being overwhelmed.*

2.  Looking at this list, how do you think some of these feelings might influence the way you parent?
    *Typical answers include:*
    *   *Make inconsistent rules and consequences because of fear of an outburst*
    *   *Fail to ask the teen to do things (chores, homework, etc.)*
    *   *Take on responsibilities for the teen that should be his or hers*
    *   *Walk on eggshells around him or her to avoid conflict*
    *   *Don't follow through on consequences*
    *   *Give in when pressured*
    *   *Become angry and return the abuse with yelling, put-downs, or name-calling*
    *   *Lose the ability to see the teen's positive behavior*
    *   *Get into a pattern of expecting negative behavior*

We discuss how many of their feelings are similar to those of any victim of abuse, but because they are the parents of the abuser, they naturally feel responsible for their teens' behavior and believe they should be able to stop it. Unfortunately, feeling responsible for the behavior gets in the way of addressing it. This is particularly true when the teen has had difficult life experiences.

One mother expressed sentiments that are very similar to what many parents tell us. "I feel badly for what my son went through when we lived with his dad, who was abusive to me. I know it has influenced his behavior, so I just try to support him and love him, hoping he will get over it. So, I don't call him on his abuse, I just stay away from him or give in because I feel bad. But it isn't helping. He is doing it more and more now."

Parents often tell us that guilt interferes with holding their teens accountable, tacitly signaling that the abusive behavior is not that serious. We emphasize that parents can support teens as they deal with past hardships, but at the same time, hold teens responsible for their hurtful behavior. This message is carried through all of our group sessions, and eventually carried by the parents into their homes.

## Thoughts, Feelings, and Responses to Teen Behavior

As parents discuss how their feelings affect their parenting behaviors, we point out the thoughts related to those feelings. For example, the mother in the above example might have thoughts about her responsibility for her son's exposure to domestic violence, such as, "It's my fault he had to see his dad's behavior with me. I should have left him sooner. My son can't help his behavior; he learned it from his dad." Such thoughts lead to guilt, and guilt can lead to excusing the abusive behavior. However, if she notices her thoughts, she can evaluate whether they are untrue or unrealistic. She can then reframe her thoughts; for example, "My ex-husband's behavior was not my fault. I was doing the best I knew how at the time. I was a good parent in many ways." Her new thoughts lead her to respond by supporting her son to change his hurtful behavior; for example, "Even though my son was exposed to his father's behavior, he does not have to repeat it. It doesn't help him if I excuse his behavior. He will be healthier and happier in the long run if I help him change. I can't help him change if I am ignoring it."

Some thoughts might be true; for example, "My son didn't have a father who was a good role model." This is not a thought that needs changing; however the conclusions drawn from it can be changed. Thoughts such as, "He's not capable of changing," can be reframed as, "Yes, his father did not give him what he needed to know about how to be a respectful man with his family. But, I have given that to him, and he can avoid following in his father's footsteps."

We explain to parents that in order to change their thinking they must first become aware of it. Many thoughts are so automatic that they do not know they have them. The next exercise is designed to increase parents' awareness of their

**Box 10.1—Thoughts, Feelings, and Behavior Worksheet**

Thoughts, Feelings, and Responses to My Teen's Behavior

    Think of some times when your teen was abusive to you. Describe how you felt, what you thought, and how you responded to your teen.

| | Teen's Behavior | My Thoughts | My Feelings | My Response |
|---|---|---|---|---|
| 1 | | | | |
| 2 | | | | |
| 3 | | | | |
| 4 | | | | |
| 5 | | | | |

thoughts and to explore how these thoughts influence feelings and parenting behavior. Parents are asked to fill in the worksheet above (Box 10.1).

    Parents share their answers with each other, discovering how similar everyone's thoughts, feelings, and behaviors are. This dialogue provides the opportunity to listen and reflect on others' experiences with an objective view, which gives them a new perspective on their own behavior. Parents often say that when other parents tell their stories, they feel as if they are looking at themselves through a new lens. One parent said, "I was giving a suggestion to another parent in group about an interaction with her teen, and later realized that it was good advice to myself! Her situation was similar to mine, but I saw it in a new light when she described it. It is a great way to learn."

## Changing Thought Patterns

### The Story of Shawn and Lisa

To get parents thinking about how thoughts and feelings influence their behavior, we use the example of Lisa and Shawn. Lisa told her son, Shawn, that he needed to do the dishes before he went over to his friend's house. Shawn started arguing with her about how he didn't have time and that he wasn't her slave and how his brother never had to do the dishes. Lisa argued back about how he was nowhere near being a slave because he didn't do any work around the house and that his brother had done the dishes several times that week. Shawn started yelling at her and picked up one of the dishes and threw it at the wall. It smashed into pieces. Lisa started screaming at Shawn and told him he couldn't go anywhere for a month. Shawn went to his room and slammed the door. Lisa did the dishes.

We ask parents the following questions to help them identify what Lisa might have been thinking and feeling, and how this may have affected how she responded to Shawn. Typical responses follow each question.

1. What do you think Lisa was thinking during the incident?
   - *"He's wrong about being a slave and that his brother never does the dishes. I have to convince him that he's wrong and I'm right."*
   - *"I have to make him change."*
   - *"He could really hurt me."*
   - *"How could I have a child who is so mean? What have I done wrong?"*
   - *"Forget getting him to do the dishes, I'll just do them. I can't deal with him anymore."*
2. What do you think she was feeling?
   *Frightened, angry, frustrated, defensive, hopeless*
3. How do you think Lisa's thoughts and feelings affected the way she responded to him?
   - *Argued with him to convince him that she is right.*
   - *Screamed at him to try to make him change.*
   - *Impulsively gave him a consequence that may be difficult to follow through on.*
   - *Did the dishes for him.*
4. How could she have changed her thinking? What could she have thought instead?
   - *"I don't need to argue with him about this. Arguing isn't helpful."*
   - *"I don't need to try to convince him of anything; I don't need to defend myself."*
   - *"I can calmly remind him of his chore, and then leave the room."*
   - *"He is responsible for breaking the dish. We can talk later when we are both calm about a plan for him to make amends and replace the dish."*
   - *"We need to be separate now. His behavior isn't safe. I'll leave the dishes for him to do later."*
   - *"He made the choice to behave this way. It is his responsibility, not mine."*

**TABLE 10.1** Negative Thinking Versus Realistic Thinking

| Negative Thinking | Realistic Thinking |
| --- | --- |
| This is my fault. I'm not a good parent. | My teen is responsible for her behavior. I am doing everything I can. |
| There is nothing I can do. I've tried everything. | There are some things I can do. I can separate from him when he is abusive. I can get help. |
| He's lazy and self-centered. | He's not motivated to do things he does not care about (like a lot of teens). An incentive or consequence might motivate him. |
| I have to make her change her behavior. | I can try to help her make good choices. But it is up to her to make the decision. |
| He's trying to manipulate me into doing what he wants. | He is using behaviors he knows to get his way. I can teach him other ways to communicate with me about what he wants. |
| I should be able to control her. | I can influence her decisions about her behavior with rules, incentives, and consequences. She is in charge of her behavior. |

## *Changing Thought Patterns*

Next, parents begin to examine their own thinking and how they can change unhelpful thoughts to positive or helpful thoughts. Negative thinking often falls into one of the following categories:

- Negative thoughts about the other person (criticism, put-downs)
- Negative thoughts about oneself (self-blame, "shoulds," self-criticism)
- Negative thoughts about the situation or the future

We begin by showing the parents a chart and discuss the examples with the group (Table 10.1).

After going over this chart, parents fill in a blank chart with their own situations with their teens and fill in their negative thoughts, and then change them into more realistic or helpful thoughts. We ask parents to pay attention to their thoughts whenever they are in conflict with their teens during the following week and to continue to add new situations to the chart, changing the negative thoughts to helpful thoughts.

## Reestablishing Leadership as a Parent

Parents want to know how to regain authority with their teens. Setting limits and holding boundaries has become a nightmare for many of them. Saying "No" turns the household into chaos, with yelling and screaming, property destroyed, little ones hiding in their rooms, and police at the door. Parents start to avoid such conflict at all costs. By the time they come to us, many feel they are no longer a parent to their teen. The first thing they want to do is figure out how to become a parent again.

When a parent decides to stop giving in to the violence and starts holding his or her ground, a power struggle begins that can go on for days. As the parent attempts to hold the boundary while the teen pushes back, they both feed on each other's charged emotions. As these emotions escalate, the parent eventually loses the ability to hold a firm boundary. Most teens need a parent who can remain firm and consistent when setting limits; teens who become aggressive need this even more. When reacting to blowup after blowup, parents hardly have a minute to collect themselves, take a break, and re-center before the next confrontation.

## The Story of Mary and Aaron

We begin this session with the story of Mary and her son Aaron. Mary took Aaron's laptop away because he hadn't been going to school and had been up most nights on his computer social networking and getting no sleep. She said he could have it back after he had gone to school for two weeks straight. This was difficult for her because she knew there was a risk of Aaron getting violent. He had been physically violent with her in the past, and often verbally and emotionally abusive towards her. Mary was anxious about it, but knew she had to finally put her foot down and stick to it. When Mary told Aaron about this, he jumped out of his chair, and loudly yelled, "You fucking bitch," along with a string of other profanities. Mary braced herself, knowing this could go on for a long time. He surprised her and walked out the door, slamming it shut. He went to school the next day. Mary thought, "Wow, I can't believe this is working." She was feeling pretty hopeful.

When Aaron came home from school he told Mary he needed the laptop for an assignment. She told him he could go to the library up the street to use a computer, and that she was sticking to the agreement. She felt fear and anxiety, certain he would blow up any moment. But she was determined to hold her ground this time. She tried to distract herself as he paced around the house, coming back in the kitchen every now and then, slamming cupboards and glaring at her. When he didn't go to the library, she started to worry he wouldn't do his assignment and began to question her decision to take the laptop. She started thinking about how he did go to school today for the first time in a while, and maybe he should have his laptop so he could do his homework.

After about 10 minutes of calm, he came to her and asked, "Can I please have my laptop back? I really do need it." Mary hesitated, not sure how to respond. She wanted to give it to him, but she remembered how she vowed to stick with it this time. She said, "You can have it in two weeks after you go to school every day." Aaron blew up. He kicked the kitchen cupboard shouting, "FUCK! You stupid bitch. I need that computer now! Give it to me! Give it to me now!" Mary felt panic. She didn't want to give in now that he was yelling at her again. She said, "Aaron, you know why I took it. Just stop. Go to the library and do your assignment." He continued to yell at her, getting in her face and screaming, "Give me the fucking computer right now or I'll tear the house apart to find it!" He began searching for the computer, tearing through closets and cupboards, throwing things all over the house.

Mary yelled at him to stop as he burrowed through her things. She was getting angrier and angrier. She started screaming at him, "Just stop and get out!" He came towards her, and she said, "Don't touch me or I'll call the police." He stopped and left the room. The police had been out before. He didn't want to deal with that again, and realized he might get arrested this time. Aaron calmed down for a while.

Mary made dinner, and they sat at the dinner table and talked about other things. Then Aaron started trying to convince her again to give him the laptop. She started to explain all of the reasons he could not have it. "You don't go to school, you are up all night on that thing face-booking or whatever, you don't sleep, you are ruining your life. What are you going to do? Quit school and sit around here on the computer for the rest of your life?!" At this point she was screaming at him and crying. She felt helpless and at a loss for what to do next. Aaron started yelling at her, telling her she was pathetic, that no one liked her, she had no friends, and she needed to get a life. By the end of the shouting match, Mary was exhausted. She had to go to work early in the morning and was tired of battling. She didn't want to be up all night. She gave up and said, "Take the damn laptop."

## What Led to Mary's Loss of Parental Control?

Scenarios like this play out regularly when parents attempt to hold their ground. Parents engage out of anger or give in out of fear or exhaustion because they don't know what else to do. Most teen violence and abuse starts with a power struggle. Next, the parents break the scenario down to identify the various dynamics that eventually led to Mary's loss of parental control. A typical discussion reveals the following points:

- Aaron starts by telling Mary he needs the laptop for an assignment. Mary says no again, and holds her ground. Mary feels fear and anxiety based on her past experience of Aaron's violence.
- Knowing his mother well, Aaron senses her fear, empowering him to continue the struggle. He ups her fear with threatening behavior. He glares at Mary and slams cupboards.
- Mary's anxiety increases. Then her feelings shift to worry when she realizes he isn't doing his assignment. She questions her decision and ponders giving in. She supports this idea by thinking about how he did go to school all day. She feels some calm when she considers letting go of the battle, knowing he will calm down and stop harassing her.

- Aaron senses Mary's internal conflict and tries again. He asks her nicely if he can have the laptop.
- Mary is not sure how to respond. She considers giving in, but remembers her firm decision. She goes back and forth in her mind. Aaron recognizes this and is sure she will give in, like she usually does. When Mary decides to say no again, Aaron is surprised.
- Aaron becomes angrier because he was sure Mary would give in this time. He escalates to almost physically attacking her.
- Mary sets a firm boundary by telling Aaron she will call the police.
- There is a break in the power struggle and some calm, but then Aaron tries for another go at getting the computer.
- Mary explains why he cannot have the computer once again, but now she is angry and yells. Aaron reacts by trying to hurt her emotionally.
- Finally, Mary is worn down and exhausted, feeling like she can't carry on with the struggle, and so she gives in.

## What Could Mary Have Done Differently?

Most parents react instead of respond to their teens' outbursts. "Reaction" is action taken in the moment, based on emotions evoked by the situation, as opposed to "response," which is action based on thought and planning. When parents have a planned response, they are seldom caught off guard and are better able to keep emotions in check. They know exactly what they will do, and when the emotions start to kick in, they can say to themselves, "Remember my plan." This helps them calm down and come across more confidently to their teen.

When parents feel confident and self-assured, teens notice it. Some teens push harder when they sense their parents are unwavering, particularly at first. But, when parents continue to hold their confidence and remain unshaken, teens get the message that no matter how hard they kick and scream, it will not get them what they want. This is much like responding to the temper tantrum of a two-year-old, when the parent says, "You can kick and scream and cry, but I cannot let you play in the street because it is dangerous."

However, these teens are not two-year-olds and can be big, dangerous, and scary. They do not settle down so easily. With teens, safety is a priority. The most important part of the response is to separate physically when the teen becomes violent or abusive. Calling the police may be needed. (See "How to Respond to Violence," Chapter 7.)

If Mary had made a plan in advance about how to respond to her son, things may have gone differently. She knew her son's pattern of response to her consequences. Thinking ahead about what would probably happen when she told him she was taking his computer gave her a chance to plan how she would respond. For example, she knew he would be angry and try to convince her. If she held her ground, she knew he would attack her verbally or physically. She knew he would be persistent, attempt to reengage in the argument, and that her own emotions of anger and frustration would be triggered. Awareness of her vulnerability to be persuaded is important. Mary felt responsible as a parent for her son's school performance. She knew it would be a challenge to keep from giving in because the consequence she set made it a little more challenging for him to do his homework. Evaluating her thoughts about this and changing her thinking would help her stick with her plan. For example, changing "I have to make sure he does his homework or he will fail" to thoughts such as, "He is responsible for his homework. He can go to the library. Even if he fails, it is more important right now for him to learn that violence does not work. This will help him stop being violent and abusive."

## Making a Response Plan for Setting a Limit

After discussing the response plan that Mary might have made, parents then work out a response plan for themselves by answering the following questions:

1.  Write down what you will say when you communicate the limit or consequence. Say it briefly, and in a calm, matter-of-fact tone.
    *Example: Because you have not been attending school and have been staying up nights on your computer, I am taking your computer until you have gone to school regularly for two full weeks.*
2.  List the ways your teen might respond.
    *Try to talk me out of it, swearing, yelling, intimidating me, punching or kicking the wall.*
3.  How do you usually respond to this?
    *I feel angry, panicky, and a need to stop him. I yell at him to stop. I try to help him calm down by explaining my reasons, which doesn't work. Sometimes I give in.*
4.  How do you want to respond to this in the future?
    *Tell him being abusive won't change my mind, separate from him, and hold my ground.*
5.  What gets in the way of responding in this way?
    *Anger, feeling inadequate as a parent, wanting to control him, wanting to get him to stop, wanting to change his mind.*
6.  What can you do to prevent this response?
    *Remind myself it's better for him if I leave him alone, and stay firm. Remember my plan.*

## Pointers for Success

- Tell your teen about your response plan ahead of time.
- When emotions are triggered, decrease their power and discomfort by acknowledging and accepting them as normal for the situation, and remembering your strengths as a parent.

- Don't expect perfection; be patient with yourself and your teen; it may get worse before it gets better.
- Acknowledge your teen's respectful and positive behavior; thank him or her for handling things well.
- Speak in a matter-of-fact tone. Be calm. Use your self-calming skills (see Chapter 6).
- Involve teens in setting rules and consequences to avoid springing consequences on them, which is often a trigger for aggression. When they know ahead of time, they are less reactive.

We use an acronym to help parents remember the skills they have learned for holding boundaries with their teens. When it's time to set a boundary, remember the word MAP.

### MAP: Make a Plan—Act with Confidence—Put It Into Place

When parents have a plan in place, they feel less hopeless and helpless. It gives them direction when they feel overwhelmed and confused about what to say and how to act with their teen. It enables them to regain leadership and become a parent again.

## Disengaging from Power Struggles with Teens

Day-to-day power struggles about anything from what cereal to buy to the amount of time on the computer can easily escalate to violent outbursts. This session teaches parents how to disengage at the first sign of a power struggle and redirect the interaction away from a win-lose battle.

### How to Disengage

- Learn to know when an interaction is becoming a power struggle.
  It is a power struggle when a parent feels controlled or feels the need to control; when either parent or teen is arguing, blaming, or demanding; or when the parent feels the need to win.

- Refuse to argue.
  When your child starts to argue about the facts—when, why, where, etc.—don't get pulled in. Teens will try to sideline conversations by disputing facts, challenging your statements, and correcting your memory of things. Once you start trying to convince them otherwise, you have been hooked. The issue is not the truth. Listen calmly without arguing.

- Separate physically from your teen.
  If your teen continues to try to engage you in an argument, leave the room. Tell him or her, "I am finished talking about it for now."

- Acknowledge the teen's feelings and opinions.
  Instead of challenging, listen with an attitude of interest to the teen's point of view. Say, "You feel really strongly about that," or "I understand why you would see it that way." When you stop challenging, they stop arguing—sometimes. You can acknowledge their point of view without agreeing with it. Sometimes just listening to teens helps them calm down.

- Notice your thinking.
  Change negative thoughts to ones that help you feel calmer, such as "I don't need to change his mind; the facts are not important. I can allow him to have his opinion and just listen." Later put attention back to the topic at hand.

- Be clear and specific about what needs to happen, and then stop talking.
  Overexplaining invites argument and power struggles. For example, you might simply say, "You need to complete all of your homework before you go out with your friends," and then separate if necessary to avoid arguing.

- Don't take your child's resistance or anger personally.
  Remember, your teen is just trying to change your mind or win the battle.

- Notice your own emotions.
  If your emotions are being triggered, and you feel angry, anxious, or fearful or have other difficult feelings, stop and separate from your teen. Talk later when you feel calmer.

- Use your self-calming skills (see Chapter 6).
  When your teen tries to engage you in a power struggle, listen while you practice self-calming techniques that work for you. Examples include deep breathing and mindfulness practices, such as being present in the moment and observing without judgment.

- Talk about the problem later when you are both calm.
  Bring up the discussion again later when you have time together and are calm. Discuss the problem using skills such as problem solving, listening, and acknowledging feelings.

- Ask yourself whether this is something you are willing to negotiate.
  Notice if you are being too rigid. Compromising and changing your mind is okay, as long as it is not in response to abuse.

## Rerouting Disrespectful Behavior

When teens speak disrespectfully, parents can help them switch to respectful words by reminding them of the skills they are learning. Similar to the way a facilitator would redirect behavior during teen groups, parents can say one of the following:

- Can you say that again in a respectful way?
- Can you say that using your assertive communication skills?
- Want to try that again as an "I" statement?
- It sounds like you are really angry. Can you tell me what else you're feeling?
- Remember what we learned about talking about feelings and how that helps? Do you want to try that instead?
- It sounds like you're on the Abuse Wheel. Can you switch to the Respect Wheel?

## What to Do After an Abusive or Violent Incident

After a teen has been abusive or violent, parents wonder how they can respond effectively and establish a consequence that matches the seriousness of the behavior. The restorative inquiry questions used during group to address violence can also be used at home (see Chapter 8).

### Using the Restorative Inquiry Questions

After the incident, once all is calm, parents can sit down with their teen and have a discussion using the restorative inquiry questions. This process gives the family a productive way to talk about what happened. It gives the teen a meaningful consequence that includes 1) taking responsibility by repairing the harm caused by the violent or abusive behavior and 2) making a plan to prevent further violence and abuse. The following scenario illustrates the use of these questions.

Greg had punched a hole in the wall and pushed his mother, Kristi, down during a conflict about his homework. His eight-year-old sister Amy heard the commotion and came into the room to find her mother on the floor. Greg lunged at Amy when she came in, and told her to get out.

The next day, Kristi told Greg she wanted to sit down and talk about what happened using the restorative questions they use in the group. He agreed, and was familiar with the questions. Kristi asked, "What was the harm done by your behavior?" Greg replied, "I hurt you physically. You were probably scared and upset that I'm acting like this again." Kristi asked, "What else?" Greg said, "I scared Amy." Kristi continued, "Let's ask Amy. Amy, what was it like for you?" Amy responded, "First I didn't know what was going on. When I saw Mom on the floor I got really scared. And then I thought you were going to hit me." Amy began to cry and said, "I hate it when you're like that." Greg looked down and said, "I'm sorry, Amy."

Kristi asked, "What other harm was caused?" Greg said, "There's a hole in the kitchen wall now, and it looks bad." Kristi agreed and continued, "How did it affect your relationship with us?" Greg said, "You probably don't trust me again. Amy probably won't want to be around me for a while."

Kristi then asked, "How did this affect you?" Greg responded, "I feel bad about myself. I was doing better. I thought I was over being like that. Now I won't have your trust so much and I have to get it back again." She replied, "I'm glad you can see that. It's a big step from how you have responded in the past."

Kristi asked, "What do you think you need to do to repair some of these harms, and make amends?" Greg said, "I know I should fix the hole in the wall. I can do chores to earn money to pay to get it fixed. Or maybe Dad can show me how to fix it." Kristi replied, "That's a good idea." Greg continued, "I want to help you trust me again and Amy not feel so scared of me." Kristi asked, "What do you think you need to do?" Greg replied, "Not get violent. Not yell at you. Try harder to use my safety plan." Then Greg asked his mother, "What do you want me to do to make amends?" Mom replied, "Be willing to talk to me about school without escalating and fighting with me about it. This all started when I asked if you turned that assignment in. The best way to make amends to me would be to sit down once a week and fill me in on where you are with your schoolwork. And be honest and respectful while we talk." Greg answered, "Okay, I can do that."

Then Greg asked Amy, "How can I make amends to you?" Amy said, "Will you take me to the park like you used to? And play on the jungle gym with me?" Greg smiled and said, "Yeah, we can do that."

Kristi then asked, "What do you think you could have done differently in that situation, instead of yelling at me and pushing me?" Greg said, "I could have just tried to tell you that school is really stressful right now, and I'm behind, and that's why I got so mad. I didn't want to talk about it. But, I know I have to. I need help with it." Kristi responded, "I'm glad you told me that. I didn't know. I want to be able to help you. I know it's hard for you to ask for help sometimes. And I could be less pushy. I will try to give you more space, if you can try to let me in and allow help."

Then Kristi said, "Now, it's time for you to make a plan to prevent this from happening again. Do you want to do it together, or on your own and then we'll go over it?" Greg said, "I'll do it and then show it to you."

Greg took a sheet of paper, reflected on the violent incident, and then wrote his answers to the final two questions of the restorative inquiry process:

- How could you have expressed your feelings or needs in a way that was not hurtful?
  *I could have told you I was stressed about school, and explained that I'm behind and don't know what to do. I could have asked for help.*

- What skills can you use next time to stay respectful and nonviolent?
  *Use my safety plan and take a break when I start to feel frustrated with you. Use my self-calming plan.*

## Supporting the Teen During the Restorative Inquiry Process

Self-blame and shame are often expressed by teens when parents ask them to talk about their hurtful behavior and its effect on family members. This may lead to expressions of denial, justification, and blaming others. Parents need to take a break if this happens and try again later.

Parents can help teens engage in this process by approaching them as allies who want to help them succeed and who believe they are capable. Parents can relay messages such as, "I am not your enemy; I am your parent and I care for you and love you. We can work together on this. I am on your side." Using the restorative "working with" mode of leadership, as described in Chapter 8, helps teens feel more open to change. Shame is reduced when teens feel supported as opposed to confronted.

Additional ways that parents can reduce a teen's shame and encourage accountability include:

- Focus on the behavior, not the person. It is a behavior that can be changed, it is not who you are.
- Avoid blame. When parents stop blaming, teens stop defending.
- Don't defend yourself. When parents defend their actions, the discussion shifts back to who is to blame.
- Give teens space to talk about feelings and behavior without comment. Allow teens to have their feelings.
- Show the teen that he or she can admit to mistakes without losing your support and love.
- Hold boundaries by not allowing disrespect or put-downs. Stop and separate if this happens.

Finally, parents need to keep their own emotions in check in order for the teen to remain open to looking at his or her own behavior instead of defending it. When parents contribute negatively to an incident, it is important for them to model accountability by taking responsibility for their behaviors. When parents acknowledge their unhelpful behaviors, it fosters mutual empathy and forgiveness, opening the way to move forward together to build a healthier relationship.

## Summary: Patience, Small Steps, and Optimism

The challenges faced by parents of teens who are violent in the home seem insurmountable at times. Some days parents walk into the parent group feeling like they want to give up. They say, "This isn't working. Nothing is helping. I can't do it anymore," spilling out an inventory of tirades by their teen during the previous week. It is also challenging for the practitioners who help these parents. We begin to feel the same powerlessness when our parenting advice fails to make a difference. These parents are on the cusp of giving up and look to us in a last effort to save the relationship. We all start to wonder, "Is this working? Maybe this is not the right approach."

Despite these feelings, the same parent who felt hopeless initially comes in a few weeks later beaming that the past week was the best week ever. We have learned to be patient and ride the waves. We have learned that it takes small steps forward, with big steps backward, over many months for real change to be established. An attitude of optimism and belief in the youths' ability to change helps parents keep going and not give up. Teens are resilient and surprise us by their ability to change their behavior when they are given support, skills, and the responsibility to do so. Helping parents have patience and optimism and to celebrate the small steps are key.

# Index

Note: Page numbers in *italics* indicate figures, tables, and boxes.